SCHOLASTIC

Grades K-3

The MEGA-BOOK of Instant Word-Building Mats

200 Reproducible Mats to Target & Teach Initial Consonants, Blends, Short Vowels, Long Vowels, Word Families & More!

M'Liss Brockman and Susan Peteete

Word-Building Mat

long e

Mat 47

Look at the picture. Then build the word.

feet
jeep
leaf
seal
tree

55

Word-Building Mat

-at

Mat 65

Look at the picture. Then build the word.

bat
cat
hat
mat
rat

73

y t r s

New York • Toronto • London • Auckland • Sydney
New Delhi • Mexico City • Hong Kong • Buenos Aires

Teaching Resources

Dedication

For Rusty, Stephen, Christopher, and Marianne and Mark, Matt and Laura for their patience and support during our many projects.

Acknowledgments

First, we extend our love and gratitude to our families for putting up with a wife and mom in the teaching profession who isn't satisfied with the status quo. This often means rearranging schedules or shuffling papers and books from the table before a family meal. Thanks for putting up with us!

We would also like to thank our principals for creating a school climate that supports and encourages new ideas and approaches. Thanks to our colleagues who have provided feedback and encouragement over the years. We are grateful to the many professionals and researchers in early literacy who have provided us with "aha" moments on how to work best with children as they learn to "crack the code" for reading and writing.

At Scholastic, we thank Liza Charlesworth for helping us find ways to make this word building book a reality.

Designed by Grafica, Inc.
ISBN-13: 978-0-439-47120-6 • ISBN-10: 0-439-47120-6

12 11 10 9 8 7 6 5 4 3 9 10 11/0

Contents

Blends & Vowel Pairs

Introduction

In today's classrooms, literacy is a top priority—but time is also of the essence! It's important to build confidence in young readers of all levels, but it can be difficult to provide independent practice with just the right skills. Not anymore! *The Mega-Book of Instant Word-Building Mats* is an easy-to-use, research-based resource that helps you build vocabulary, phonemic awareness, phonics, and fluency skills—independently. These engaging activities invite children to work with words hands-on, giving them ownership of the language as they manipulate letters. Plus, they're lots of fun to use! So get children ready to see it, say it, build it—and give them a headstart on the road to reading success!

How the Mats Support Young Readers

Research has shown that the following experiences are significant factors in helping children to internalize letter-sound relationships:

- Hearing the sounds in a spoken word
- Using concrete manipulatives to see the letters and build the word
- Reading the word

The reproducible mats in this book are designed to take children through each of these experiences, while teaching them essential spelling rules for words with common sounds. The more experience children have with these spelling patterns, the more proficient they will become at reading and writing hundreds of words! By manipulating letters and sounds to create words, children receive hands-on practice examining the roles that letters and sounds play within words. This leads to increased reading and writing vocabulary and improved spelling skills, while also fostering the development of reading and writing fluency. The activities in this book invite children to see, say, solve, and build words as they study each target sound in depth, making the mats a key component of any literacy program.

What's Inside

The Mega-Book of Instant Word-Building Mats provides you with an endless supply of essential literacy manipulatives. You'll find ready-to-use activities for each of the following target skills:

- initial consonants
- short and long vowels
- word families (words that end with the same sound and spelling pattern)
- blends
- digraphs

... plus blank mats to customize for any skill!

You'll also find that each mat comes in two versions, allowing you to differentiate for children of all skill levels. Children who need extra scaffolding can build words by matching letter tiles to preprinted letter guides. More advanced readers can work on their own to sound out words by placing letter tiles on blank squares. For even more flexibility, the mats are designed to be a perfect fit for use with Little Red Tool Box Word-Building Tiles—or with the included reproducible letter tiles on pages 21–24. All you need is a copier, and you're ready to go!

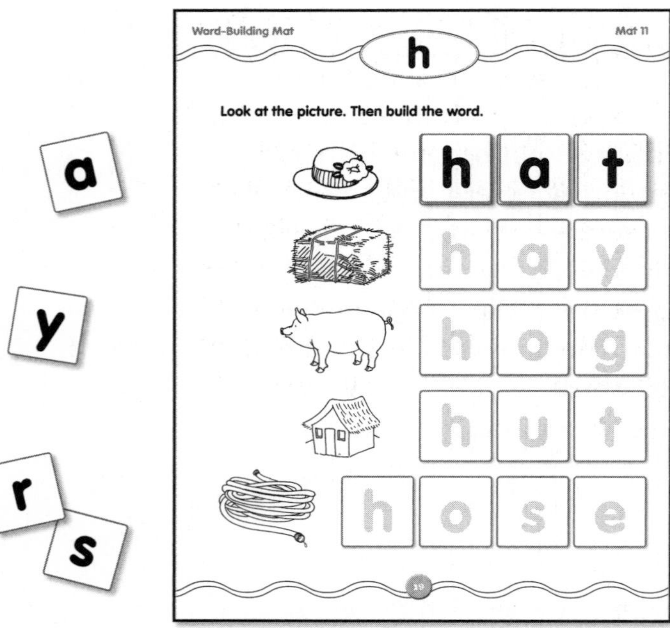

Teaching With the Mats

Setting Up

The mats in this book are easy to set up and use—in an instant! Follow these guidelines for using the mats in your classroom.

- To create a learning center, simply copy the mats that focus on your selected target skills—you'll find each skill printed in bold type at the top of the sheet. If you like, you may laminate the sheets for durability. If using the included reproducible letter tiles, simply copy a few sets of letters (you can laminate these, as well) and cut apart to create the tiles. Depending on children's skill level, you might allow them to choose from all the tiles, or set out just the ones they'll need to complete a particular mat. If using Little Red Tool Box letter tiles, place the activity mat on any magnetized surface (such as a cookie sheet, or Little Red Tool Box Jumbo Fold-Out Magnetic Mats) and have children place the tiles on top to build words. Place the tiles in a bag or basket, and children are ready to start word-building!
- To create take-home packs for homework, copy one or two mats for skills you'd like children to focus on. (Again, you may wish to laminate them to allow for prolonged use.) Place the mats in a self-sealing bag, along with a set of reproducible tiles (or Little Red Tool Box letter tiles). If you like, you can also include a short note to families. Now you have an instant take-home literacy activity!
- To create customized word-building mats, copy a blank activity sheet (you'll find one for building four-letter words and one for five-letter words). Write your selected target skill in the oval at the top of the sheet. Then add a picture representing the target word next to each set of letter boxes. You can draw your own pictures, or use clip art. Depending on children's skill level, you can leave the boxes blank, or print letter guides. Copy your customized activity sheet, and you've got a whole new word-building mat!

Modeling the Activities

When you first introduce the activities to children, model the steps in the process. First, read the directions on the mat aloud. Then have children look at the first picture and say its name. Next, show children how to use the letter tiles to build the word by placing one tile in each square. When the word is complete, read it aloud. Then move to the next word and repeat the process. When the mat is completed, read the list of words aloud. Once children are familiar with the steps, they'll be able to use the mats independently.

Tracking Progress

Add a writing component—and track progress—by inviting children to record their word lists. Children can write their name, the date, and the target sound at the top of any lined or unlined piece of paper. Then have children reproduce the completed mat by writing the words they built on the sheet of paper. Another option is to have children create their own word booklets. Provide each child with a small notebook, or create one by stapling several sheets of paper together to form a booklet. Then invite children to record each group of words on a different page and add to it throughout the year.

b

Look at the picture. Then build the word.

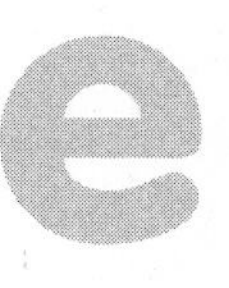

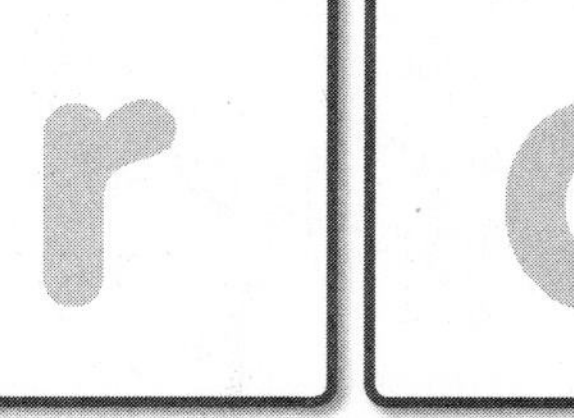

b

Look at the picture. Then build the word.

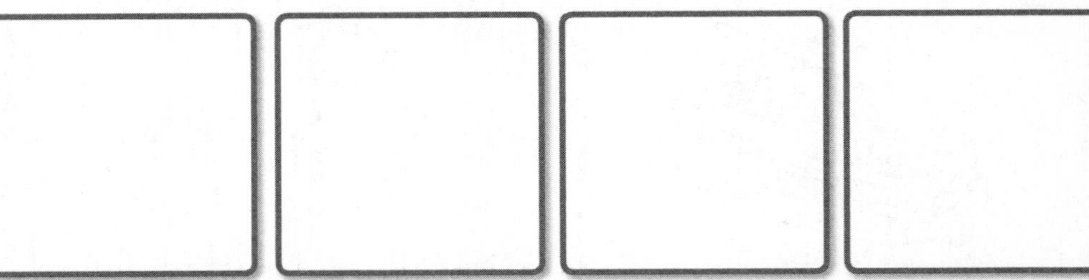

c

Look at the picture. Then build the word.

c

Look at the picture. Then build the word.

d

Look at the picture. Then build the word.

d

Look at the picture. Then build the word.

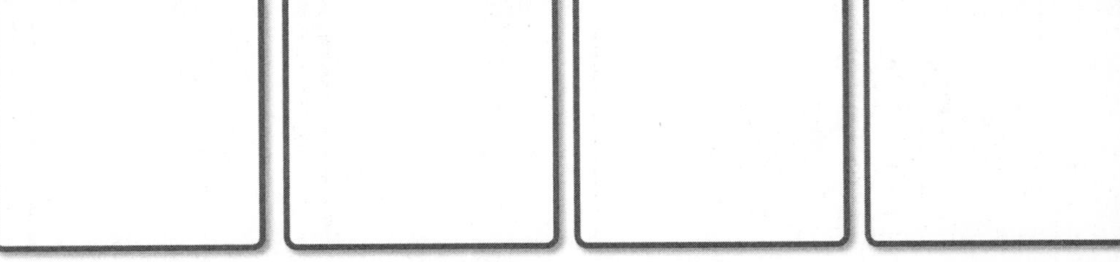

Look at the picture. Then build the word.

f	a	n

f	o	x

f	i	r	e

f	i	s	h

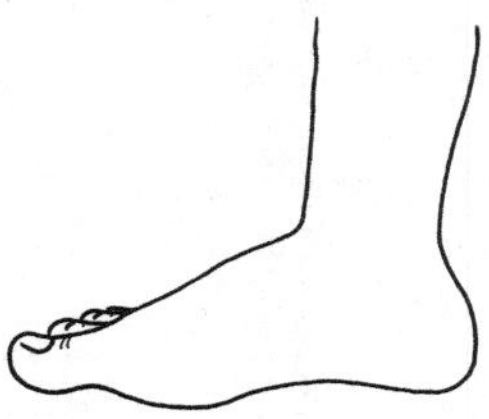

f	o	o	t

f

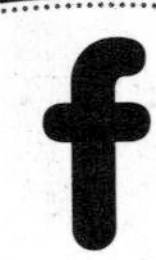

Look at the picture. Then build the word.

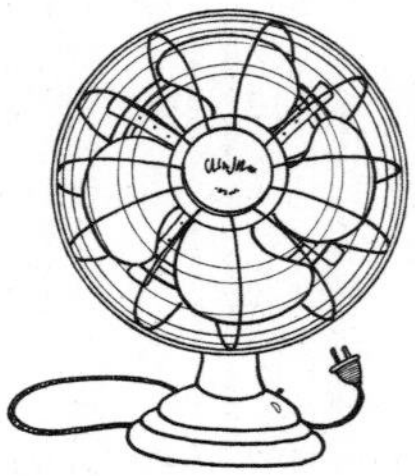

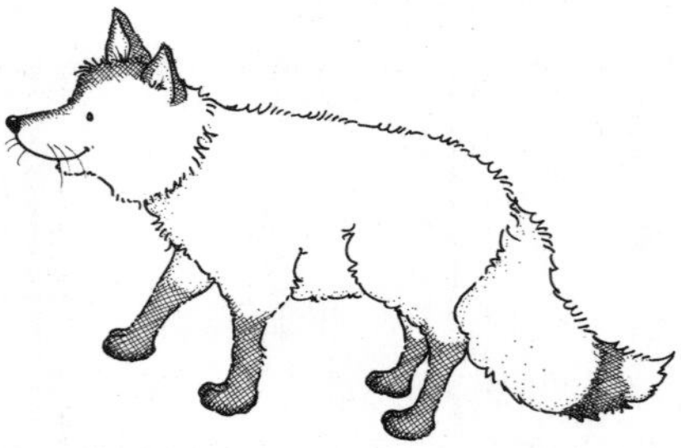

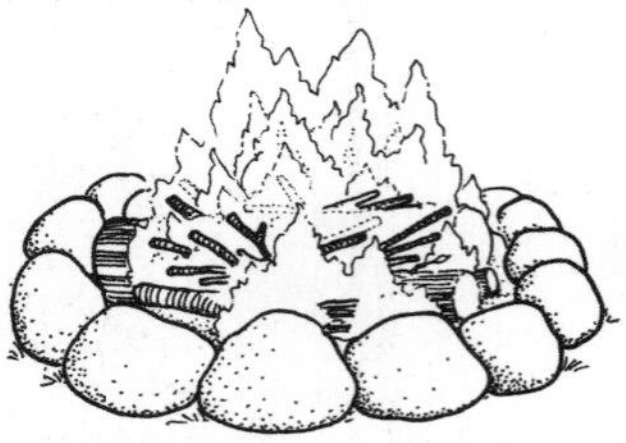

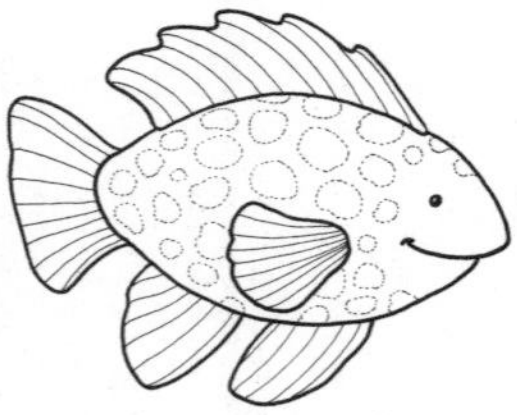

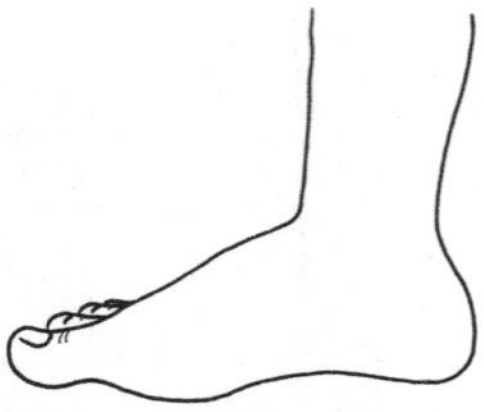

g

Look at the picture. Then build the word.

g  

   e

   t

g   

g

Look at the picture. Then build the word.

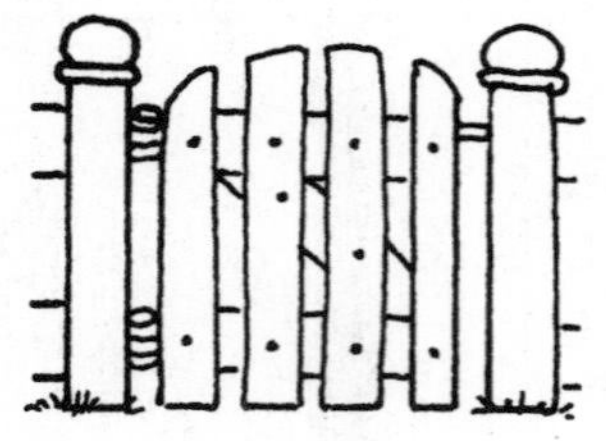

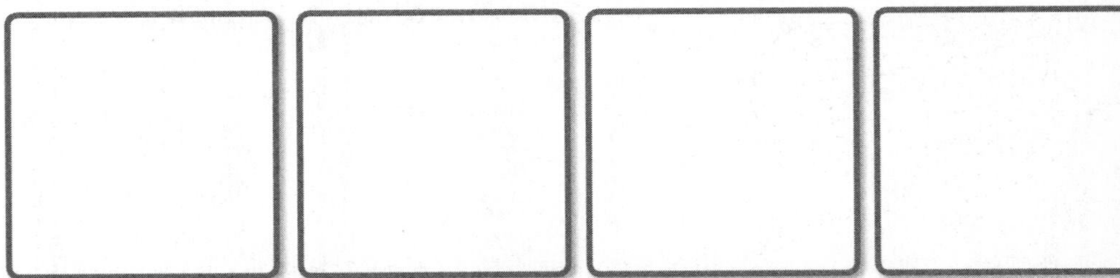

h

Look at the picture. Then build the word.

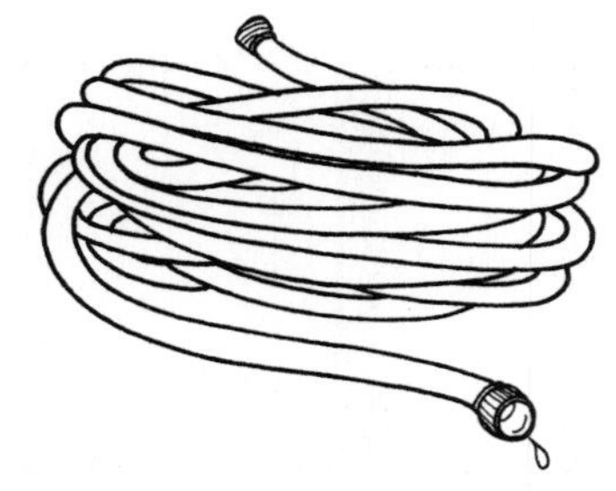

h

Look at the picture. Then build the word.

j

Look at the picture. Then build the word.

j

Look at the picture. Then build the word.

k

Look at the picture. Then build the word.

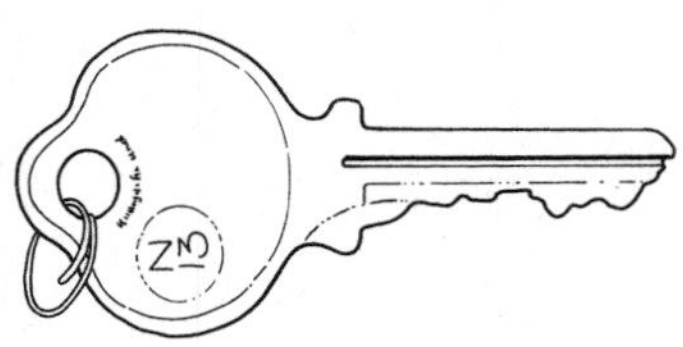

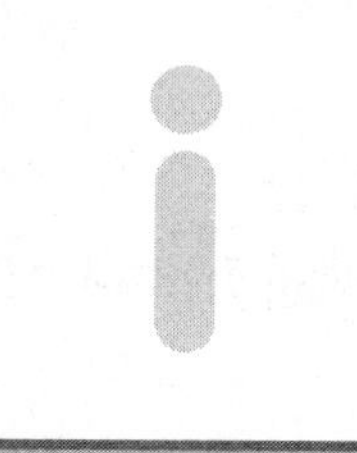

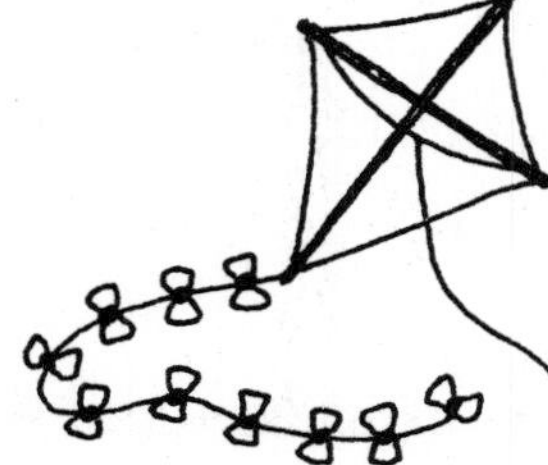

k

Look at the picture. Then build the word.

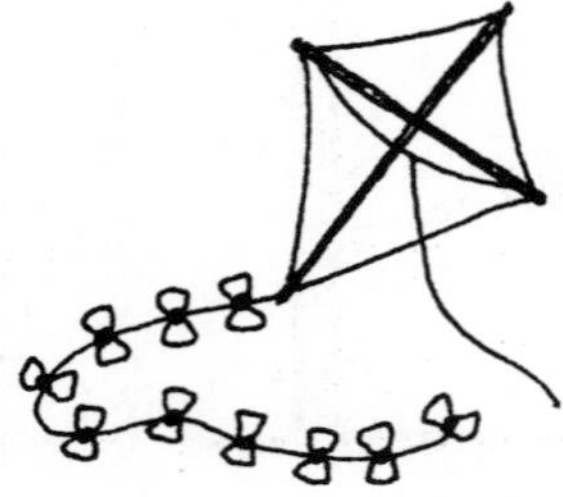

l

Look at the picture. Then build the word.

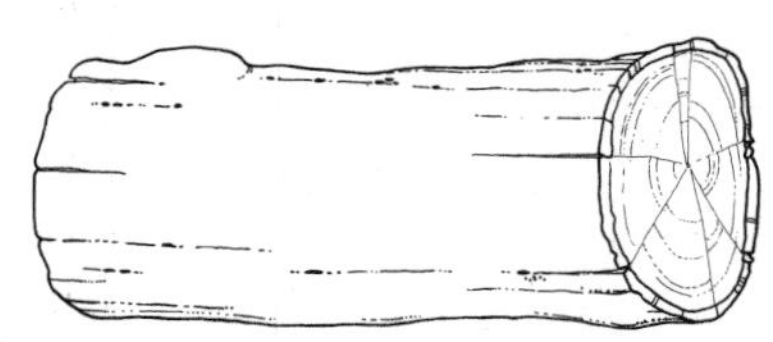

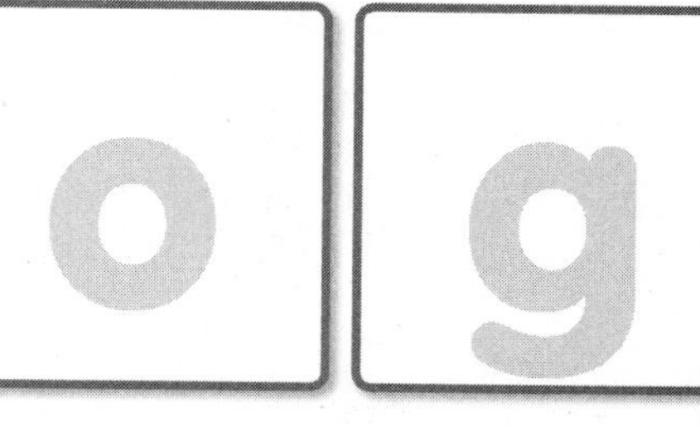

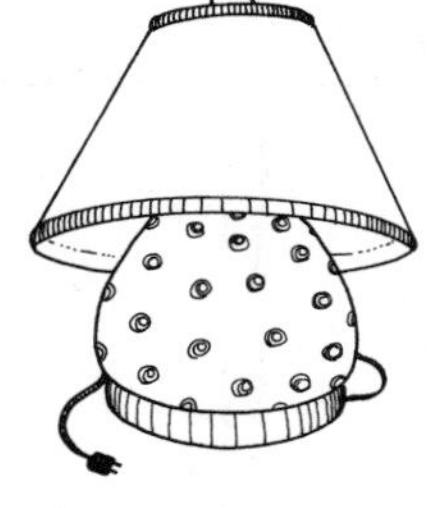

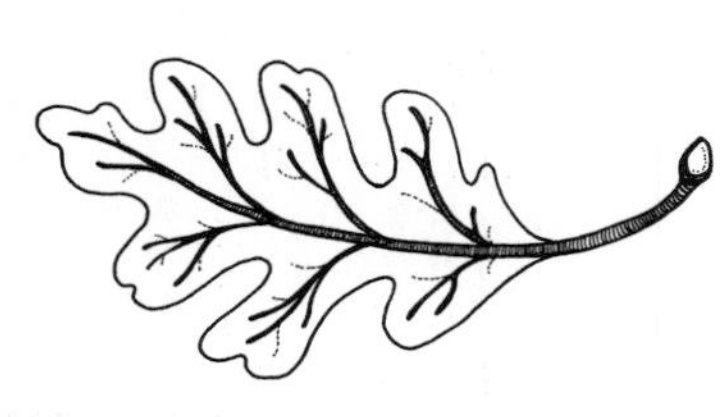

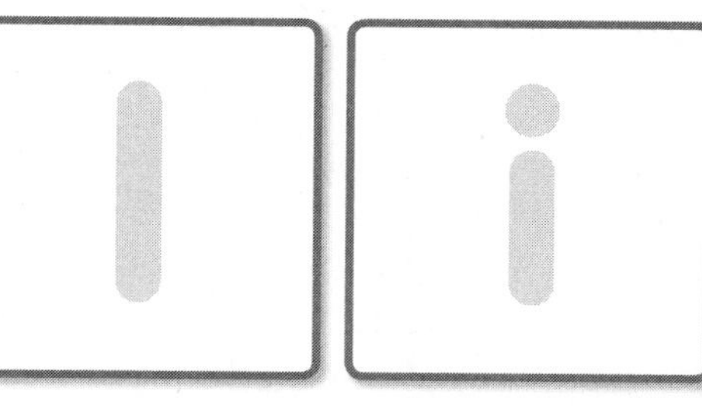

l

Look at the picture. Then build the word.

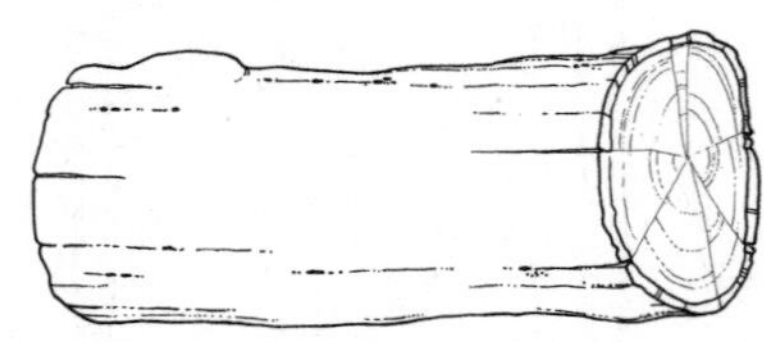

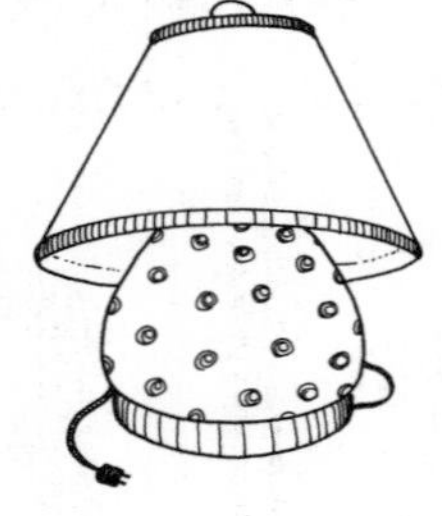

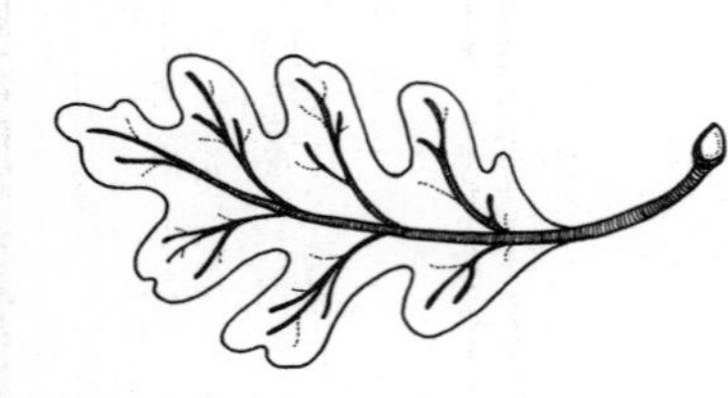

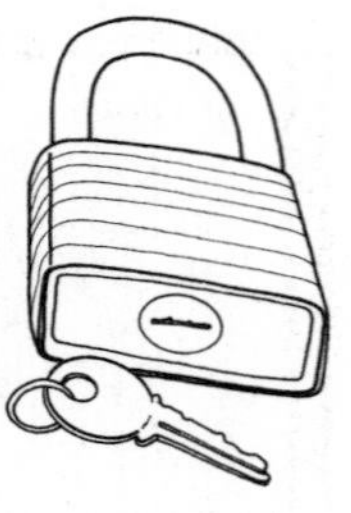
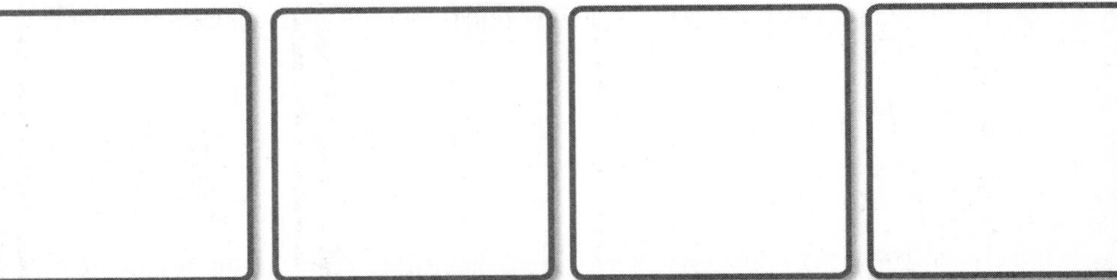

m

Look at the picture. Then build the word.

m

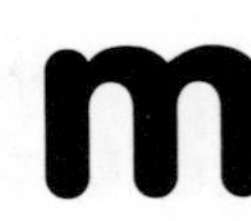

Look at the picture. Then build the word.

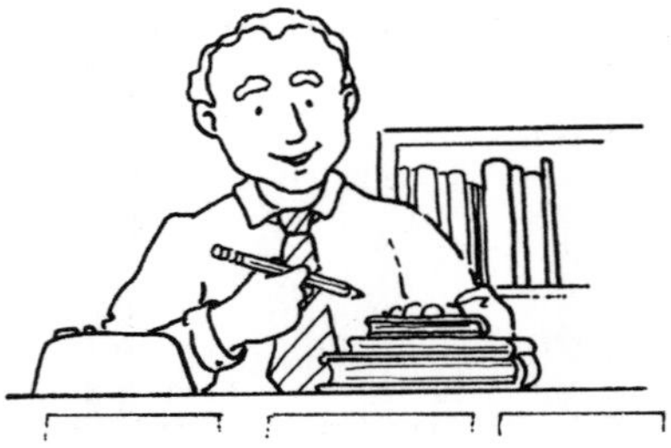

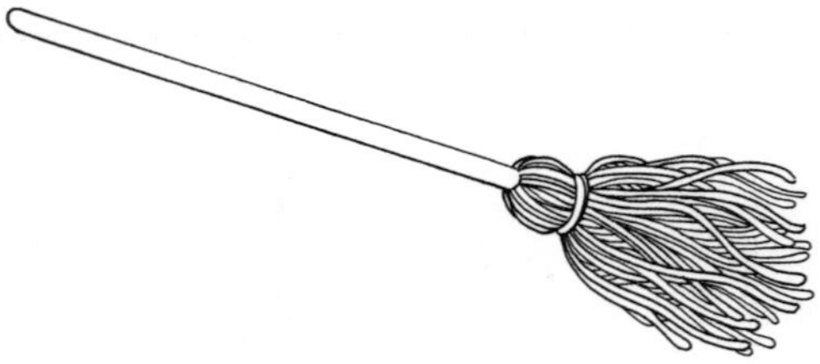

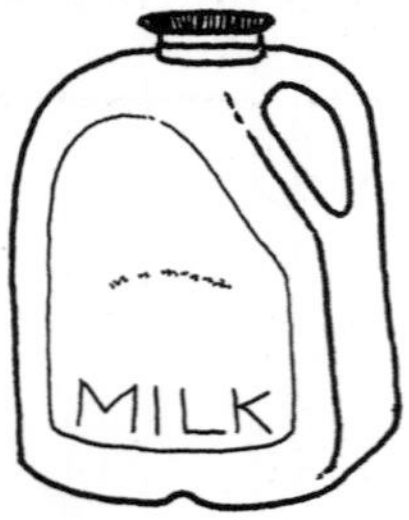

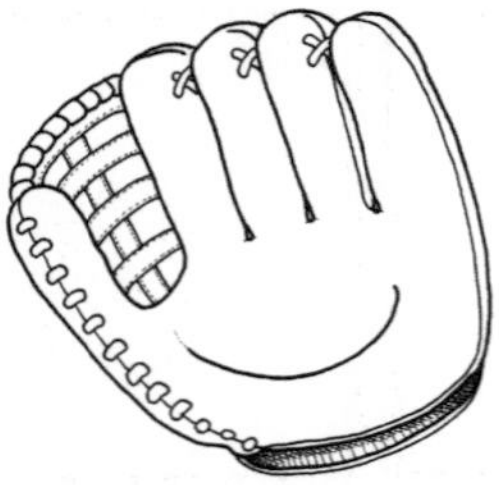

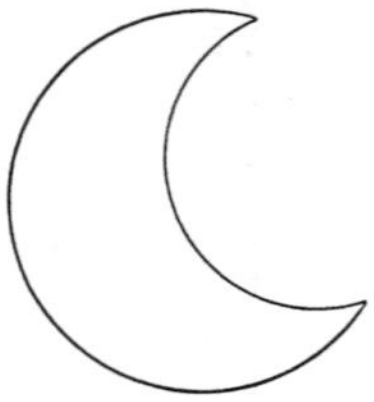

n

Look at the picture. Then build the word.

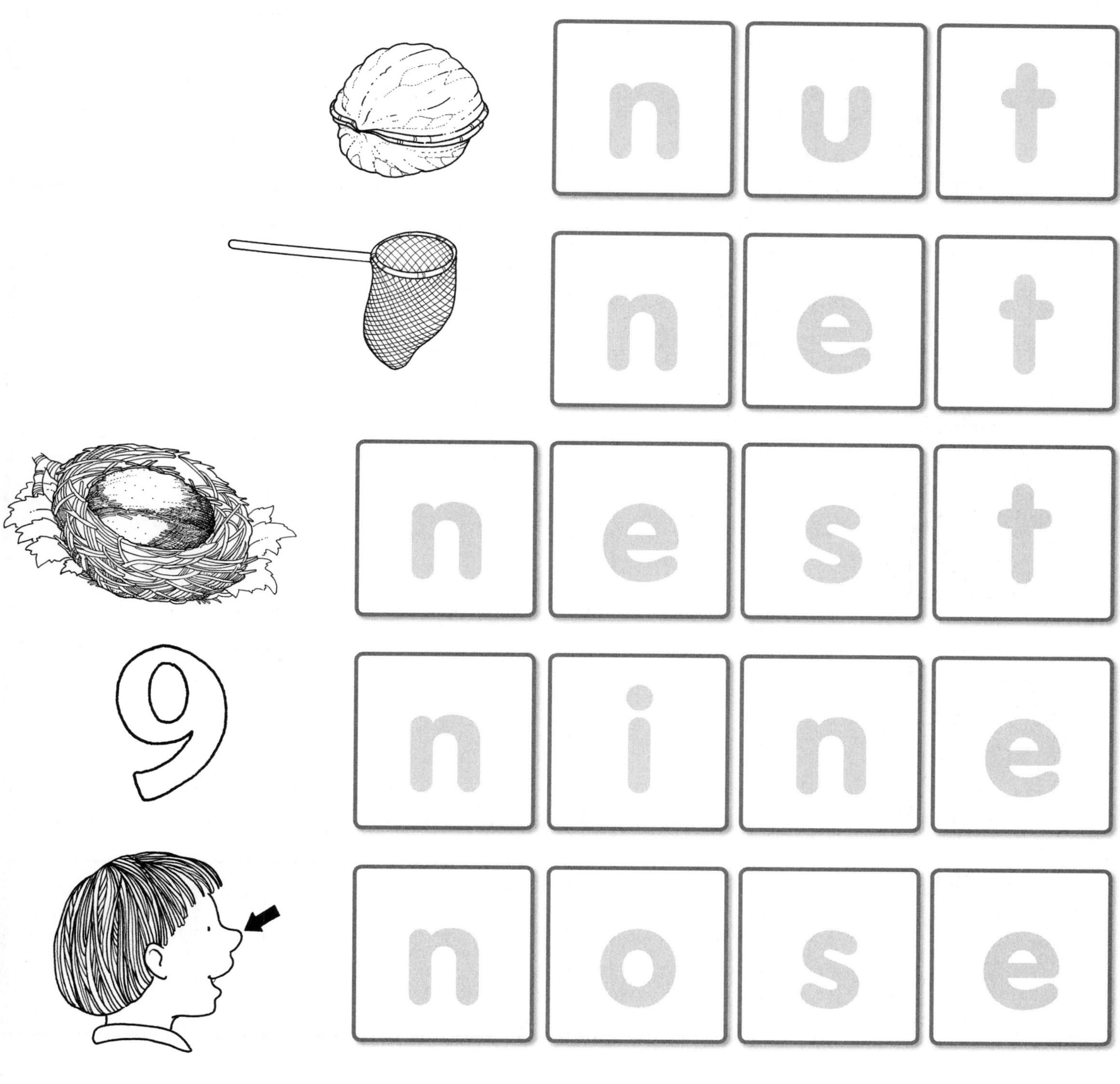

n

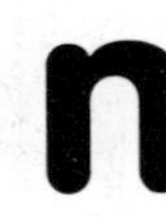

Look at the picture. Then build the word.

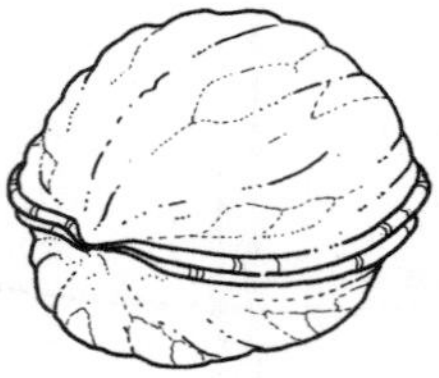

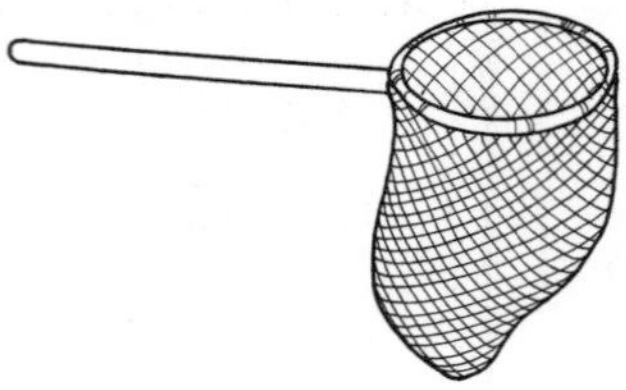

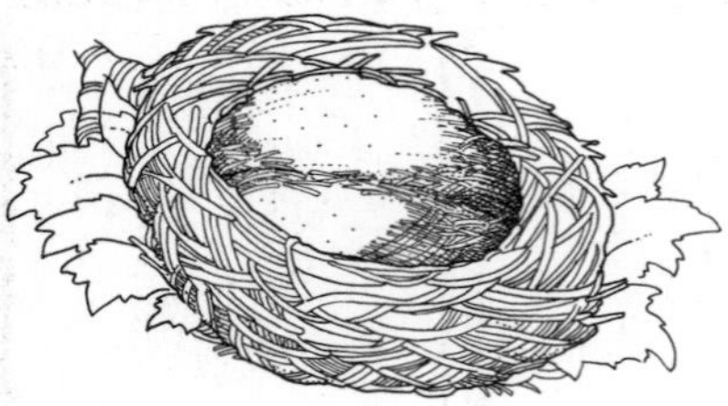

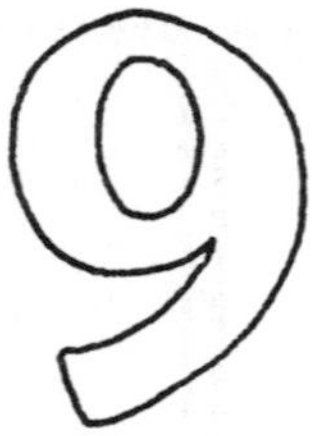

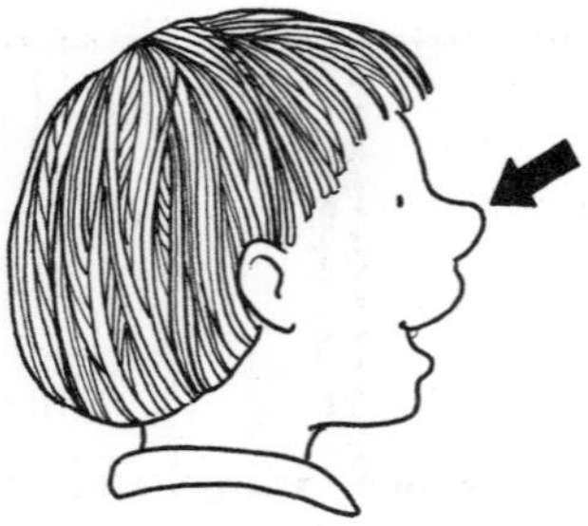

p

Look at the picture. Then build the word.

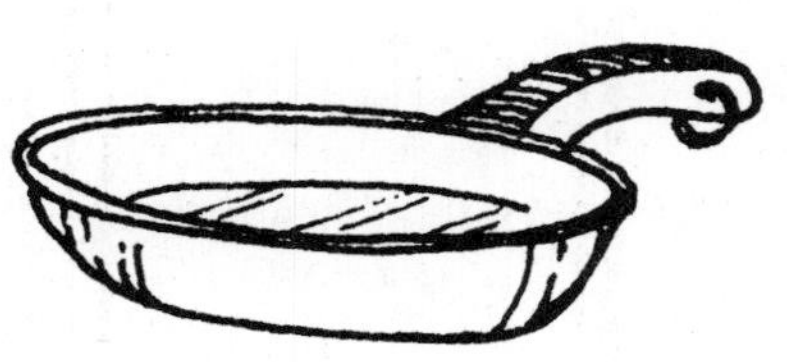

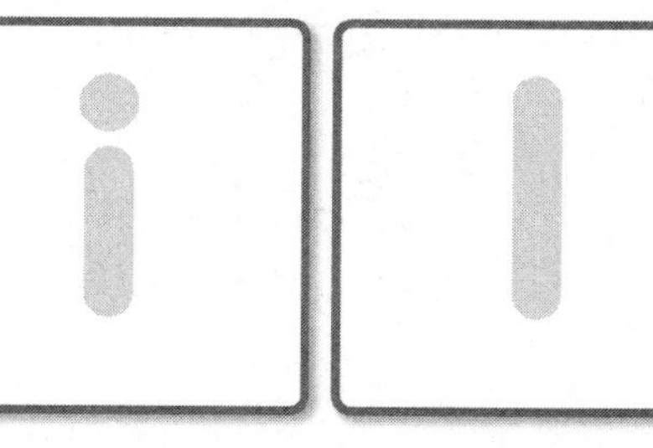

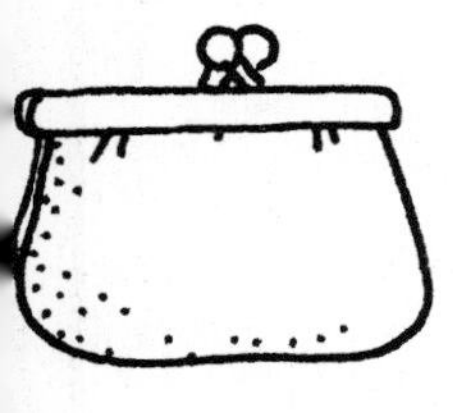

p

Look at the picture. Then build the word.

Look at the picture. Then build the word.

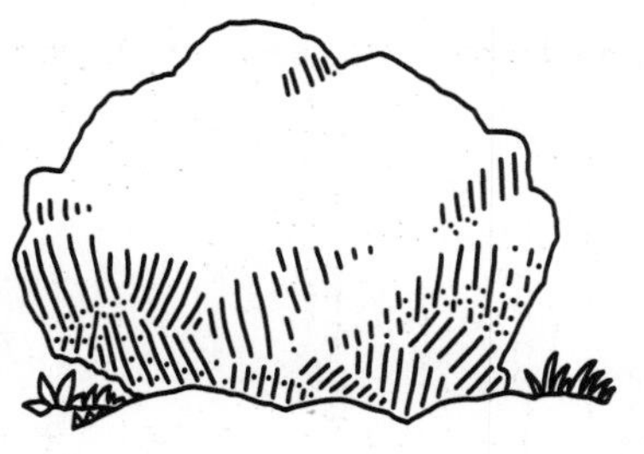

r

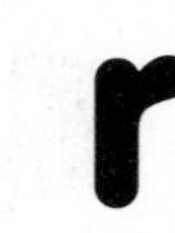

Look at the picture. Then build the word.

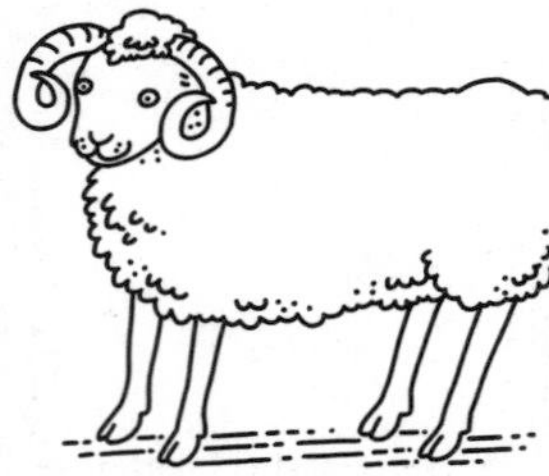

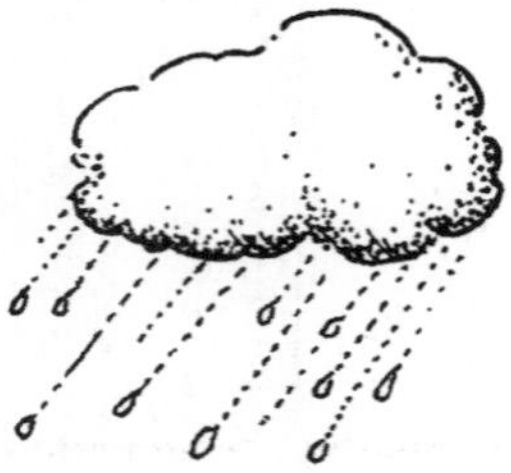

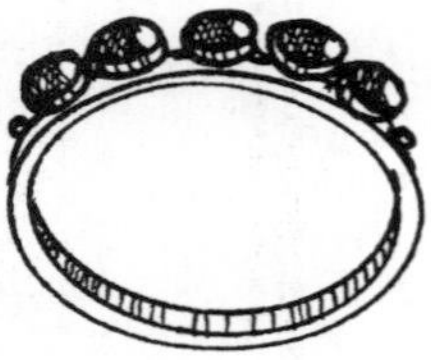

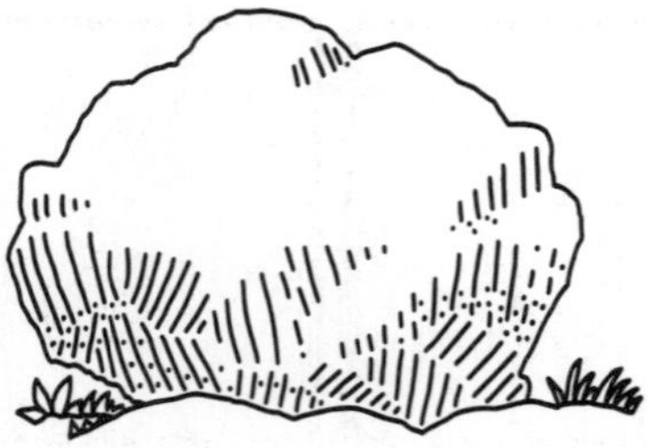

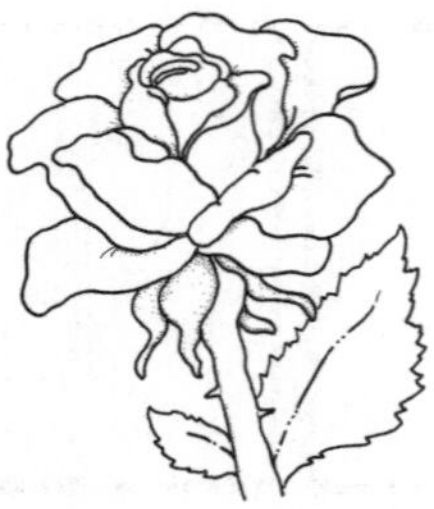

s

Look at the picture. Then build the word.

6 s 

s 

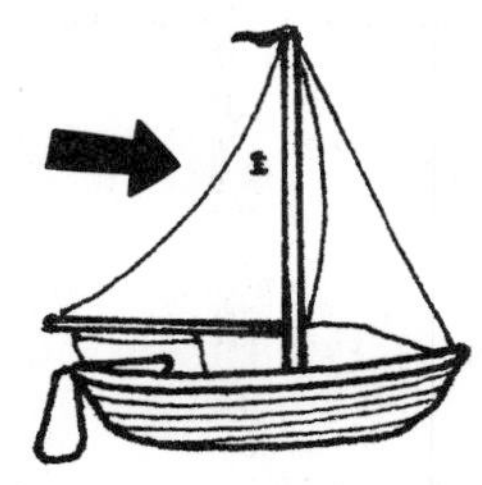

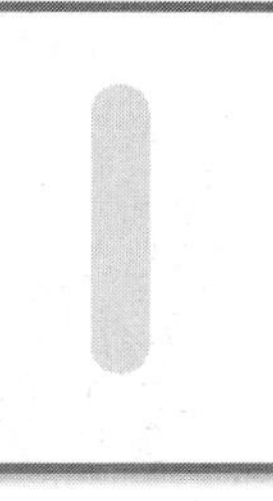

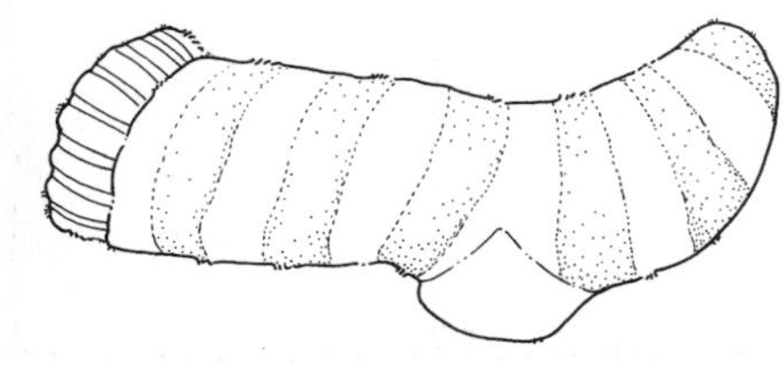

s

Look at the picture. Then build the word.

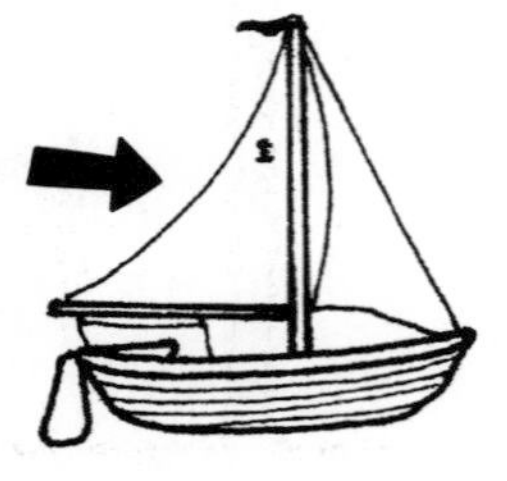

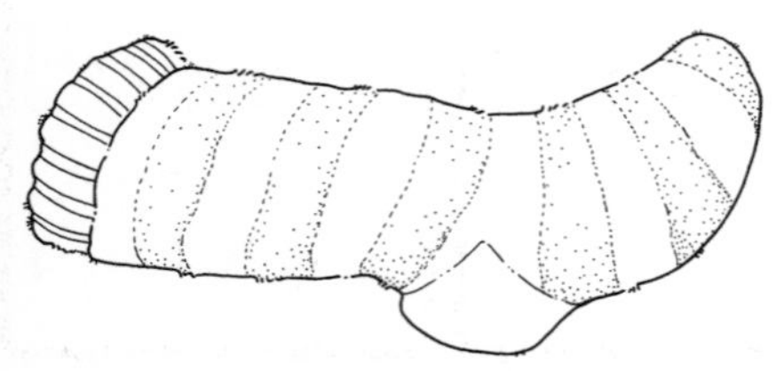

Look at the picture. Then build the word.

t o p

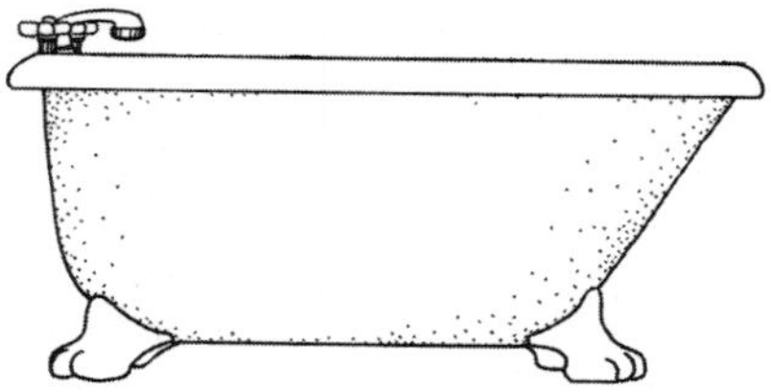

t u b

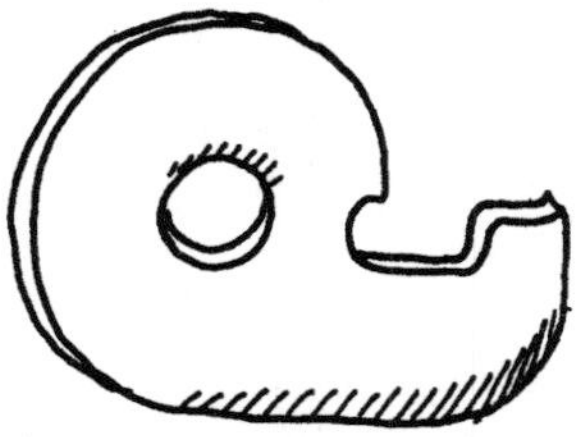

t a p e

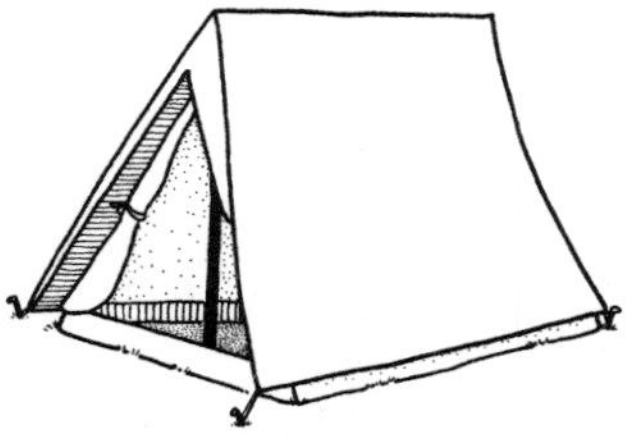

t e n t

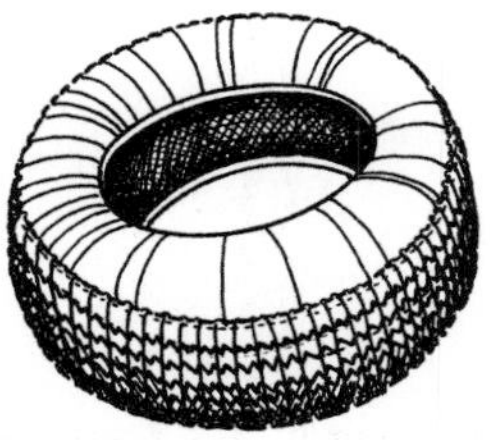

t i r e

t

Look at the picture. Then build the word.

Look at the picture. Then build the word.

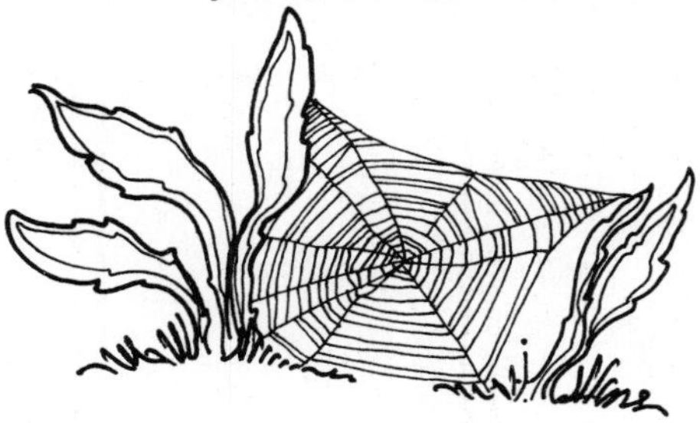

w e b

w i g

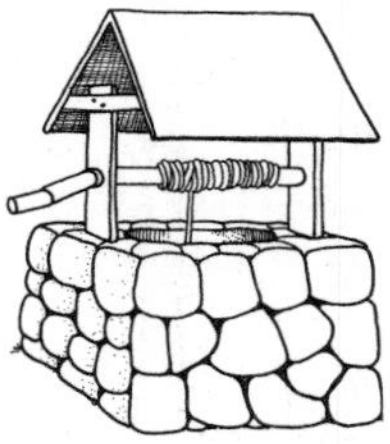

w e l l

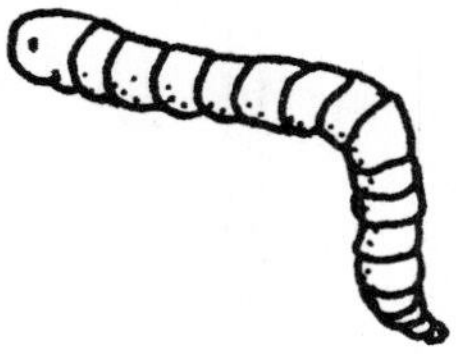

w o r m

w a g o n

W

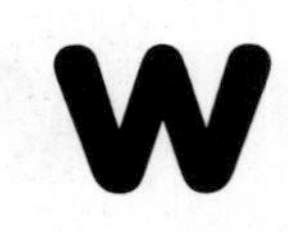

Look at the picture. Then build the word.

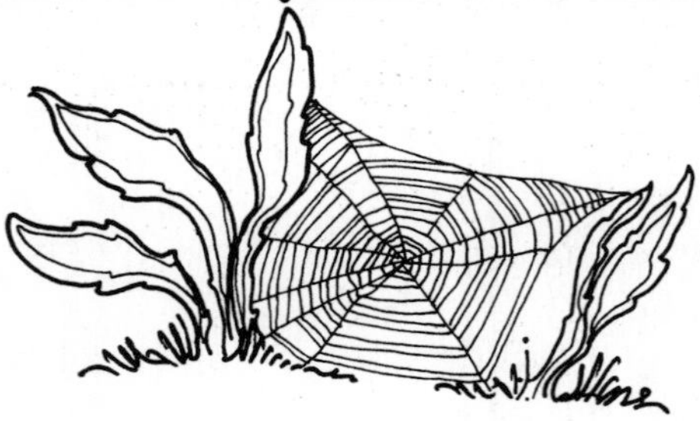

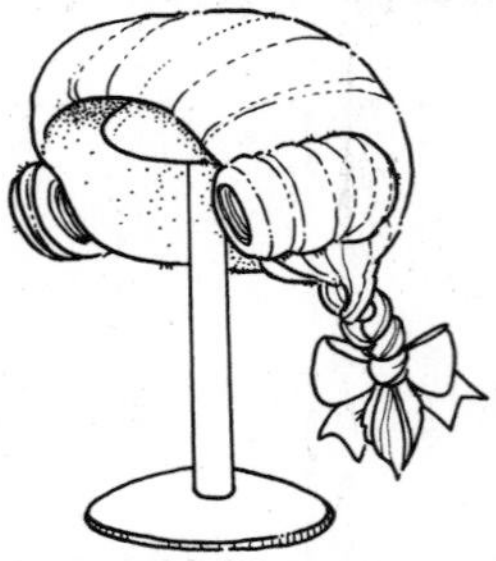

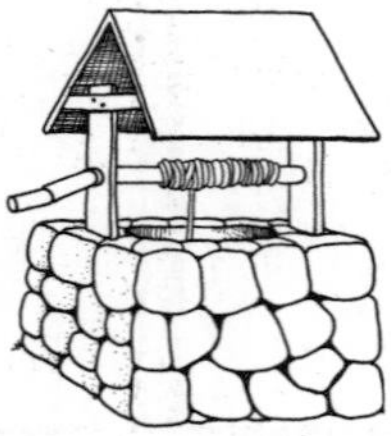

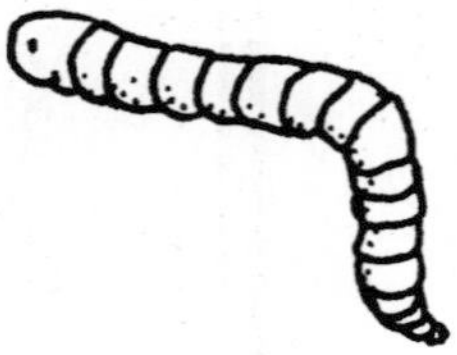

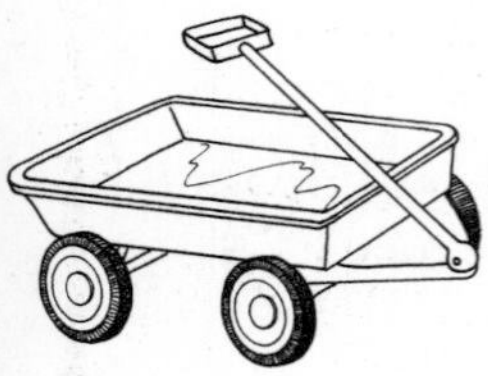

y

Look at the picture. Then build the word.

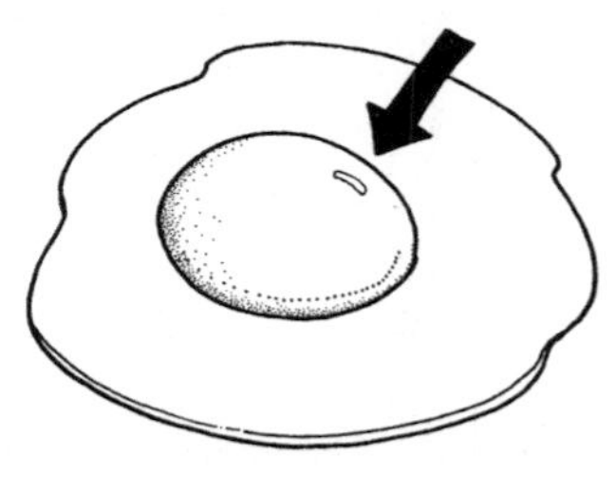

y

Look at the picture. Then build the word.

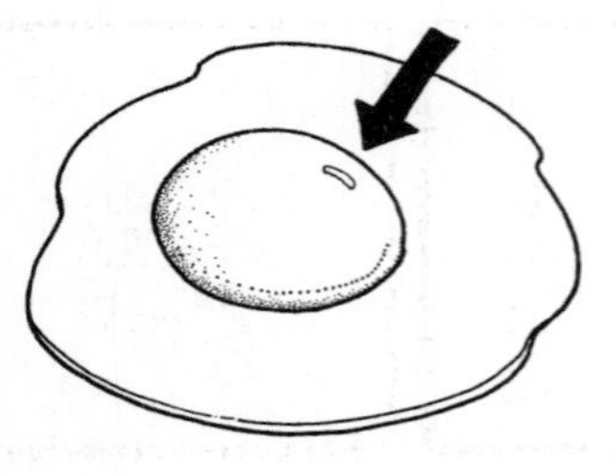

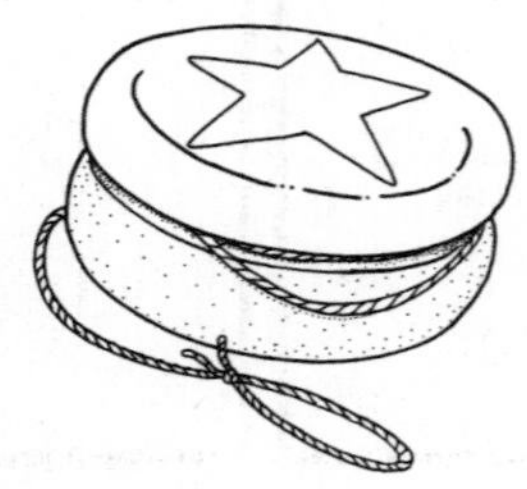

short a

Look at the picture. Then build the word.

short a

Look at the picture. Then build the word.

short e

Look at the picture. Then build the word.

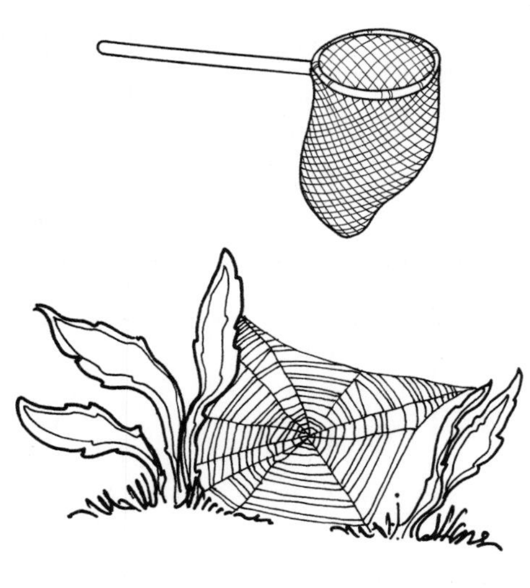

n e t

w e b

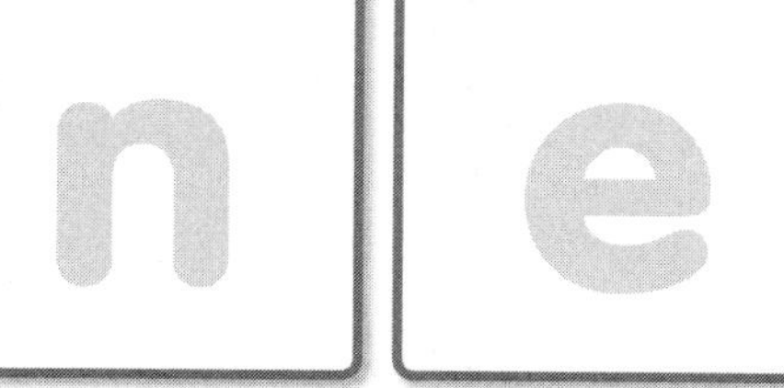

n e s t

w e l l

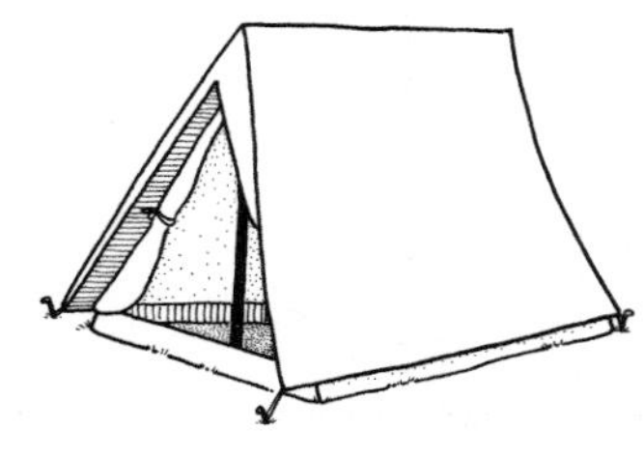

t e n t

short e

Look at the picture. Then build the word.

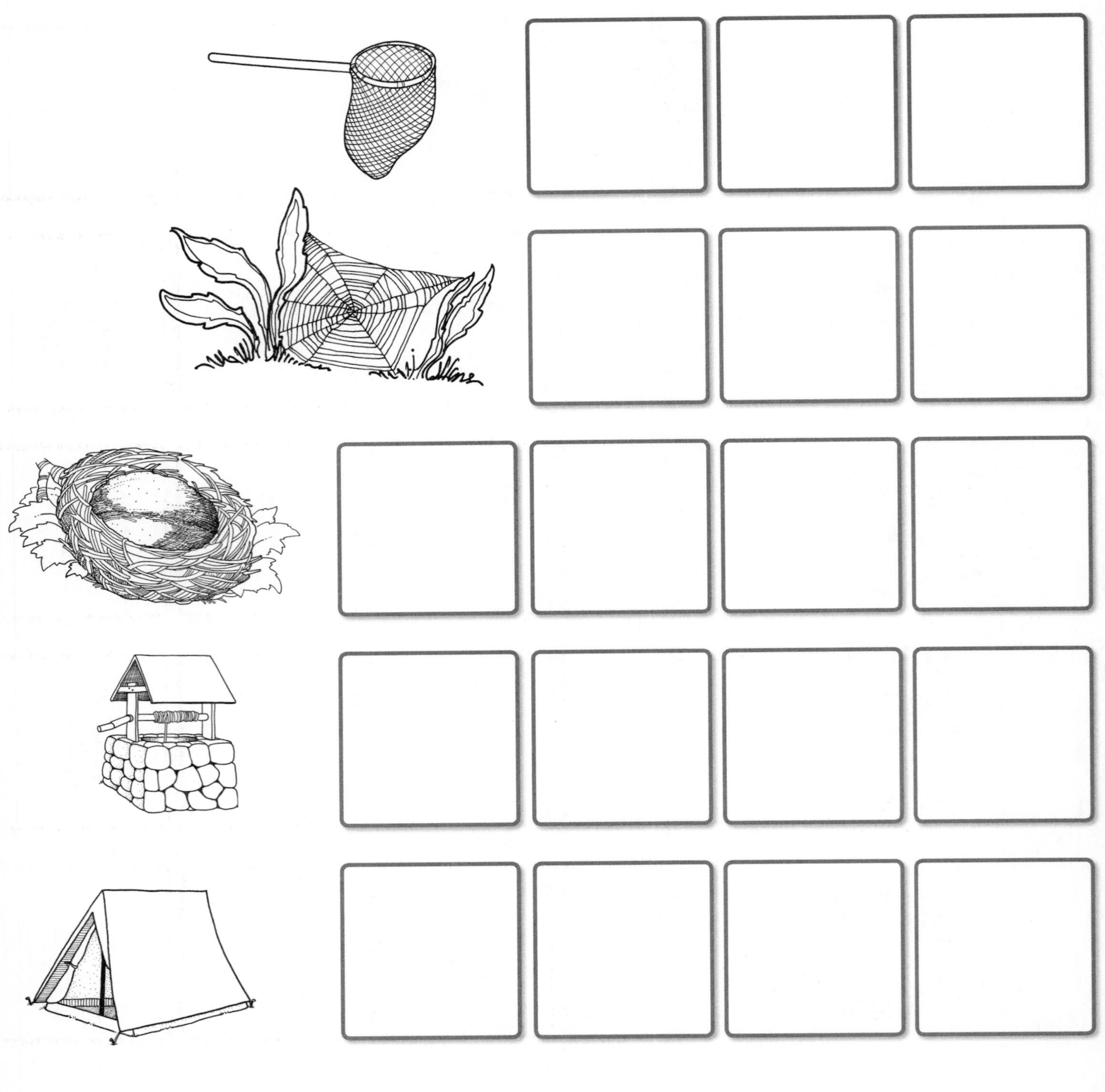

short i

Look at the picture. Then build the word.

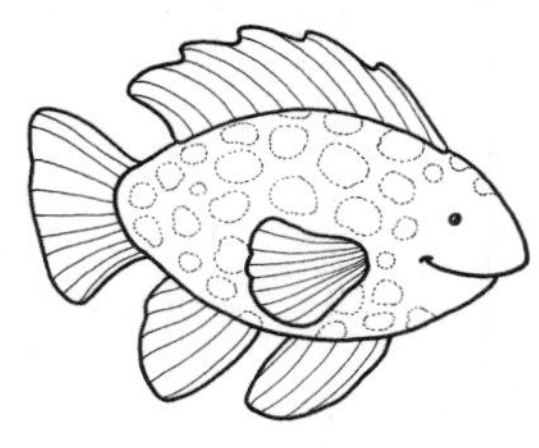

short i

Look at the picture. Then build the word.

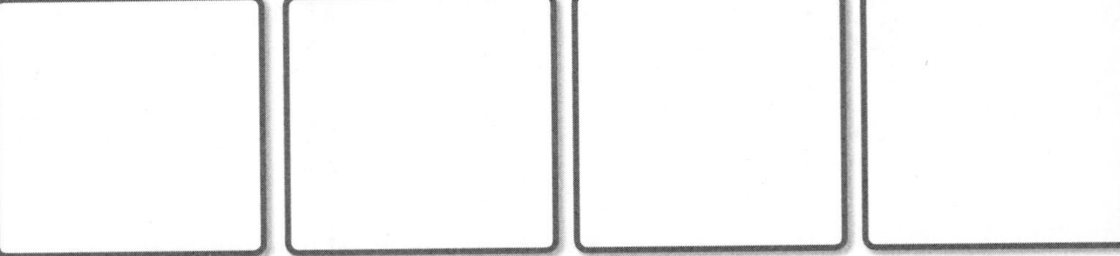

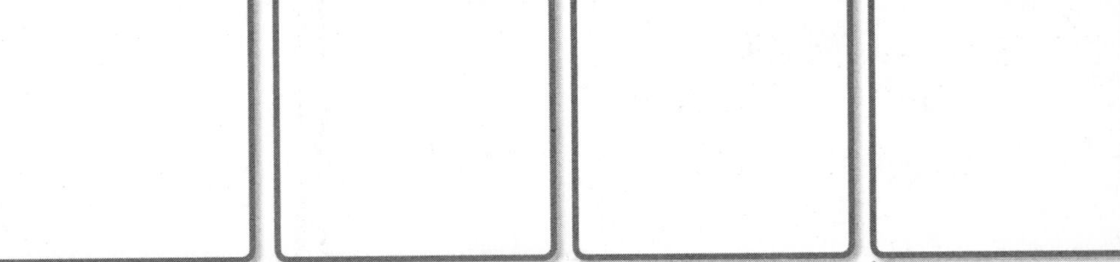

short o

Look at the picture. Then build the word.

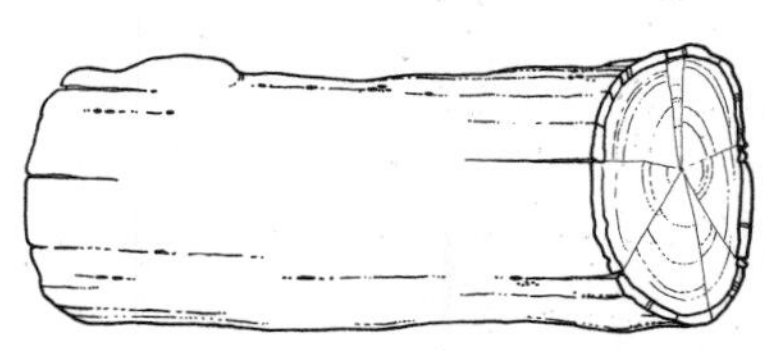

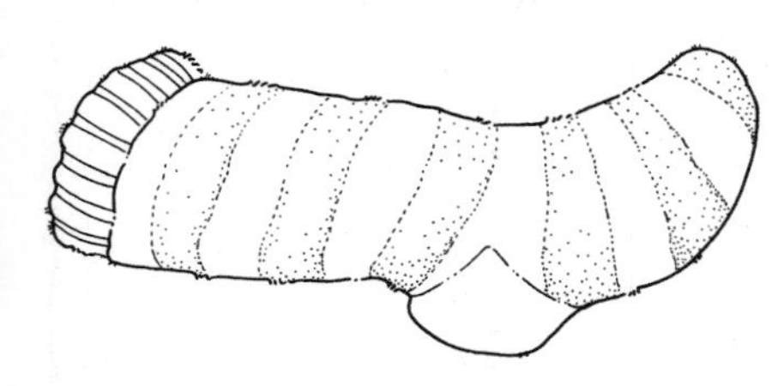

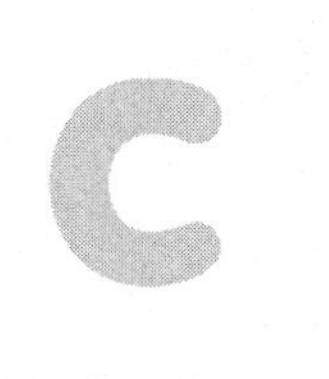

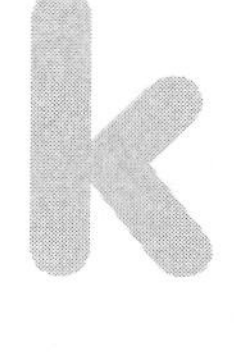

short o

Look at the picture. Then build the word.

short u

Look at the picture. Then build the word.

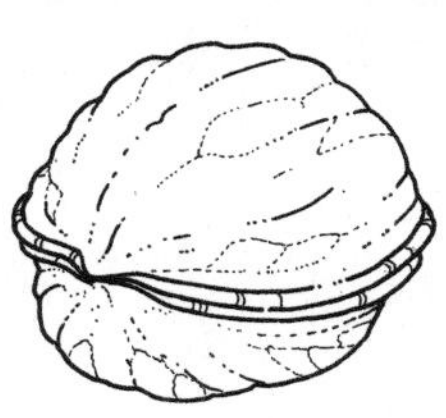

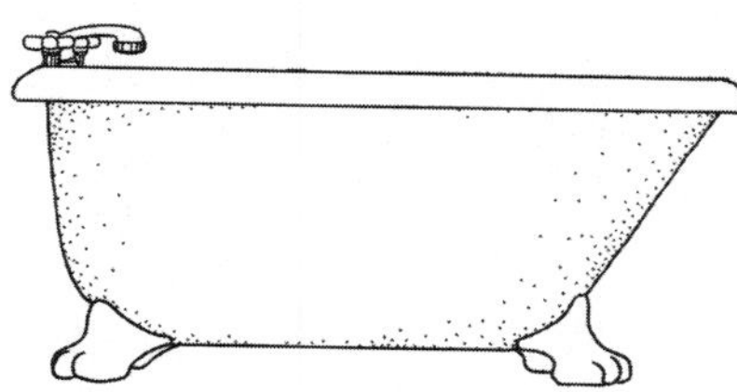

short u

Look at the picture. Then build the word.

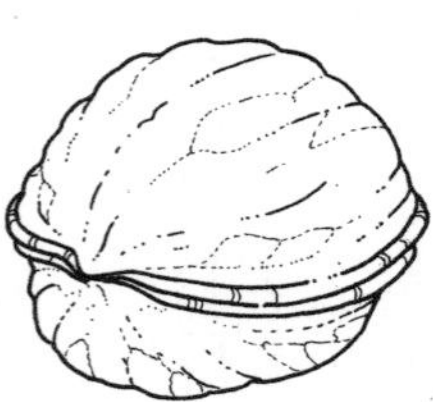

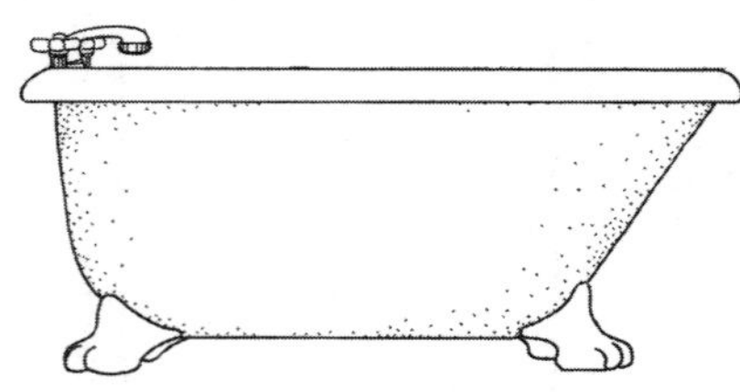

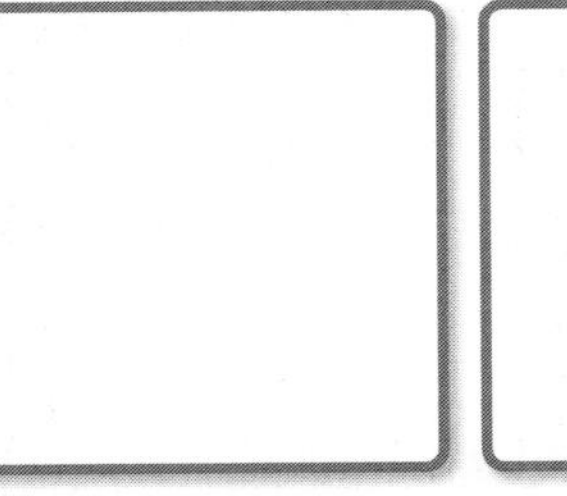
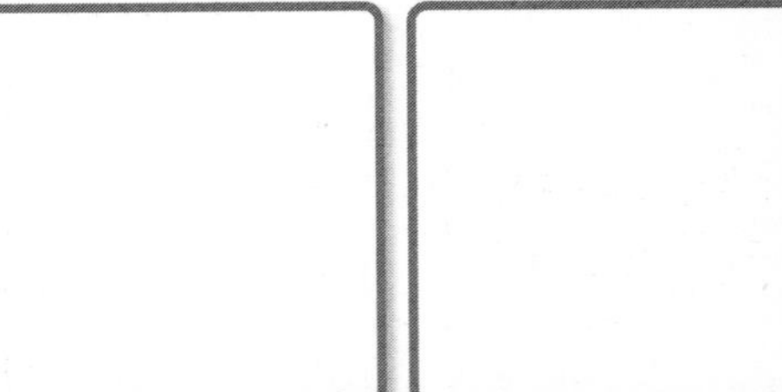

long a

Look at the picture. Then build the word.

h a y

c a k e
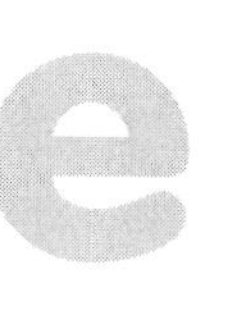

g a t e

f r a m e
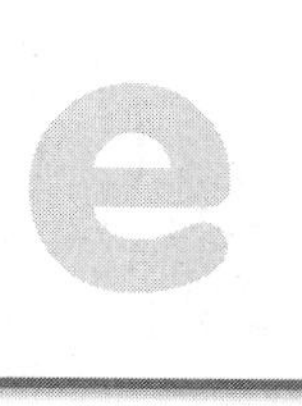

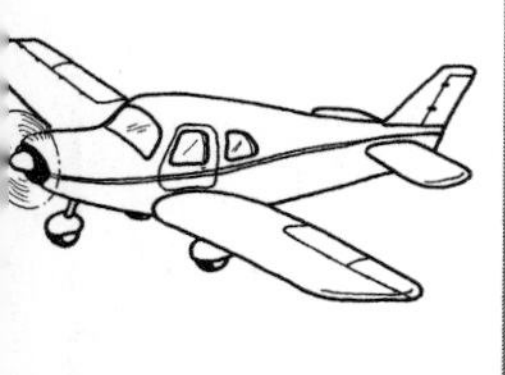

p l a n e

long a

Look at the picture. Then build the word.

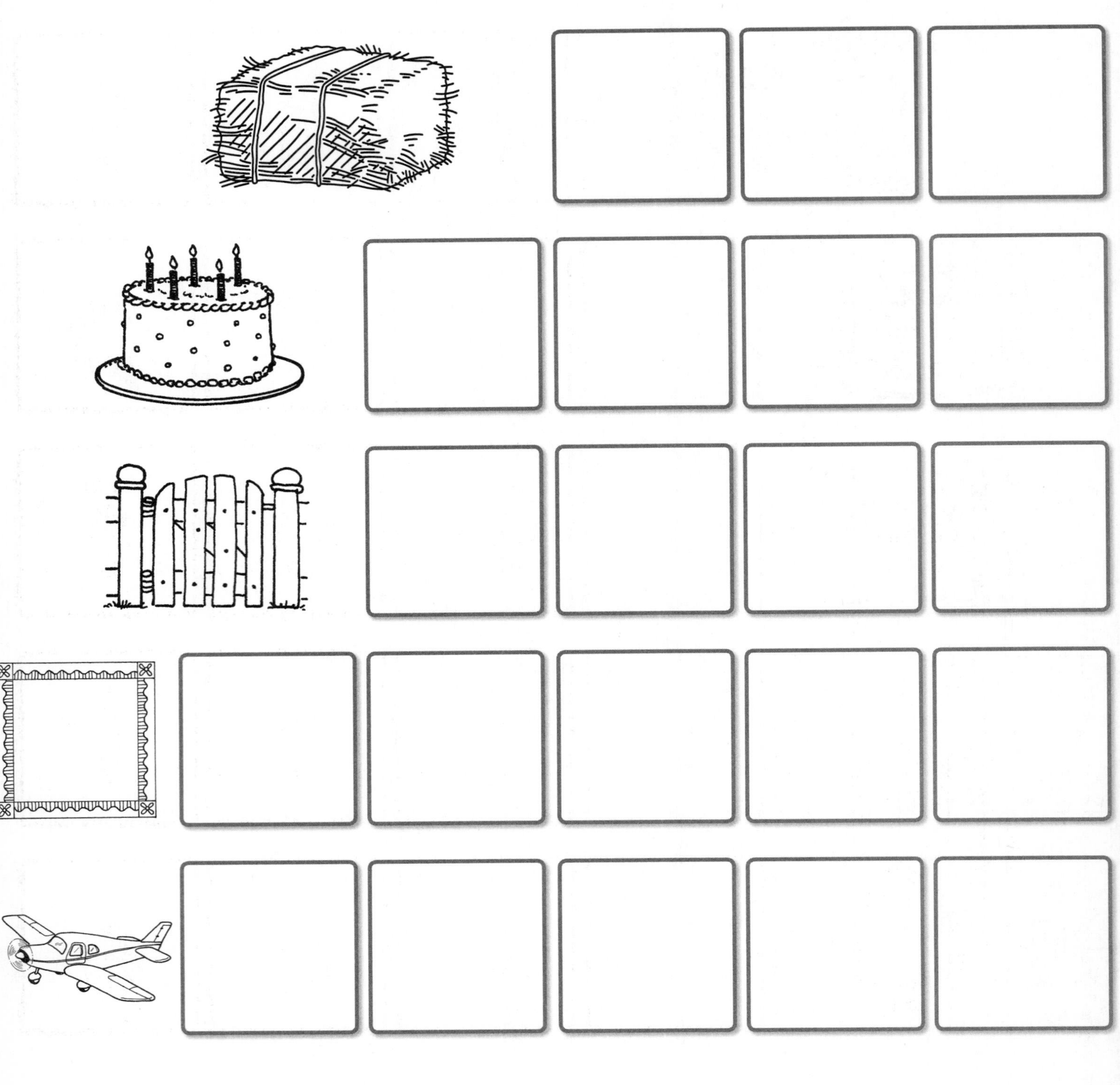

long e

Look at the picture. Then build the word.

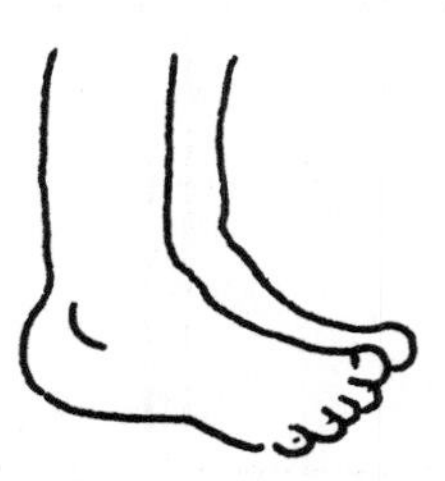

long e

Look at the picture. Then build the word.

long i

Look at the picture. Then build the word.

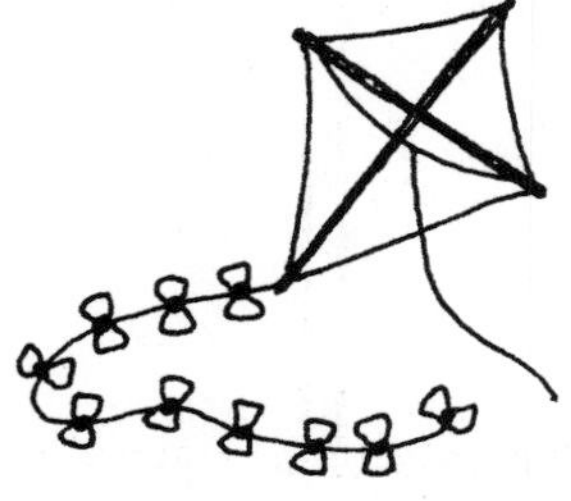

long i

Look at the picture. Then build the word.

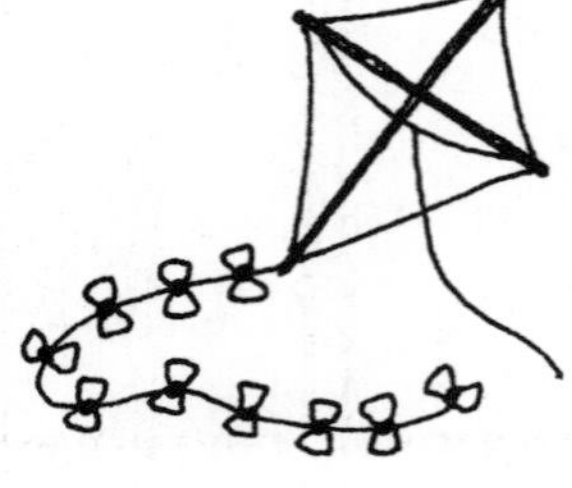

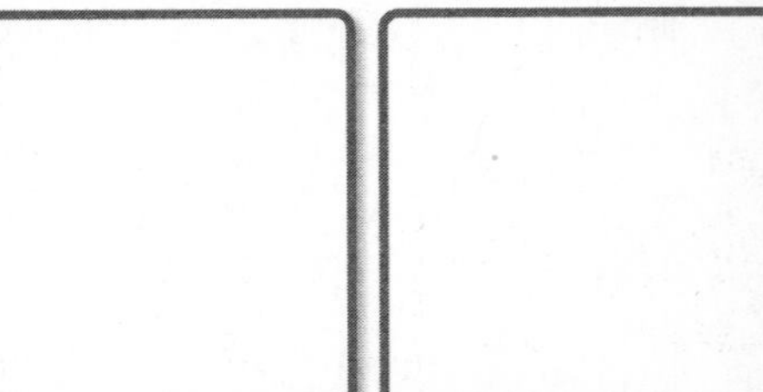

long o

Look at the picture. Then build the word.

b	o	a	t 

c	o	m	b 

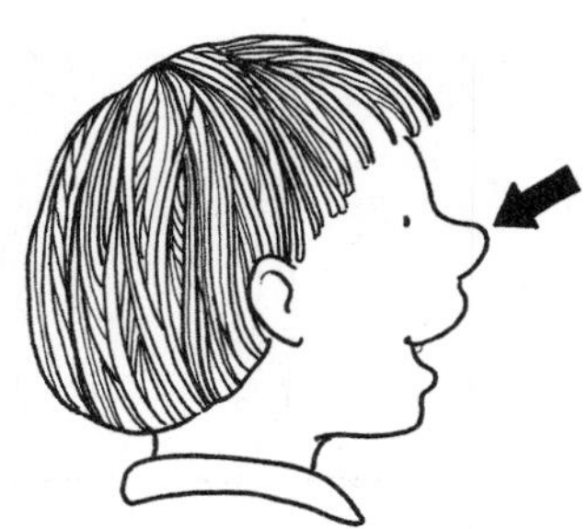

n	o	s	e 

y	o	y	o 

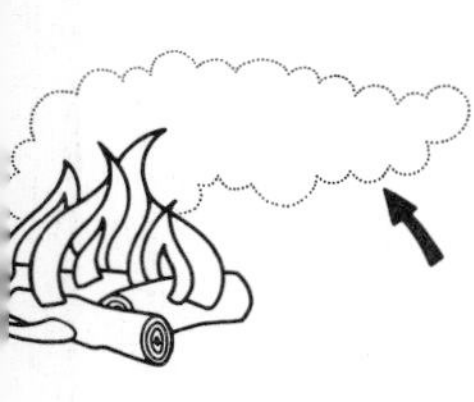

s	m	o	k	e

long o

Look at the picture. Then build the word.

long u

Look at the picture. Then build the word.

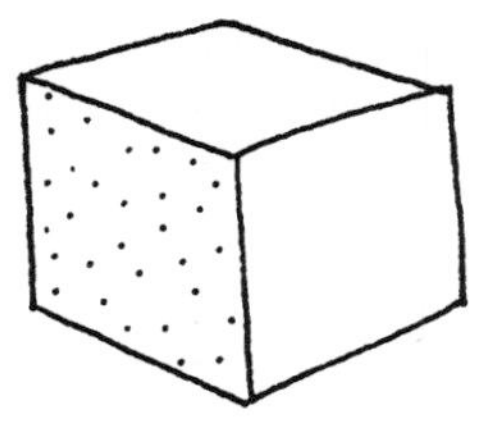

c   

m   

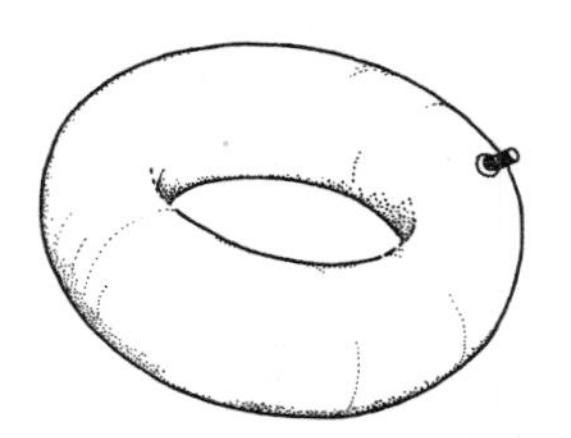

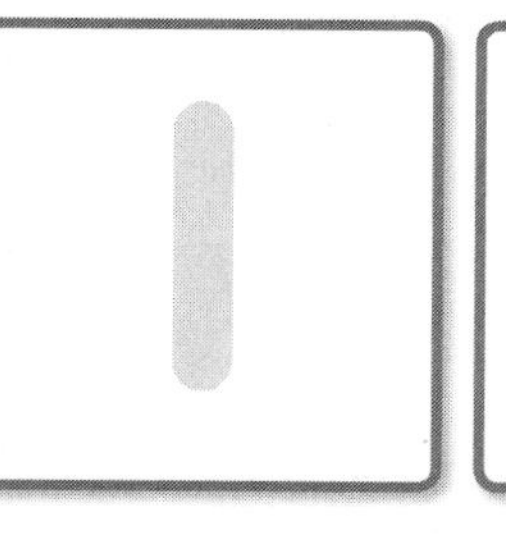   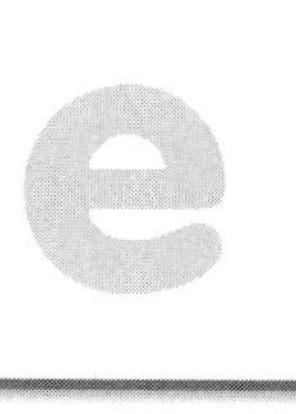

f

long u

Look at the picture. Then build the word.

-ad

Look at the picture. Then build the word.

d a d

m a d

p a d

s a d

g l a d

-ad

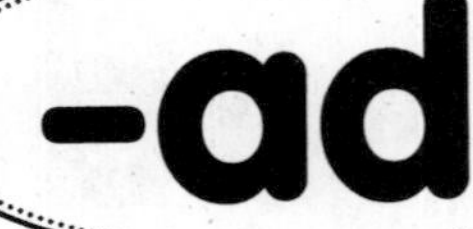

Look at the picture. Then build the word.

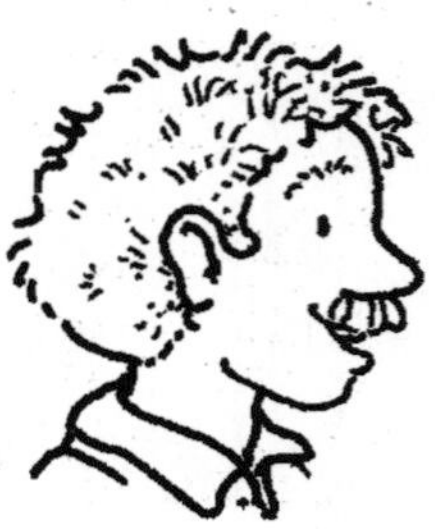

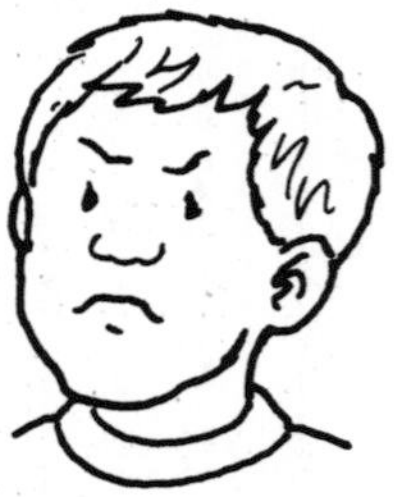

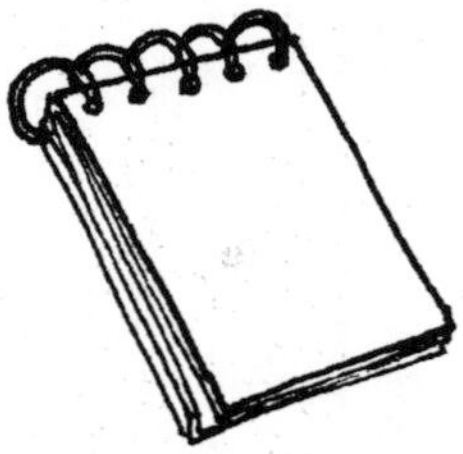

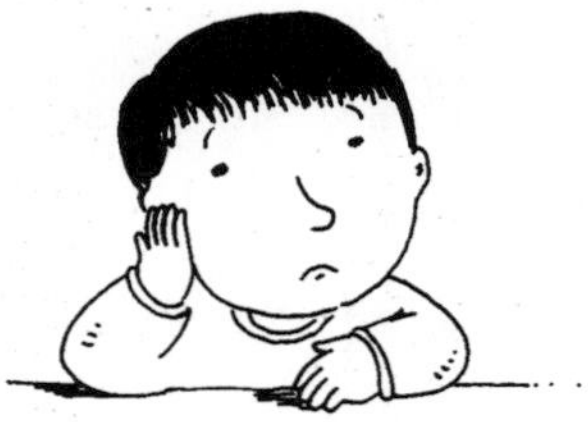

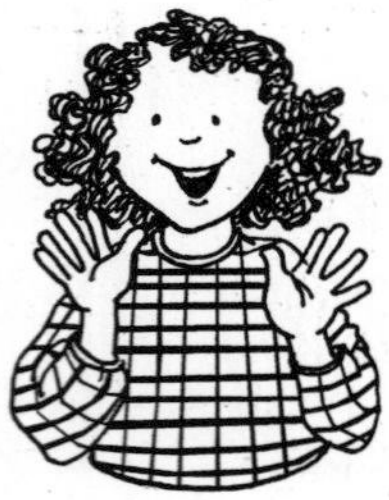

Look at the picture. Then build the word.

-ag

Look at the picture. Then build the word.

-am

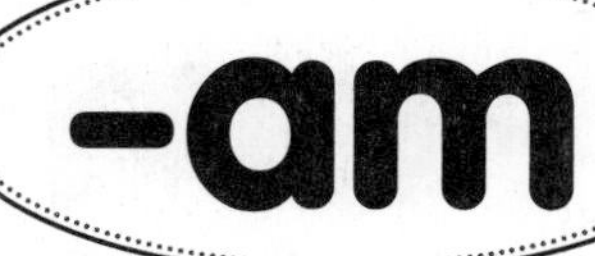

Look at the picture. Then build the word.

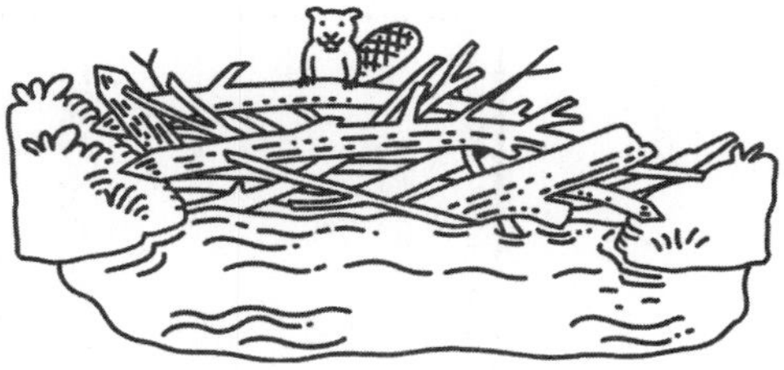

d	a	m

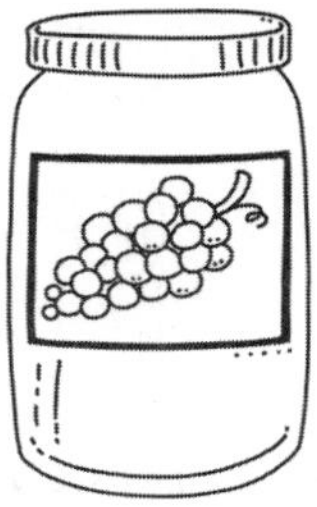

j	a	m

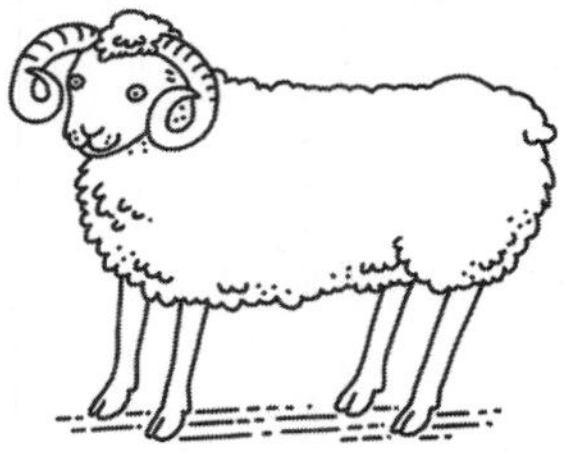

r	a	m

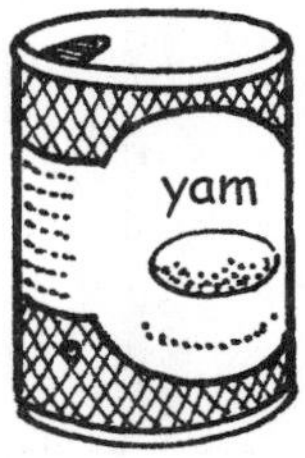

y	a	m

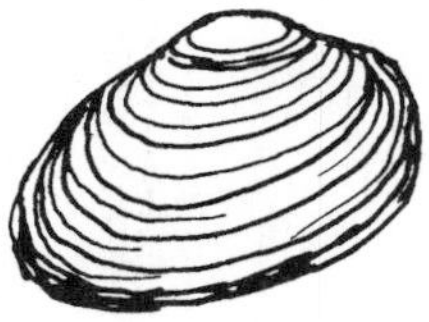

c	l	a	m

-am

Look at the picture. Then build the word.

yam

-an

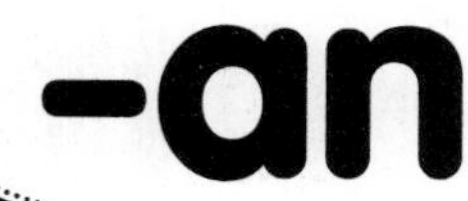

Look at the picture. Then build the word.

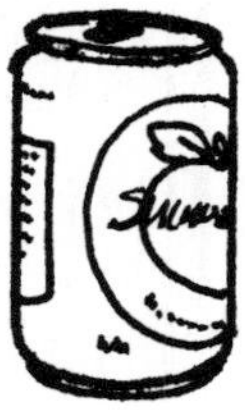

c a n

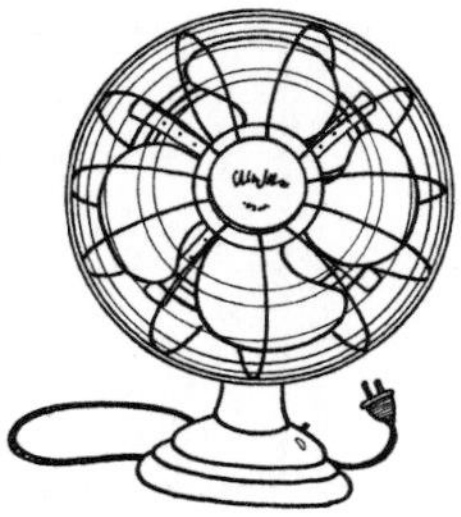

f a n

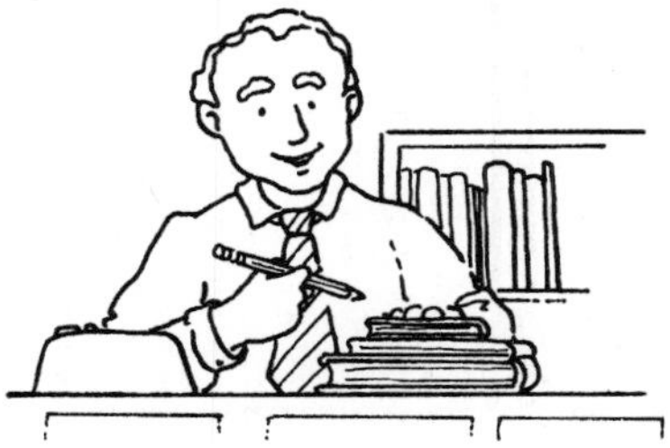

m a n

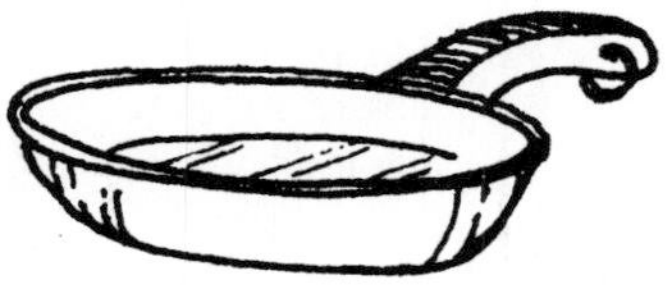

p a n

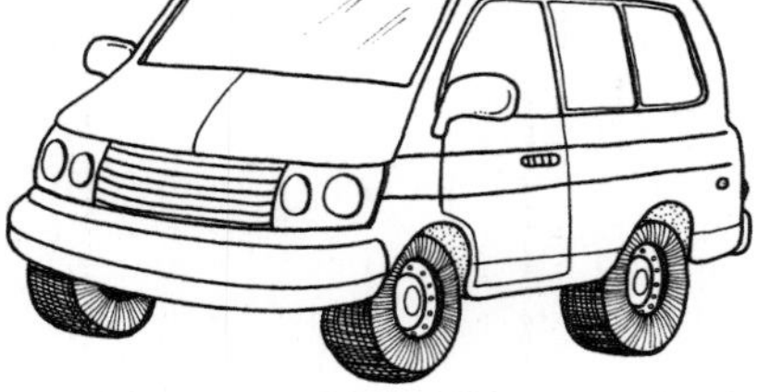

v a n

-an

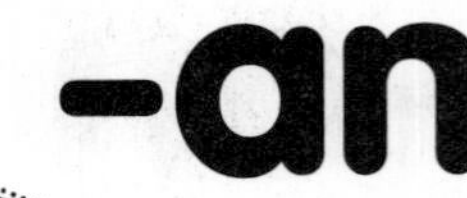

Look at the picture. Then build the word.

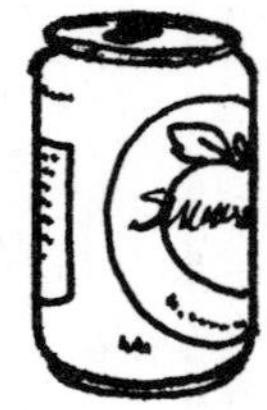

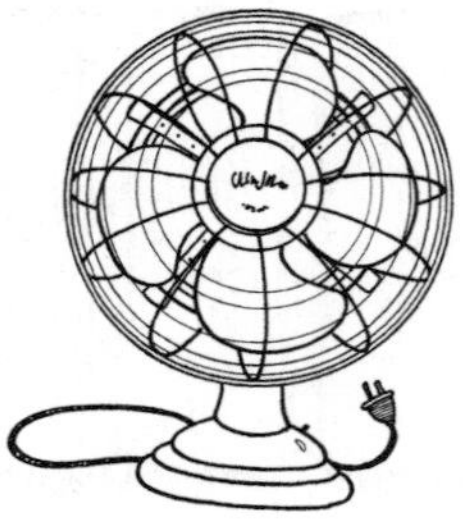

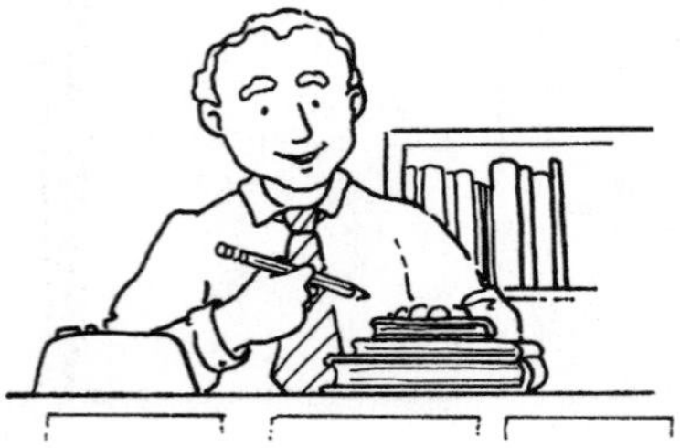

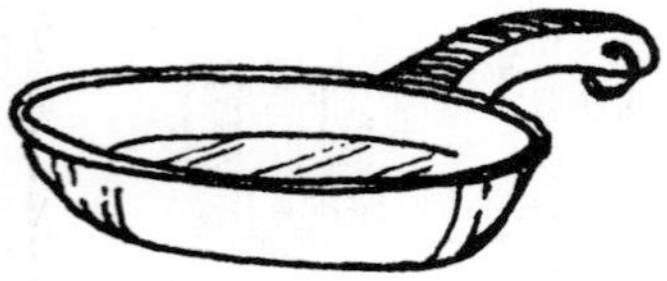

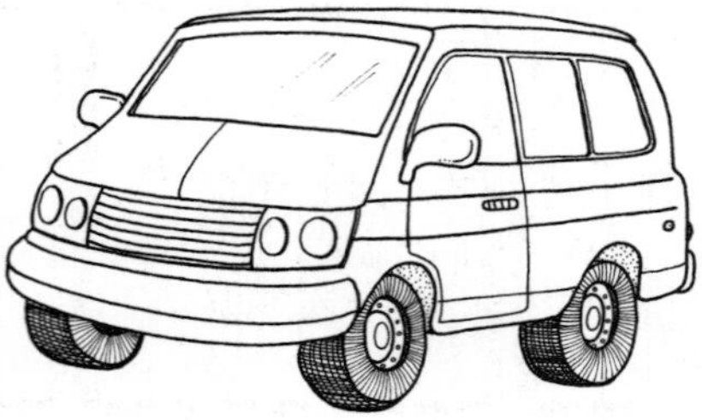

-ap

Look at the picture. Then build the word.

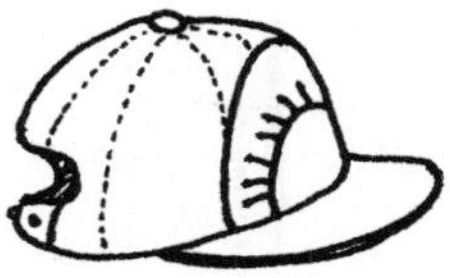

	c	a	p
	m	a	p
	n	a	p
	t	a	p
c	l	a	p

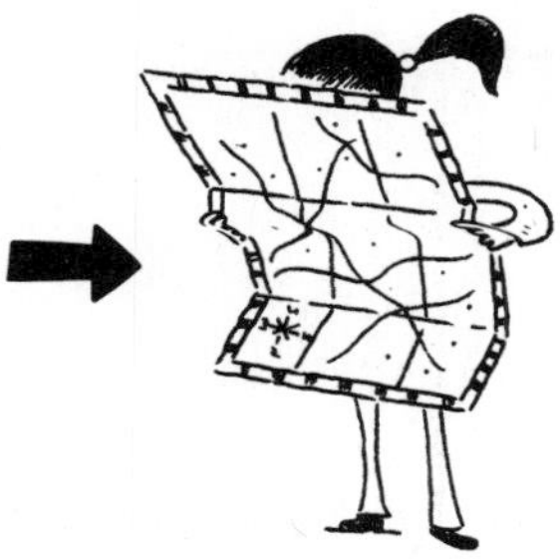

-ap

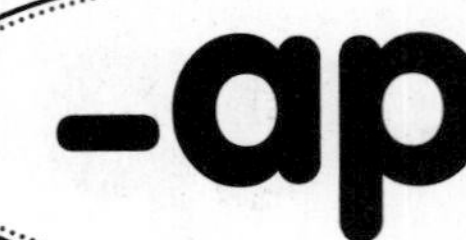

Look at the picture. Then build the word.

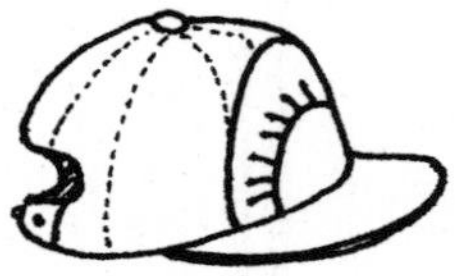

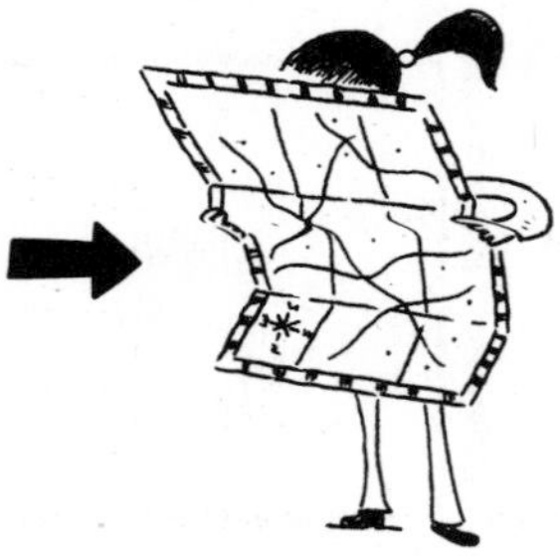

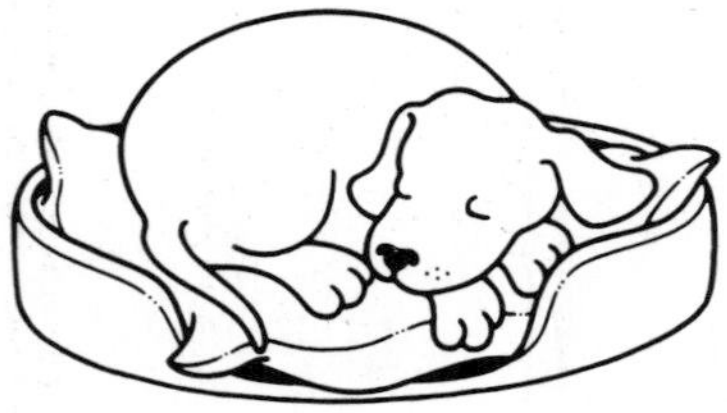

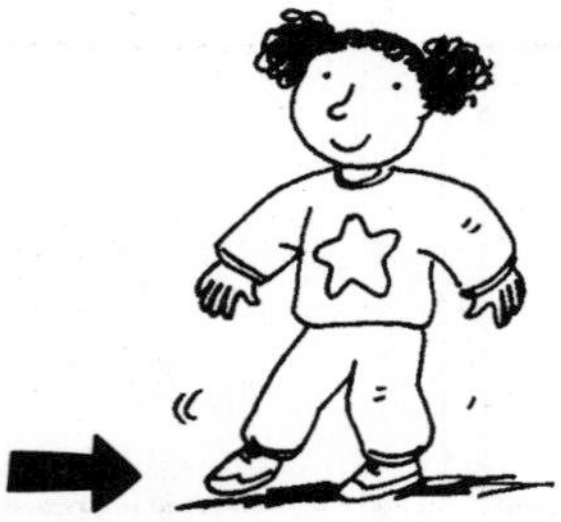

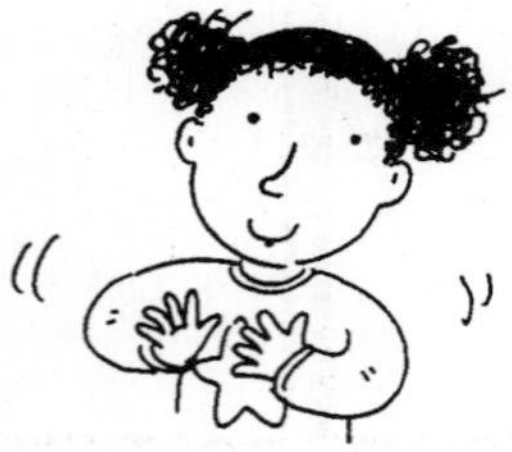

-at

Look at the picture. Then build the word.

	b	a	t
	c	a	t
	h	a	t
 WELCOME	m	a	
	r		

-at

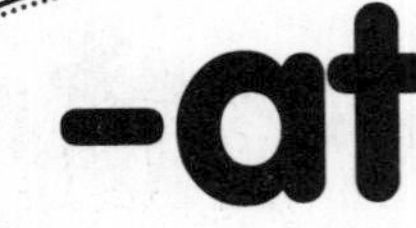

Look at the picture. Then build the word.

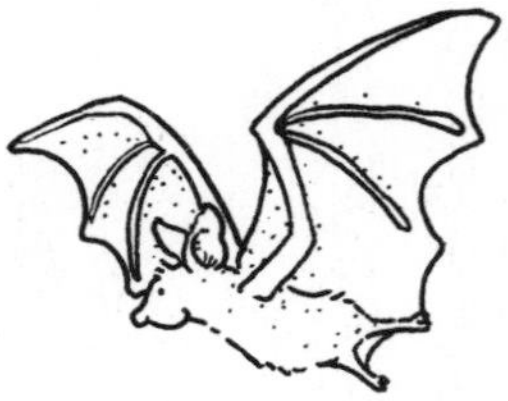

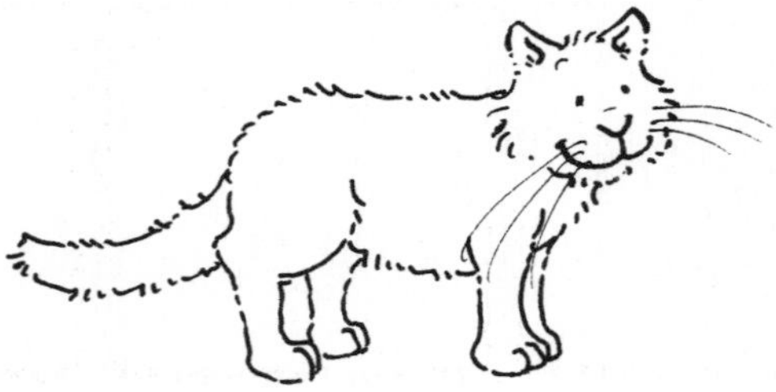

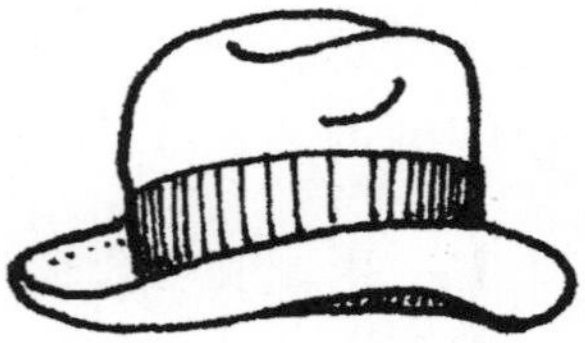

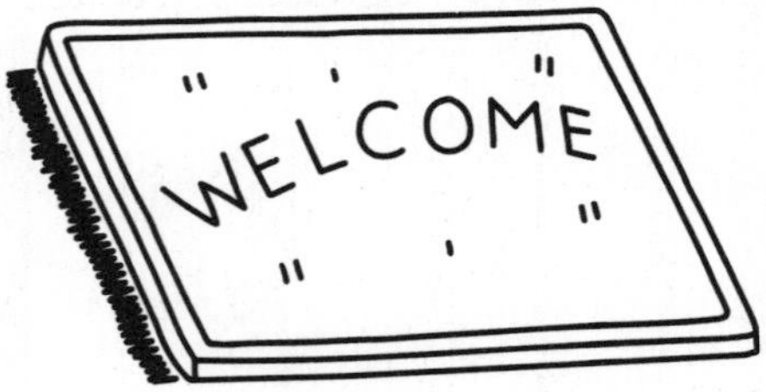

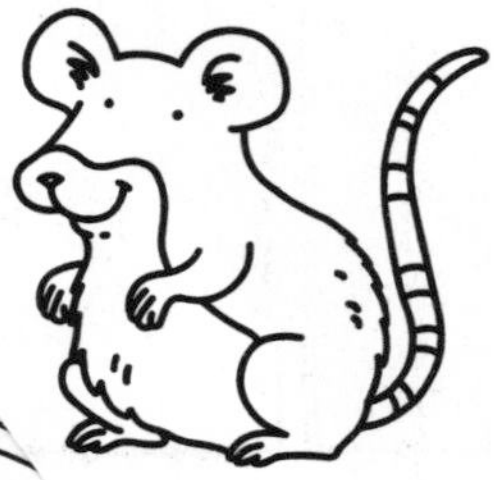

-aw

Look at the picture. Then build the word.

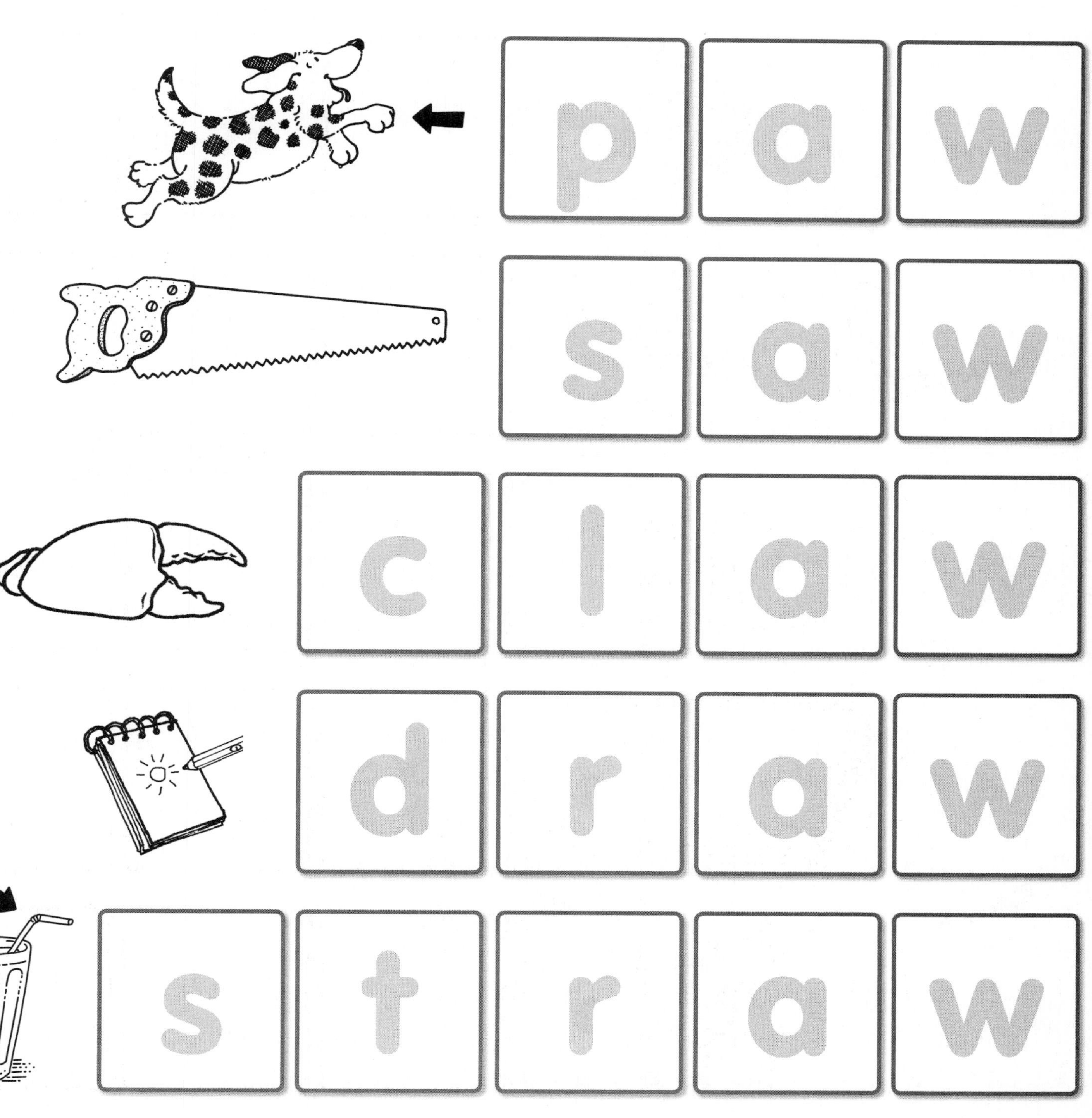

-aw

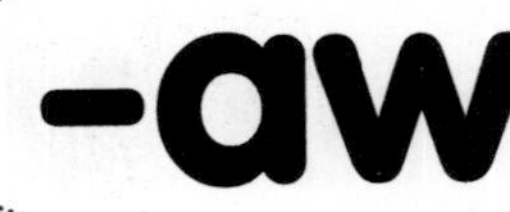

Look at the picture. Then build the word.

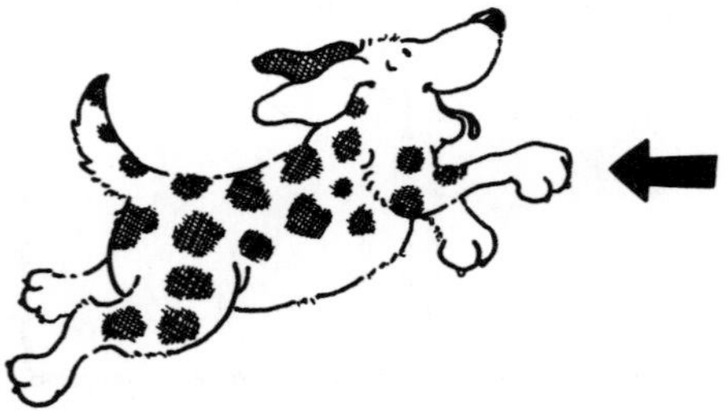

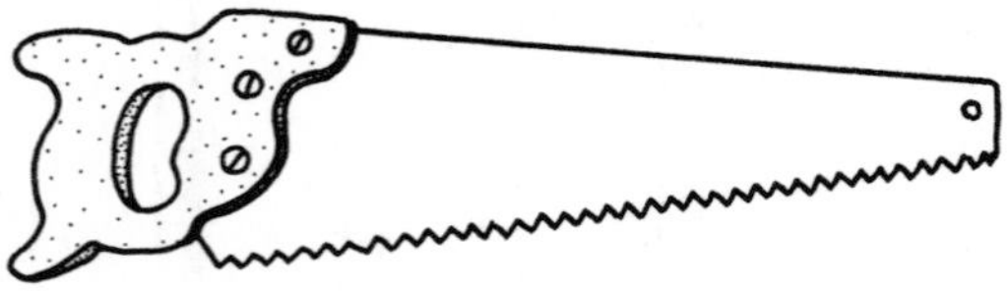

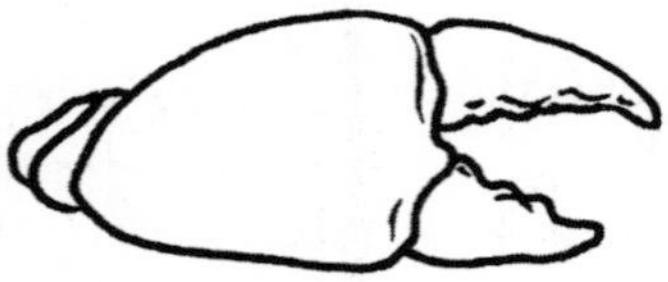

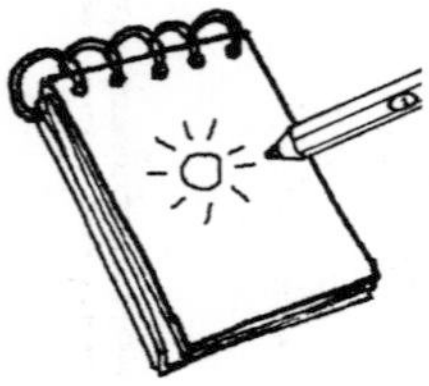

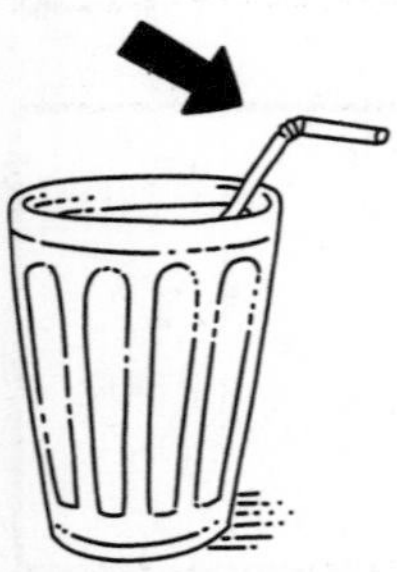

-ay

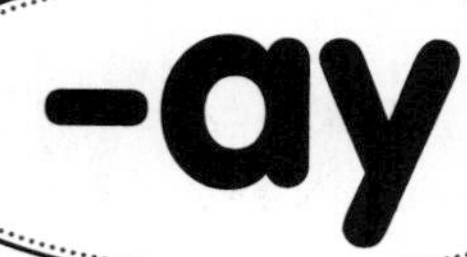

Look at the picture. Then build the word.

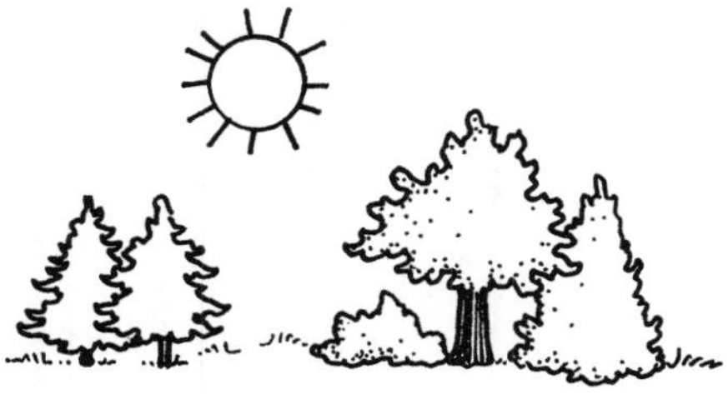

d a y

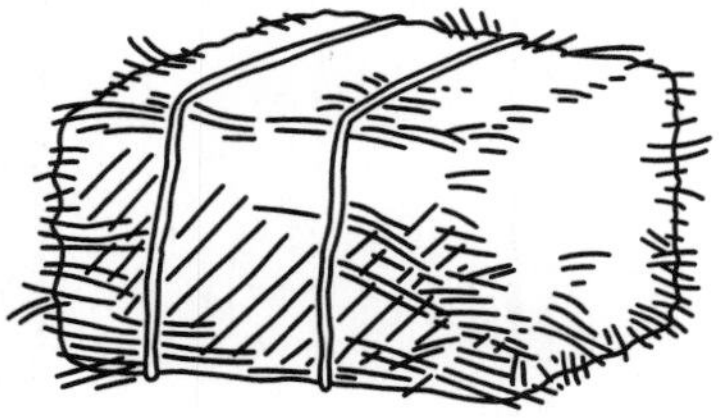

h a y

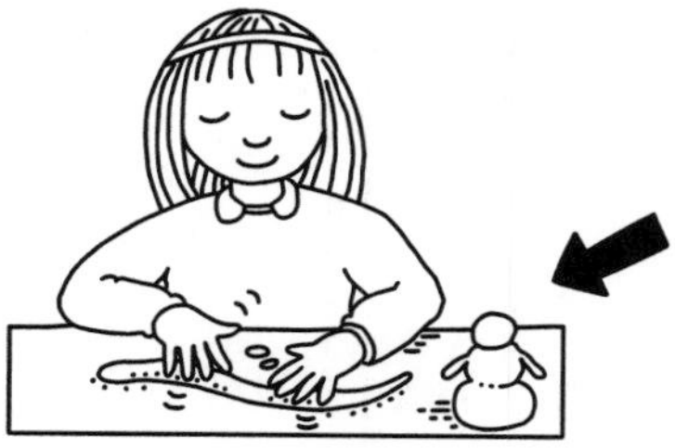

c l a y

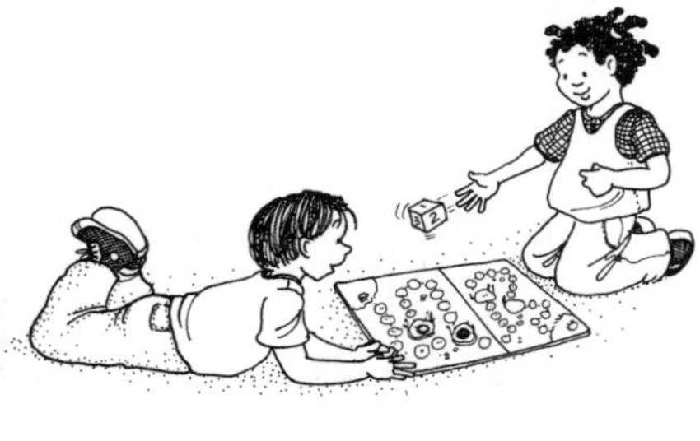

p l a y

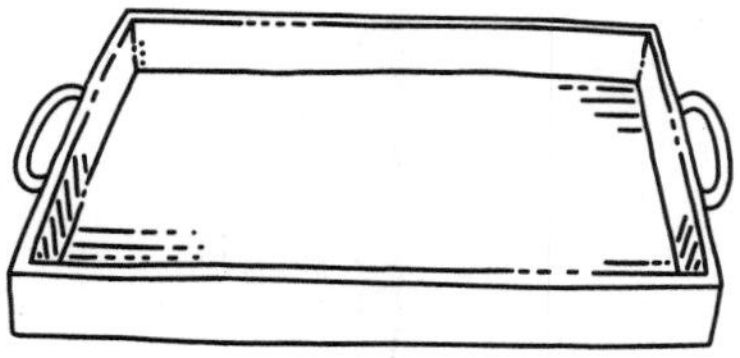

t r a y

-ay

Look at the picture. Then build the word.

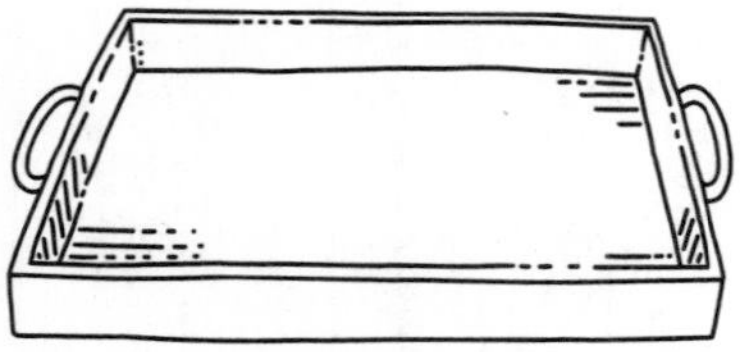

-ace

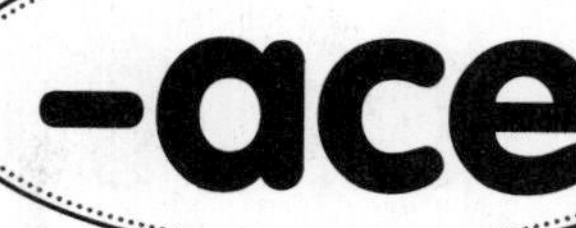

Look at the picture. Then build the word.

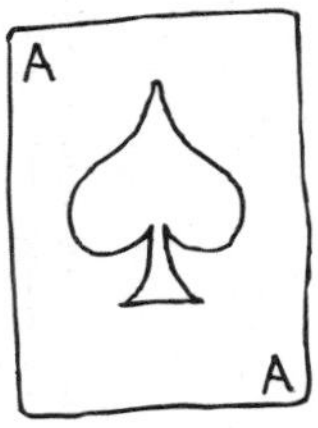

a c e

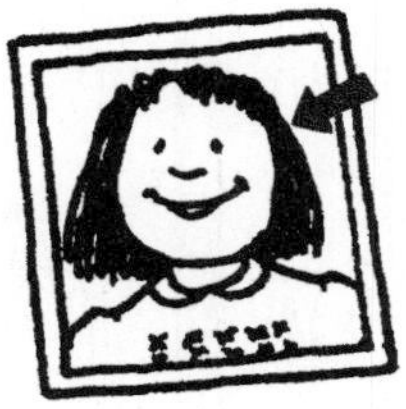

f a c e

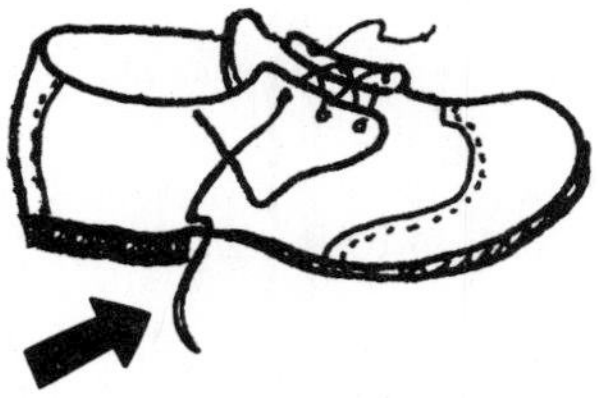

l a c e

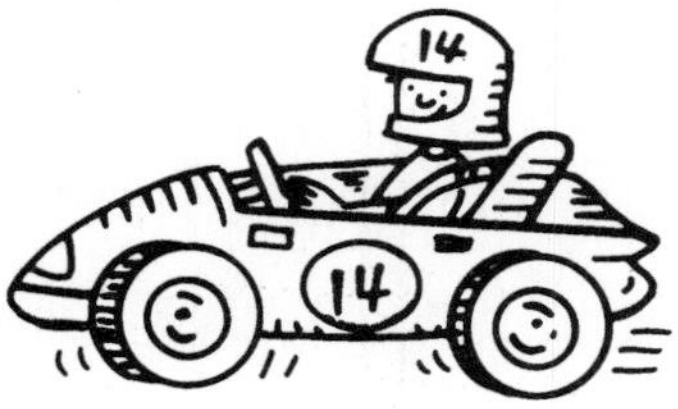

r a c e

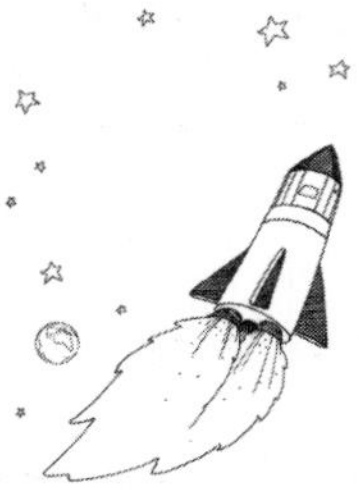

s p a c e

-ace

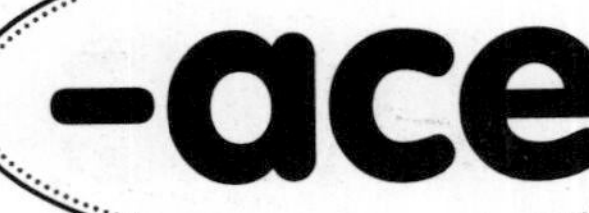

Look at the picture. Then build the word.

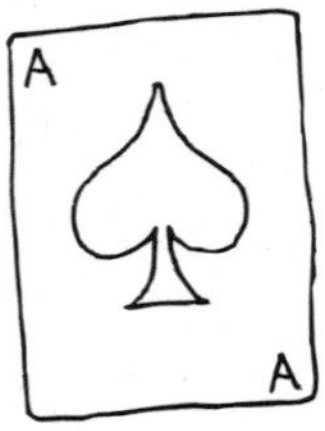

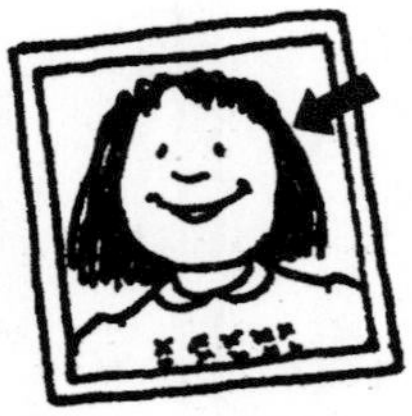

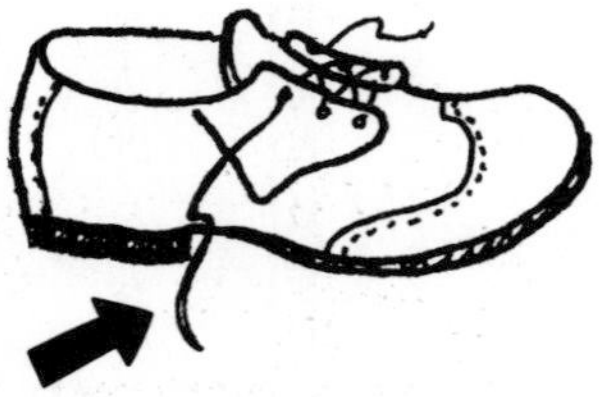

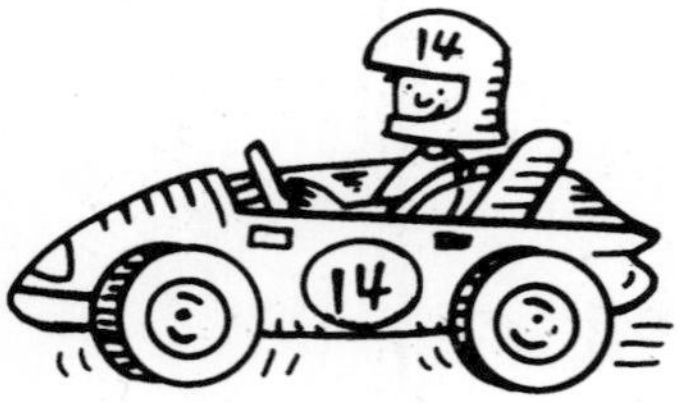

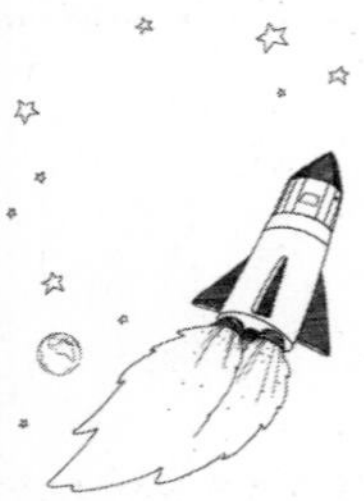

-ack

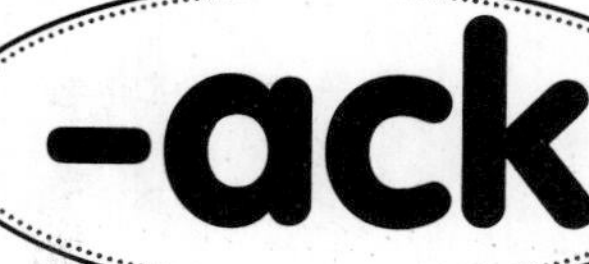

Look at the picture. Then build the word.

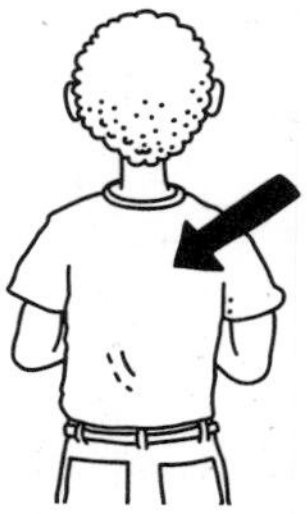

b	a	c	k

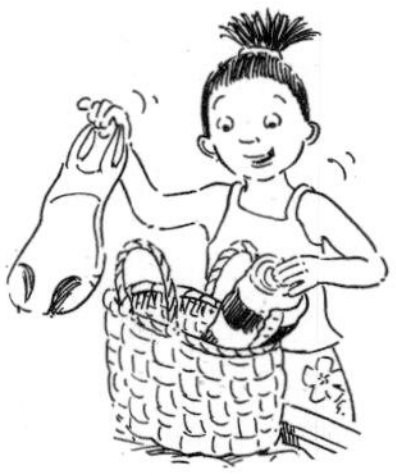

p	a	c	k

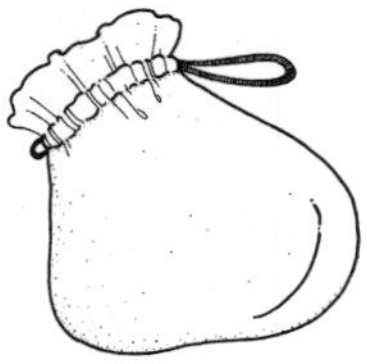

s	a	c	k

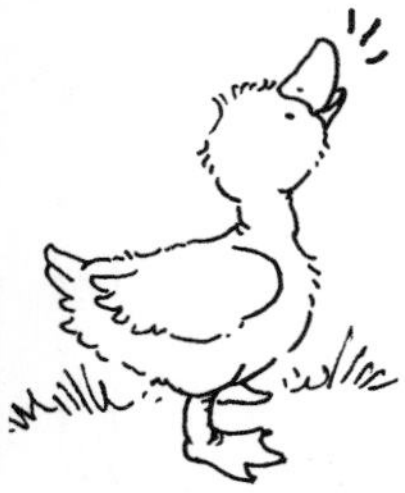

q	u	a	c	k

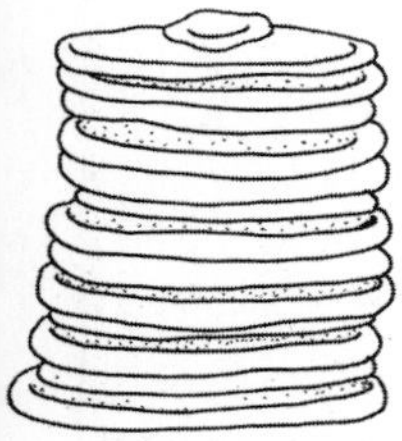

s	t	a	c	k

-ack

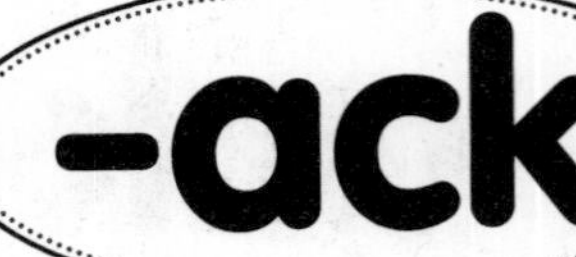

Look at the picture. Then build the word.

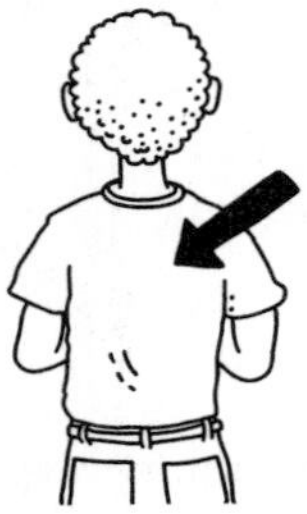

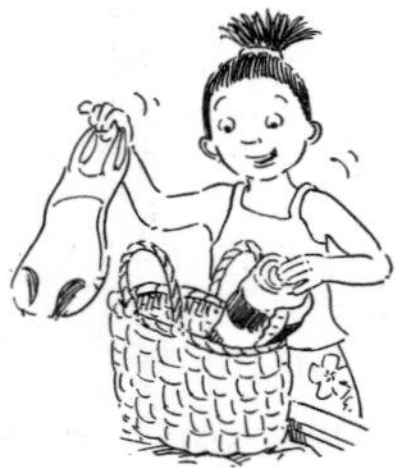

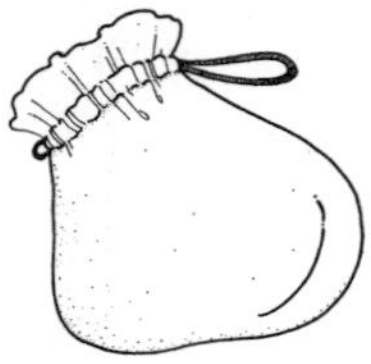

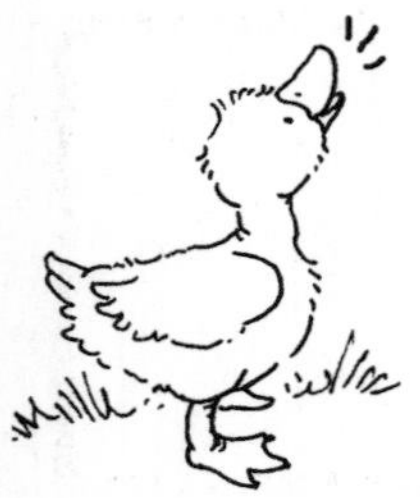

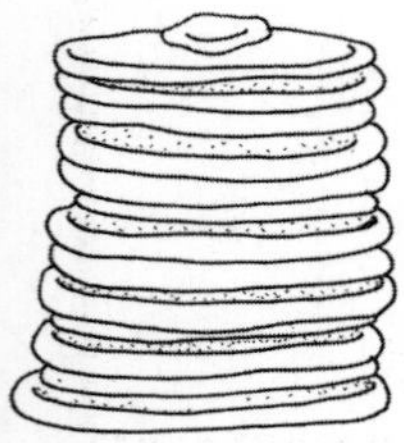

-ail

Look at the picture. Then build the word.

   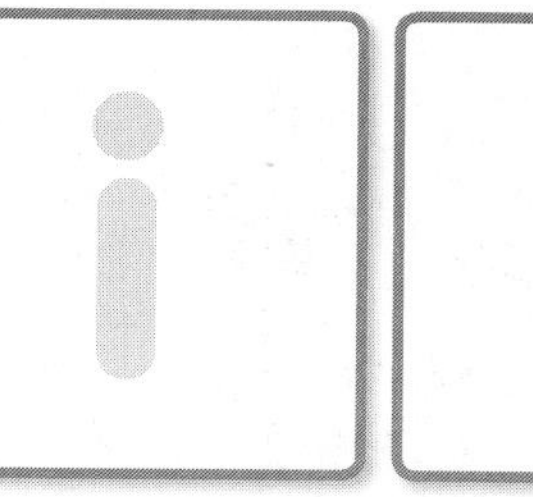 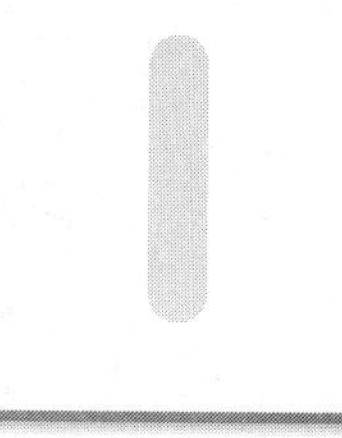

m a i l

n a i l

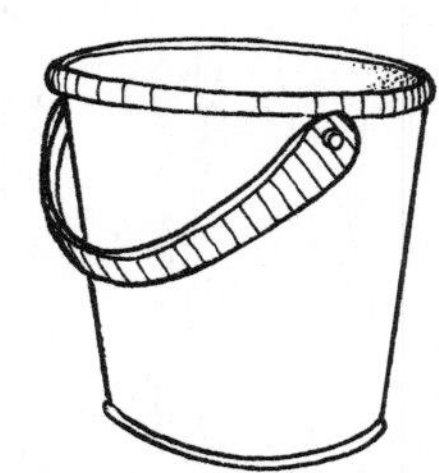  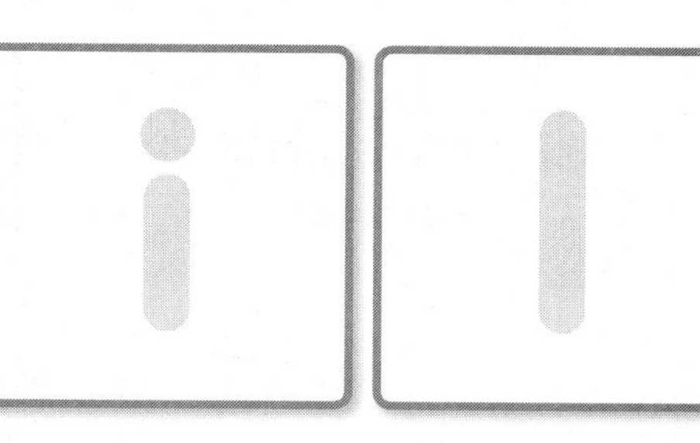

p a i l

  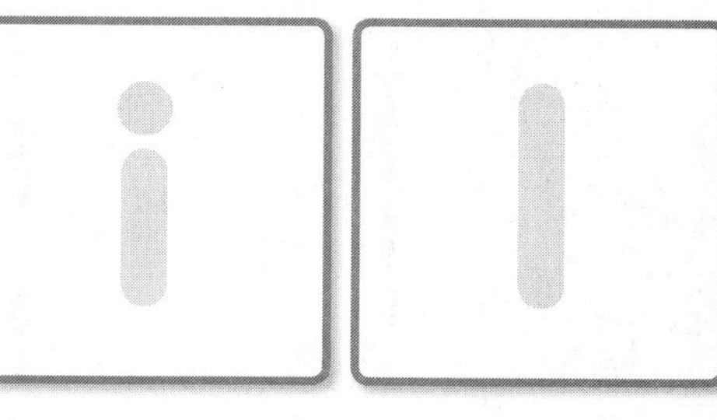

q u a i l

s n a i l

-ail

Look at the picture. Then build the word.

Look at the picture. Then build the word.

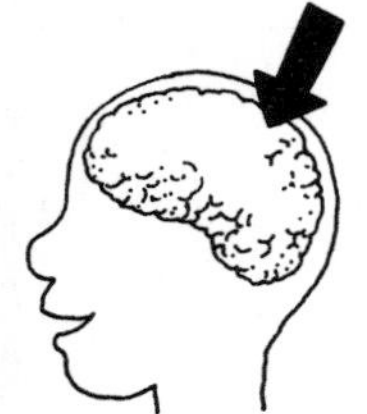
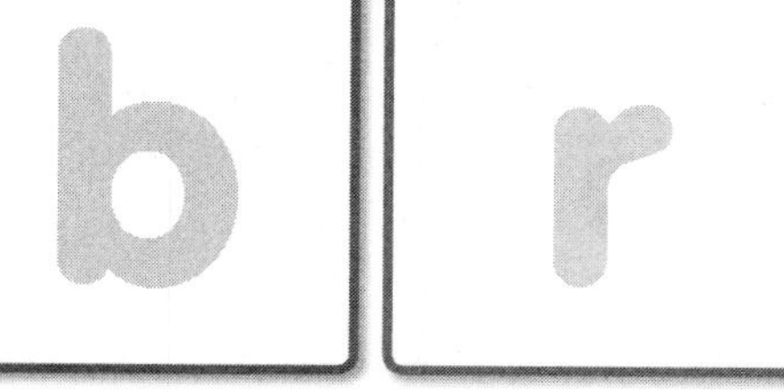

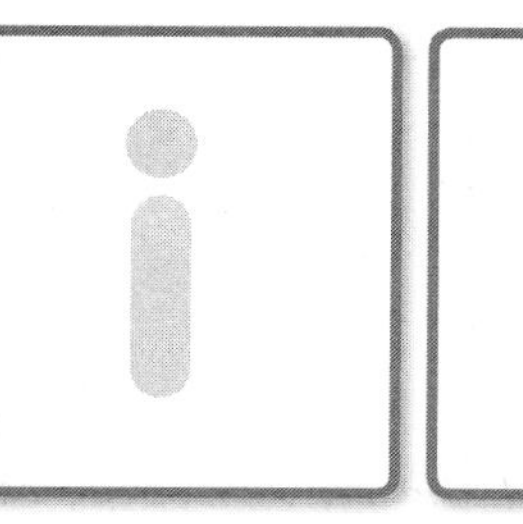

-ain

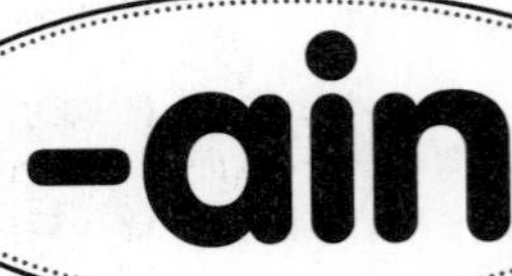

Look at the picture. Then build the word.

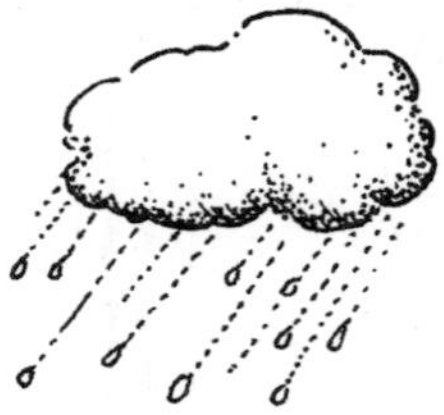

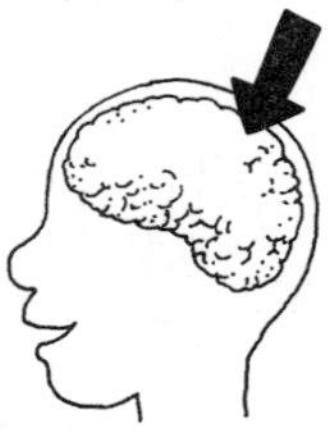

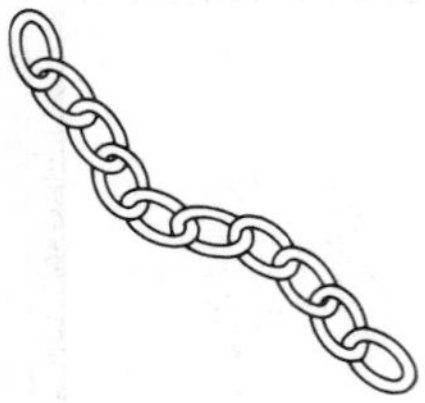

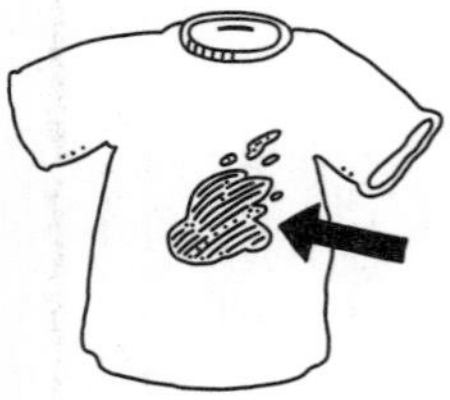

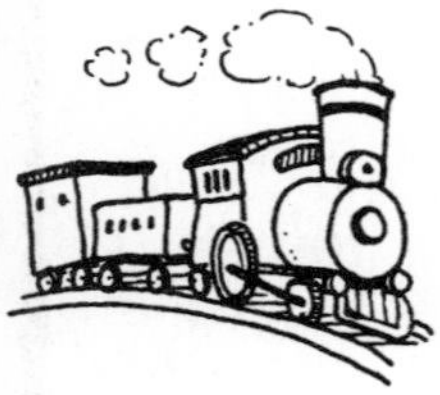

-ake

Look at the picture. Then build the word.

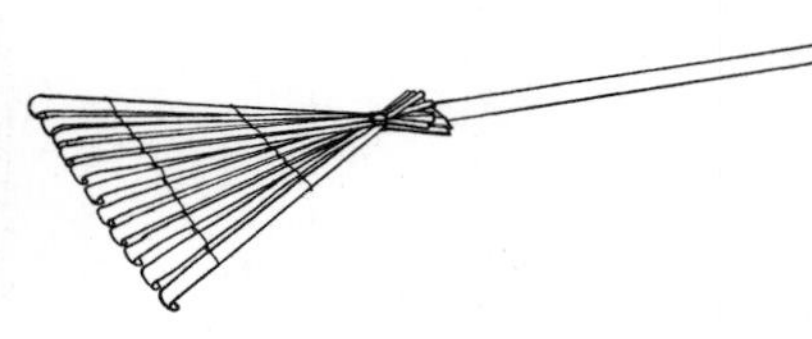

-ake

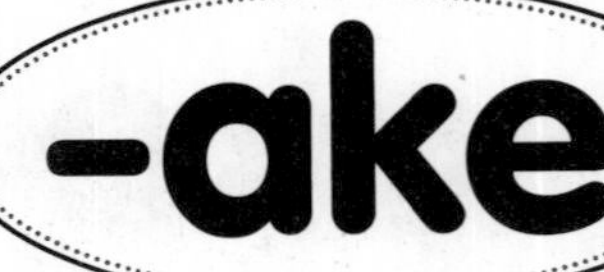

Look at the picture. Then build the word.

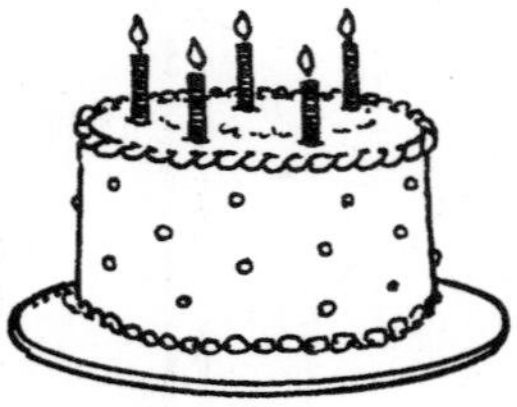

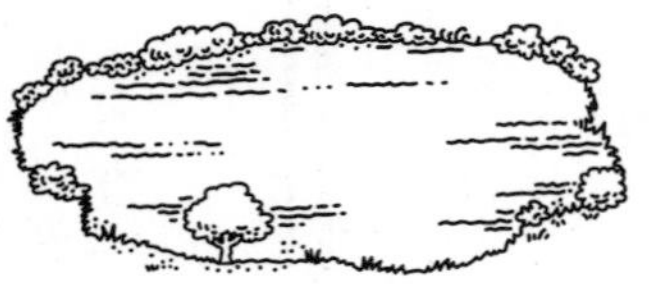

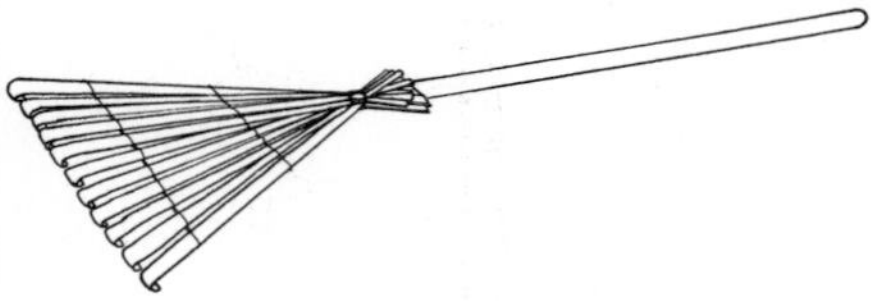

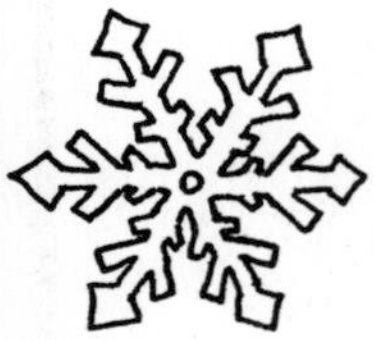

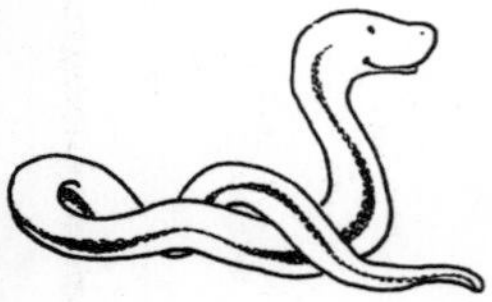

-ame

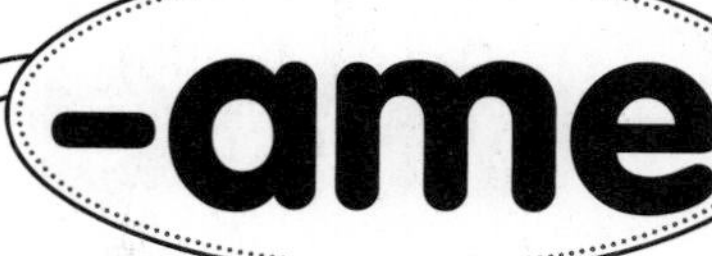

Look at the picture. Then build the word.

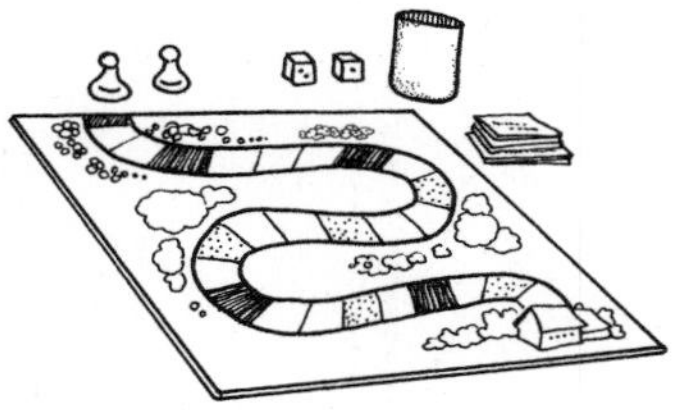

g	a	m	e

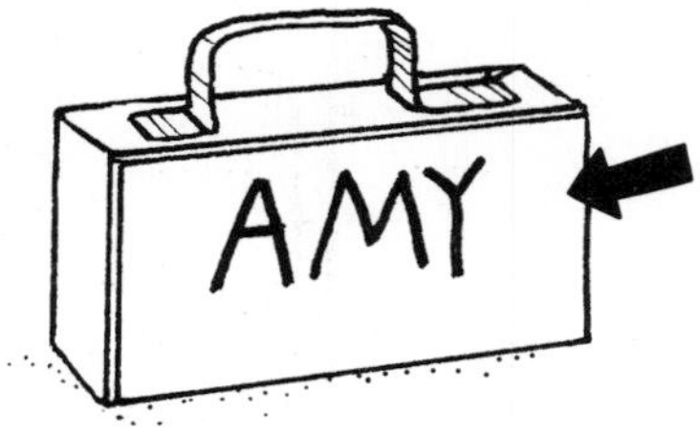

n	a	m	e

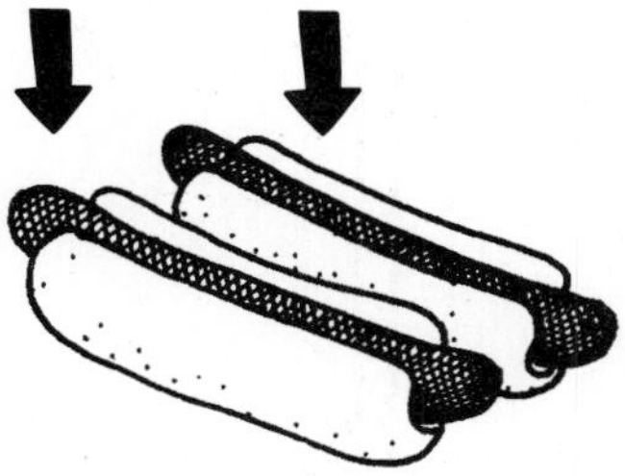

s	a	m	e

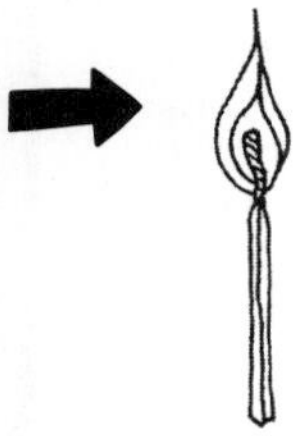

f	l	a	m	e

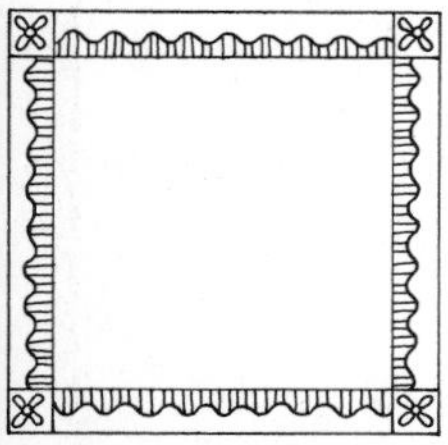

f	r	a	m	e

Look at the picture. Then build the word.

AMY

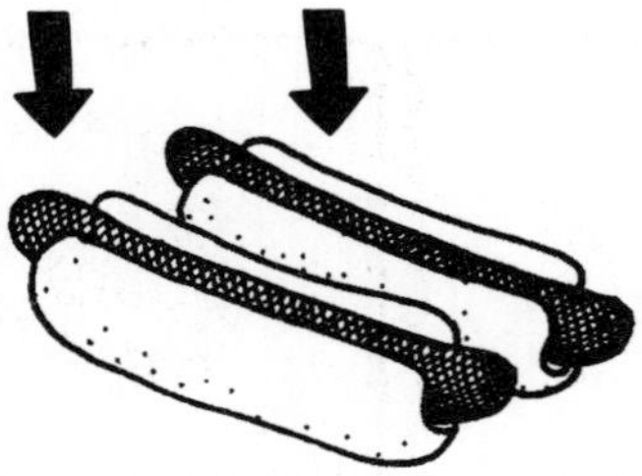

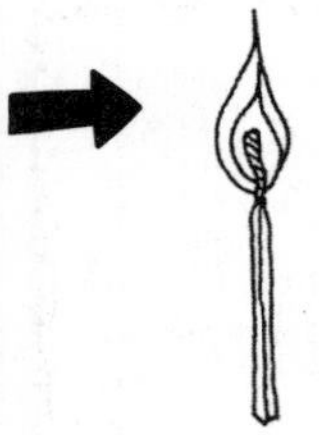

Look at the picture. Then build the word.

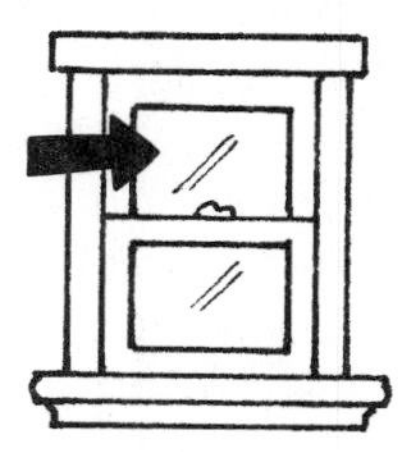

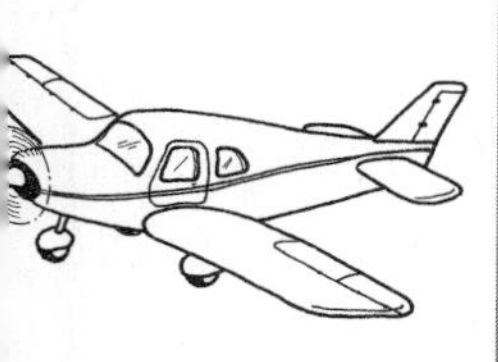

-ane

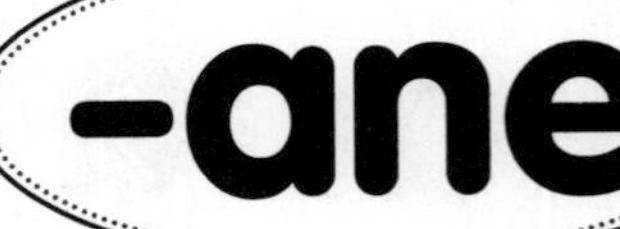

Look at the picture. Then build the word.

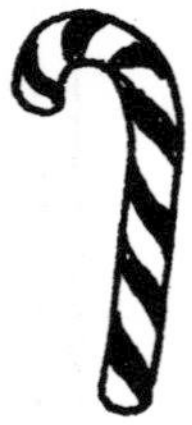

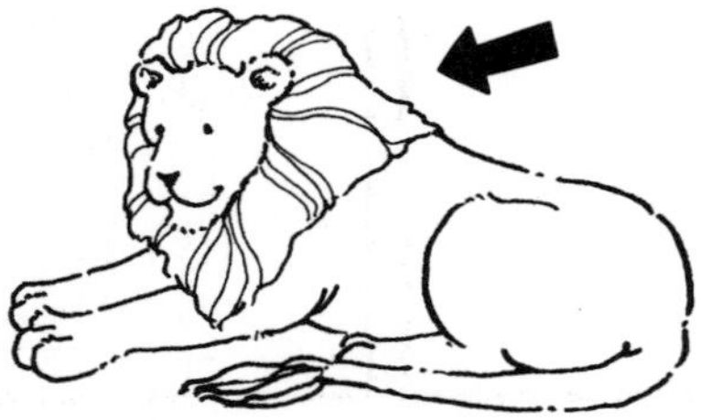

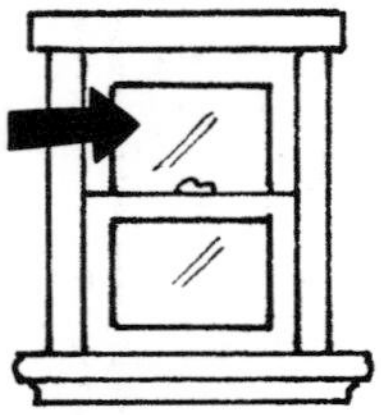

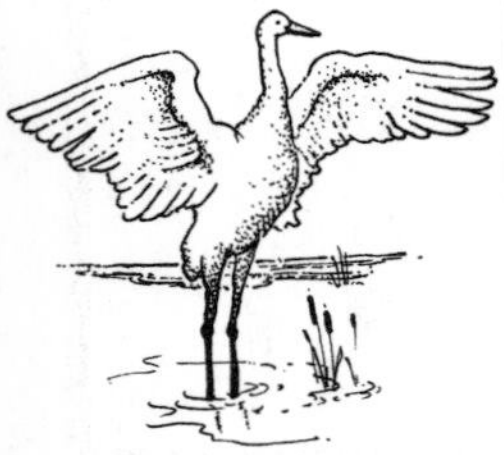

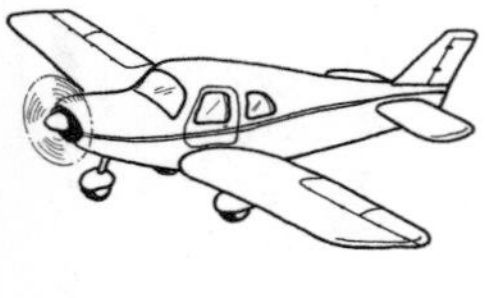

Look at the picture. Then build the word.

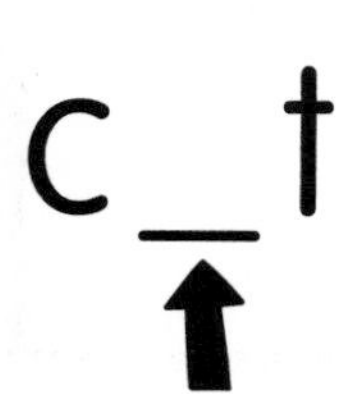

-ank

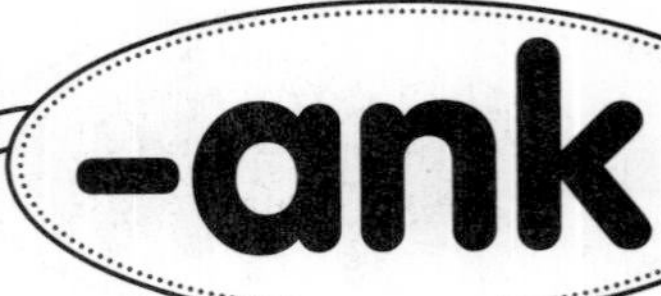

Look at the picture. Then build the word.

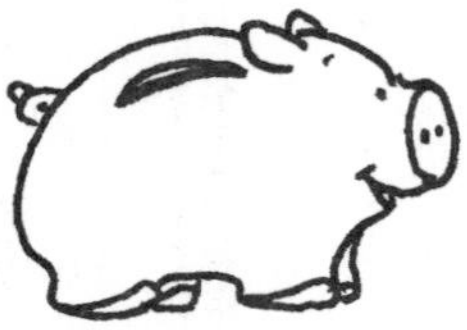

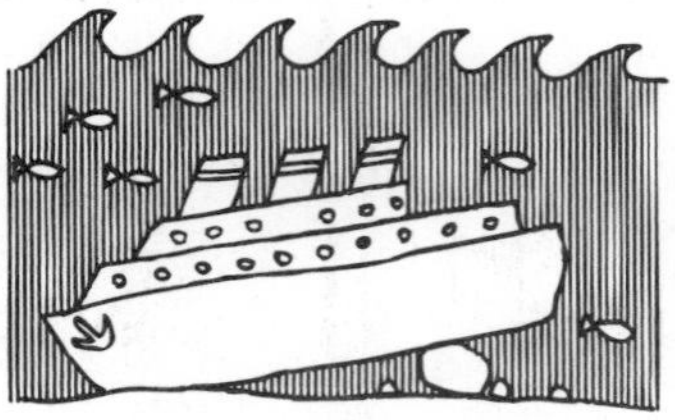

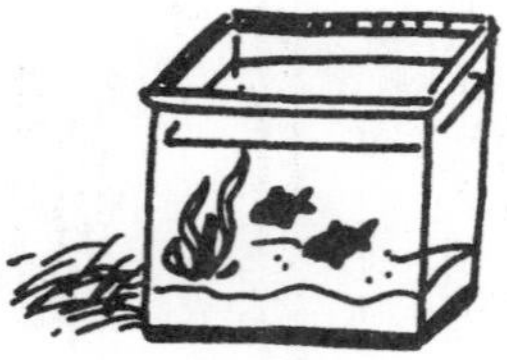

c _ t

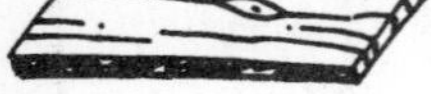

Look at the picture. Then build the word.

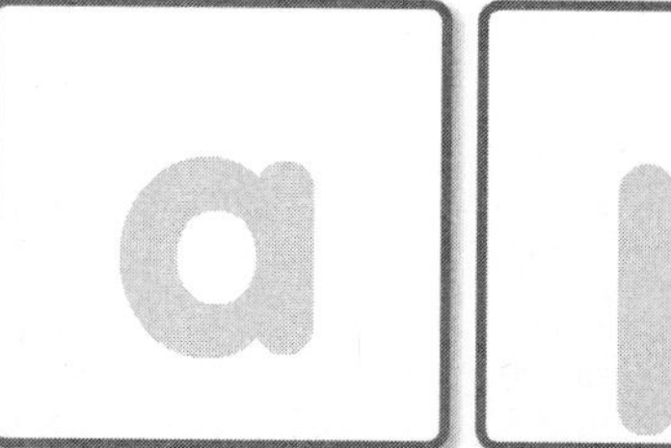

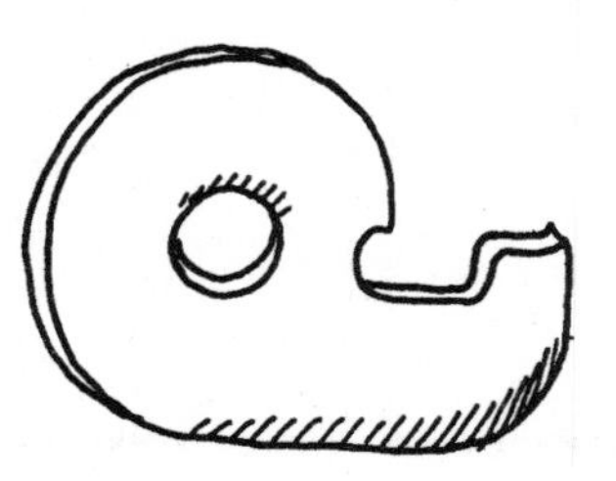

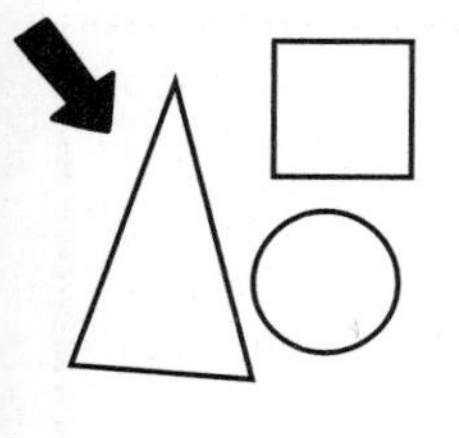

-ape

Look at the picture. Then build the word.

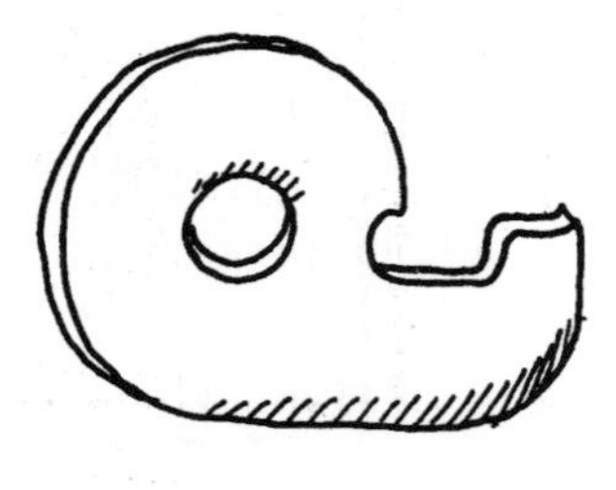

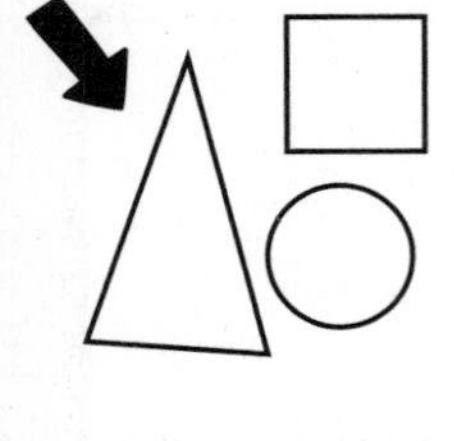

-art

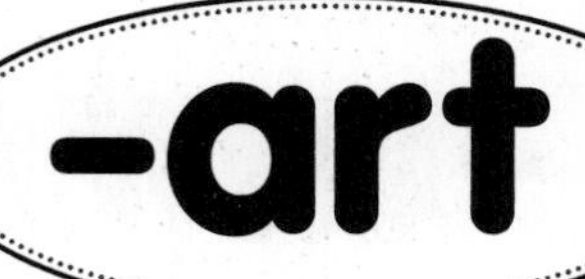

Look at the picture. Then build the word.

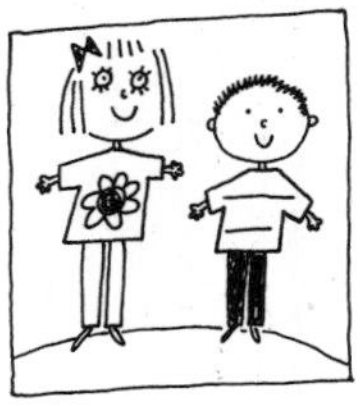

a r t

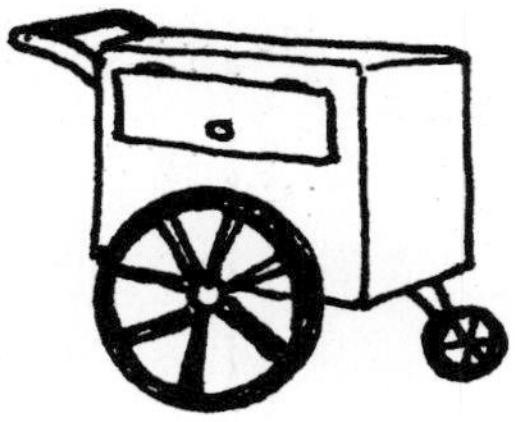

c a r t

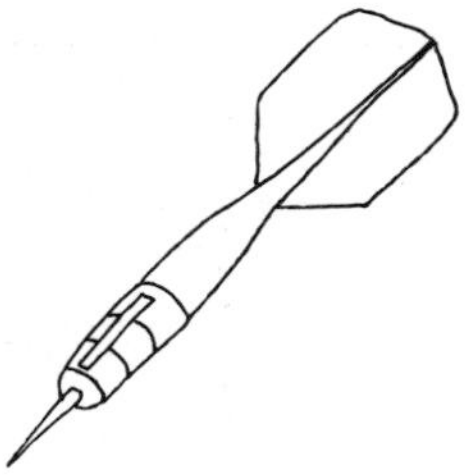

d a r t

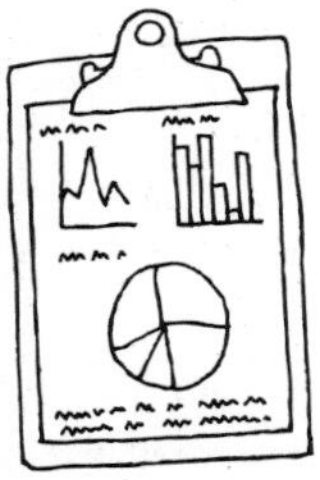

c h a r t

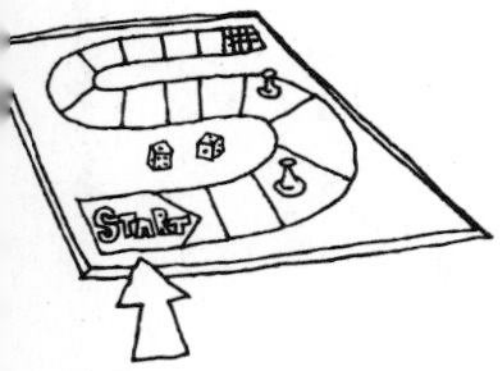

s t a r t

Look at the picture. Then build the word.

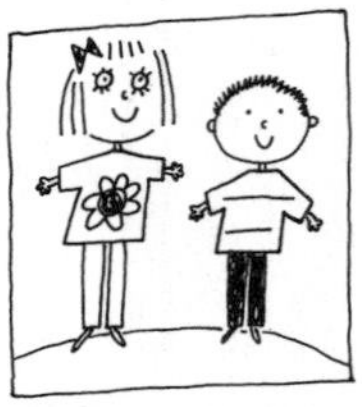

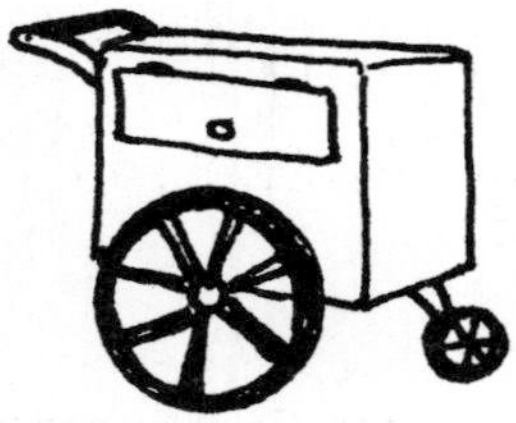

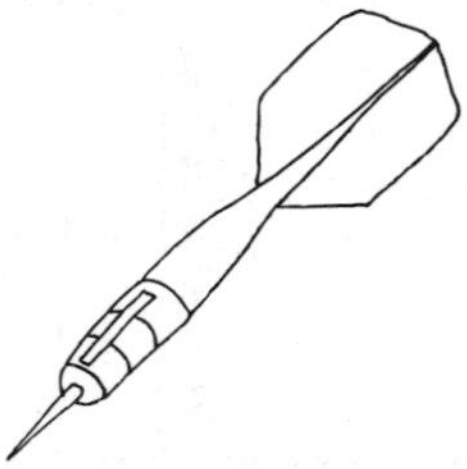

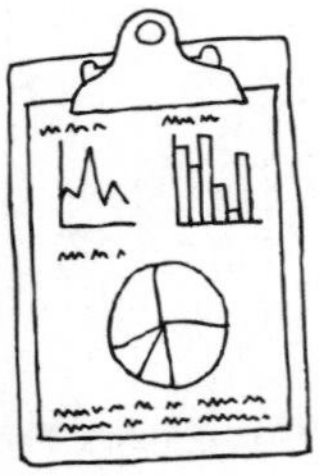

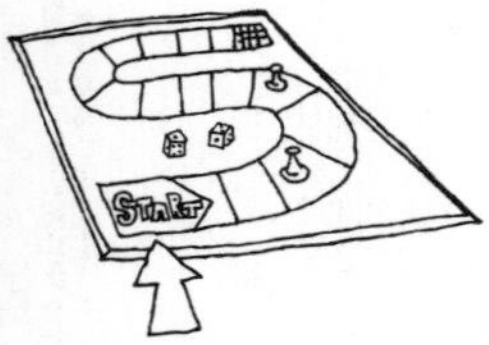

-ash

Look at the picture. Then build the word.

Look at the picture. Then build the word.

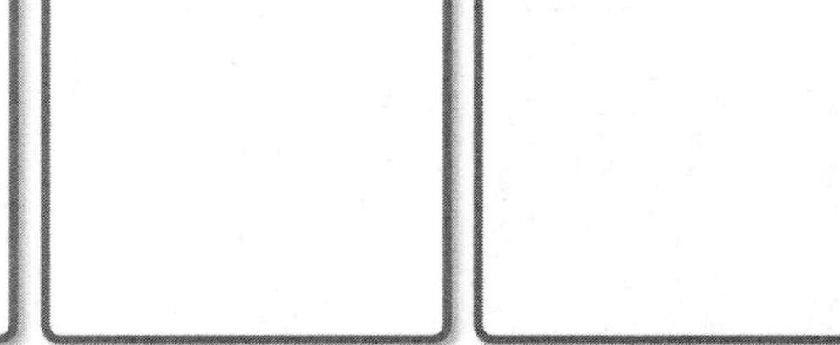

-ate

Look at the picture. Then build the word.

d	a	t	e

g	a	t	e

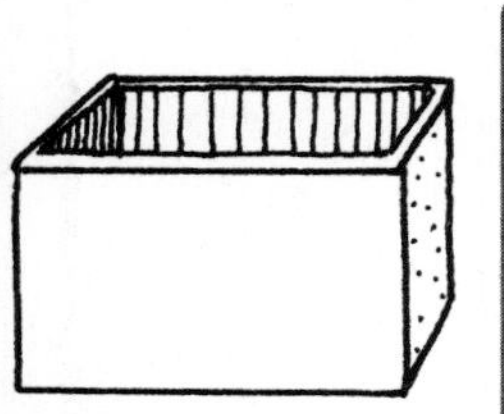

c	r	a	t	e

p	l	a	t	e

s	k	a	t	e

Look at the picture. Then build the word.

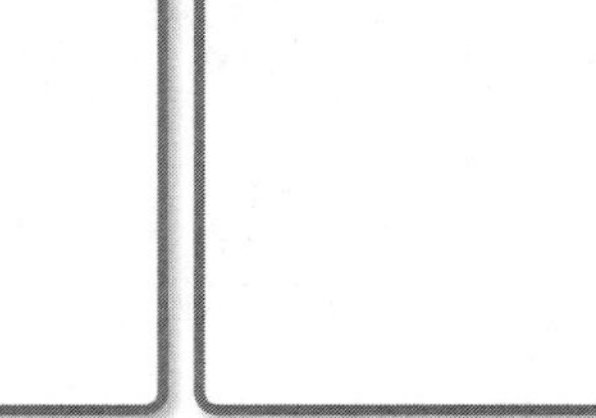

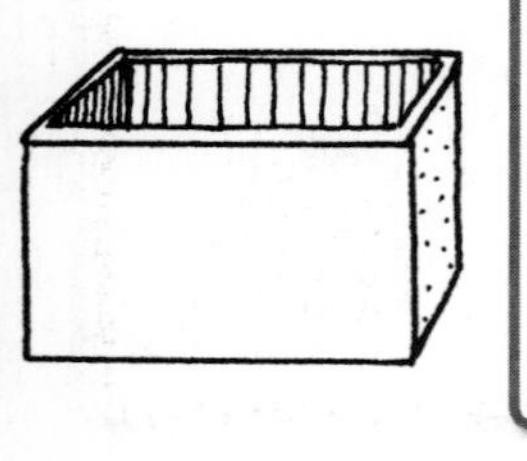

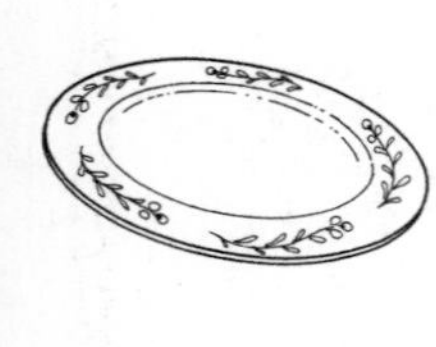

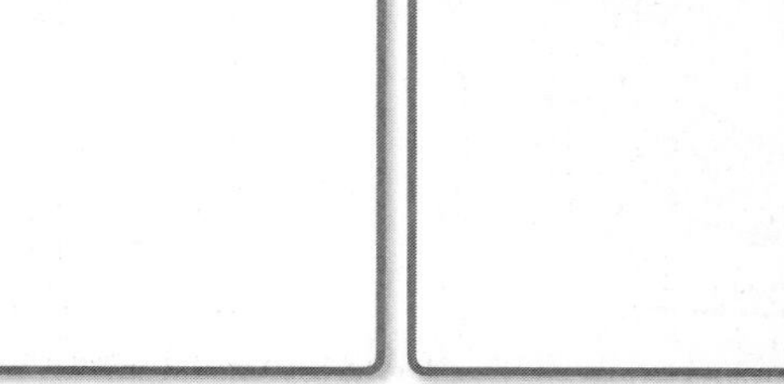

-ave

Look at the picture. Then build the word.

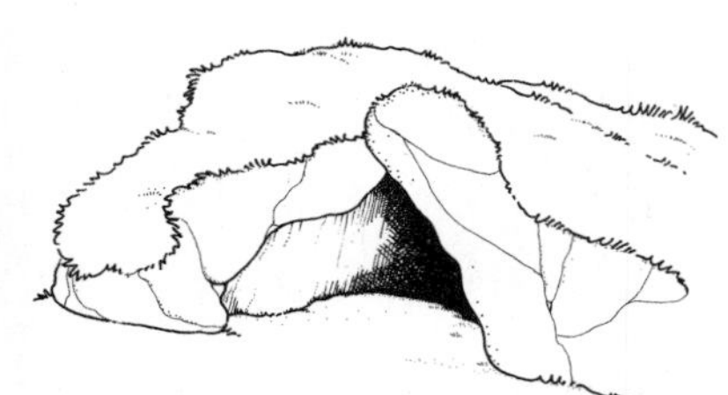

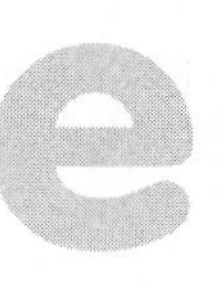

c	a	v	e

g	a	v	e

w	a	v	e

b	r	a	v	e

s	h	a	v	e

-ave

Look at the picture. Then build the word.

-ed

Look at the picture. Then build the word.

-ed

Look at the picture. Then build the word.

-ee

Look at the picture. Then build the word.

-ee

Look at the picture. Then build the word.

-en

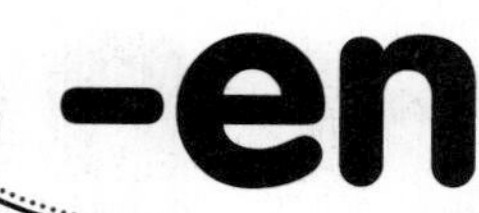

Look at the picture. Then build the word.

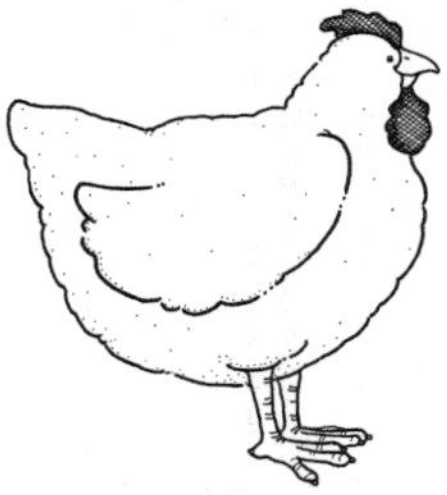

| h | e | n |

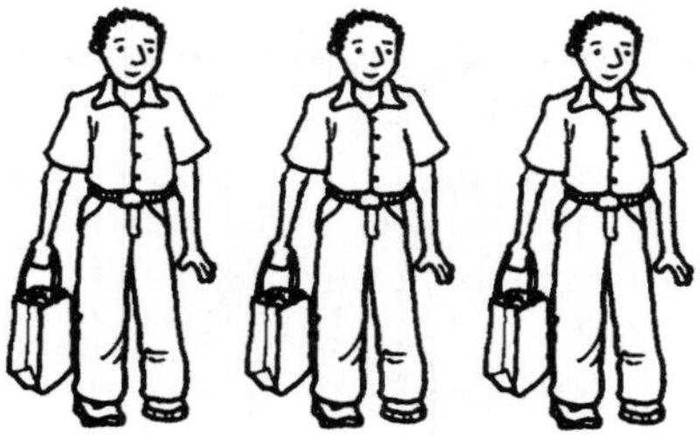

| m | e | n |

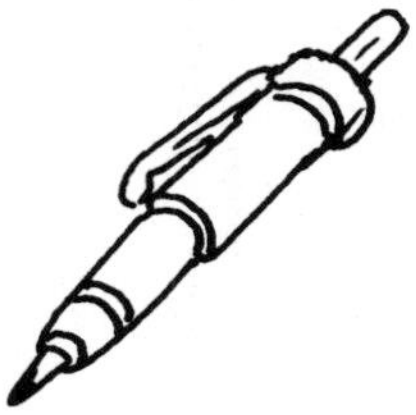

| p | e | n |

10

| t | e | n |

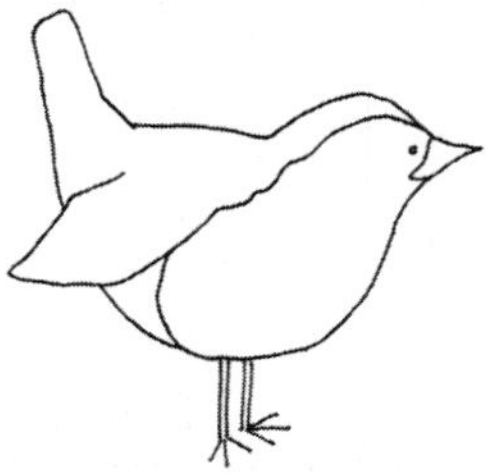

| w | r | e | n |

-en

Look at the picture. Then build the word.

10

-et

Look at the picture. Then build the word.

j	e	t
n	e	t
p	e	t
v	e	t
w	e	t

-et

Look at the picture. Then build the word.

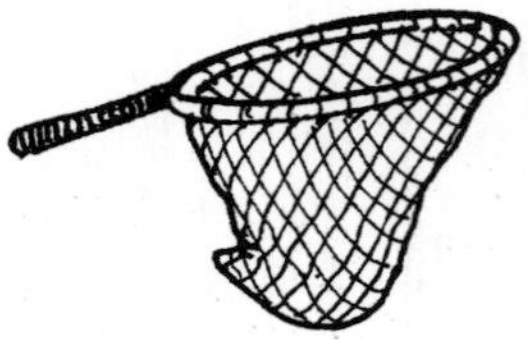

Look at the picture. Then build the word.

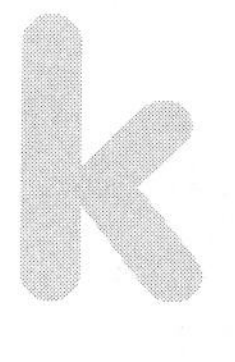

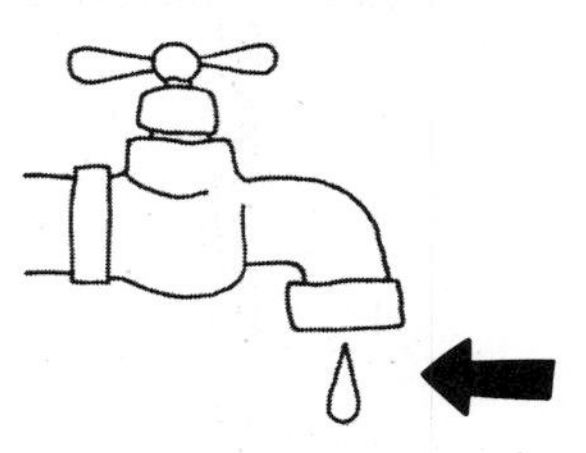

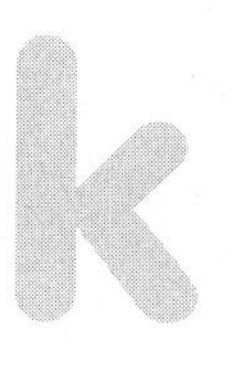

-eak

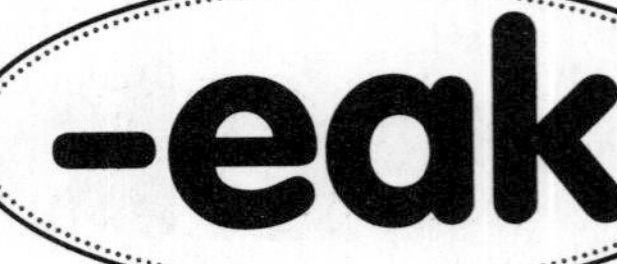

Look at the picture. Then build the word.

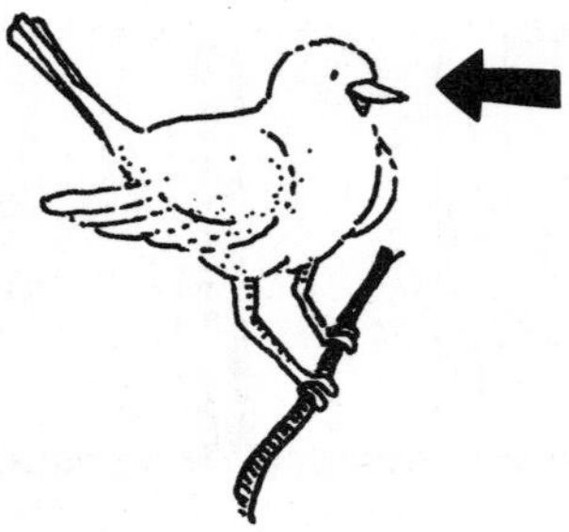

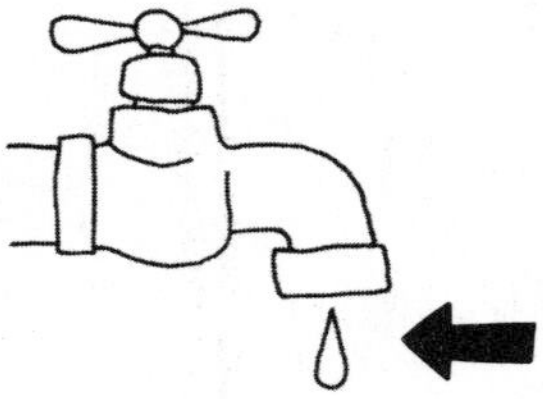

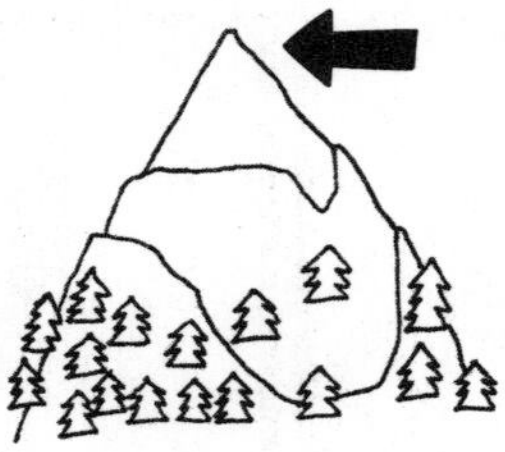

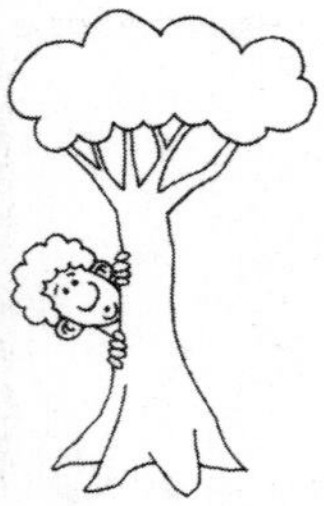

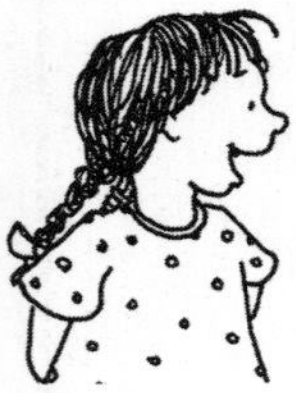

-ear

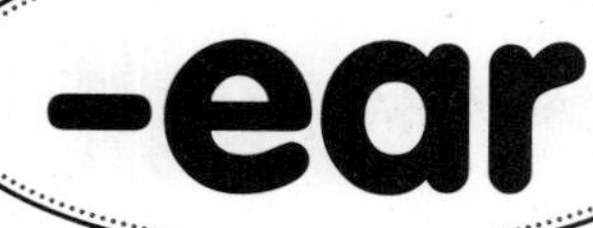

Look at the picture. Then build the word.

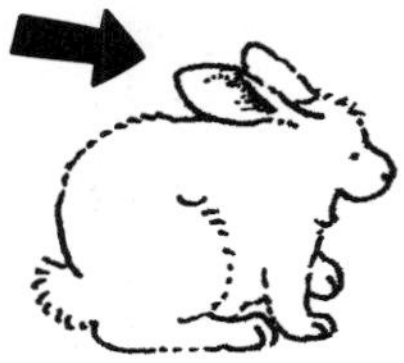

e	a	r

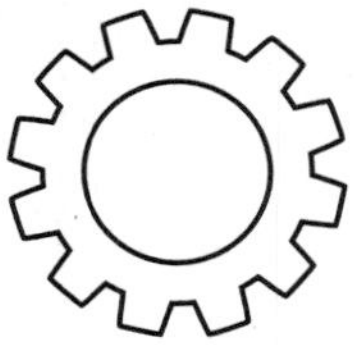

g	e	a	r

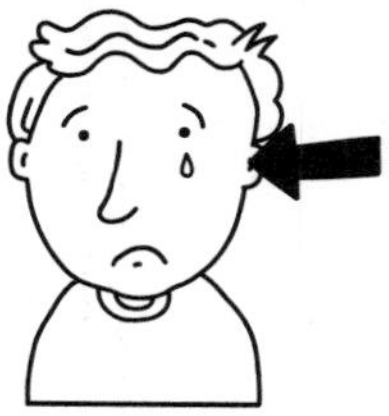

t	e	a	r

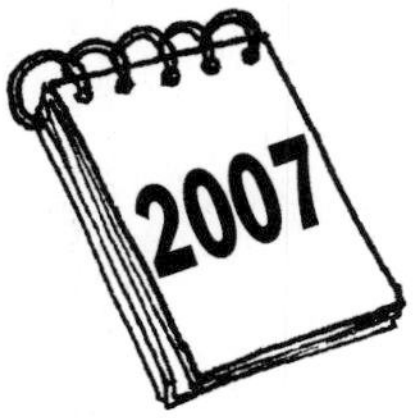

y	e	a	r

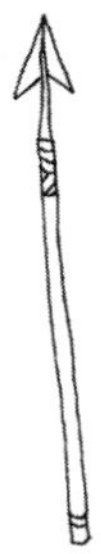

s	p	e	a	r

-ear

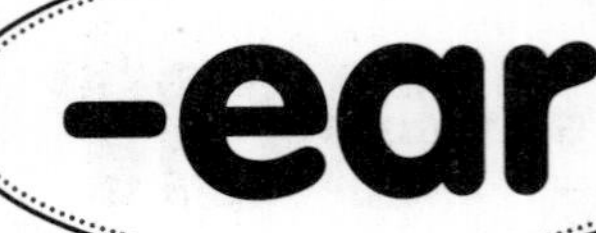

Look at the picture. Then build the word.

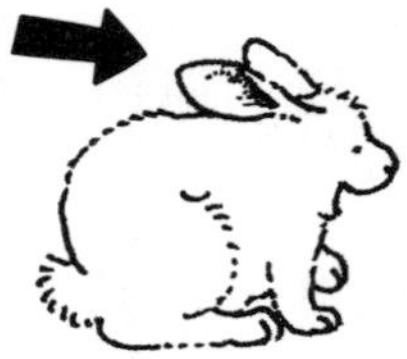

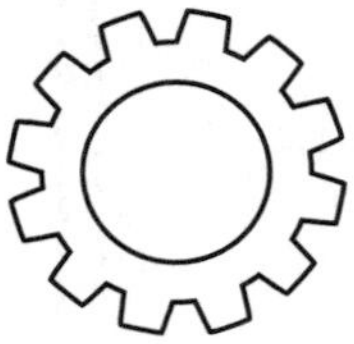

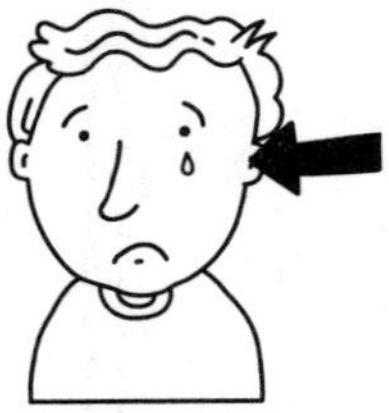

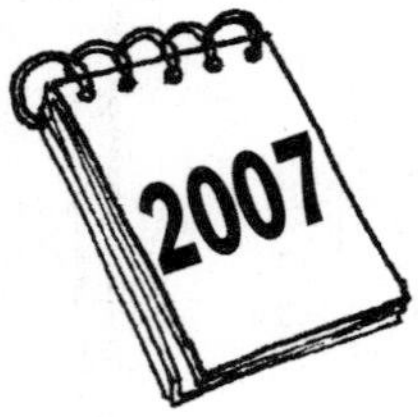

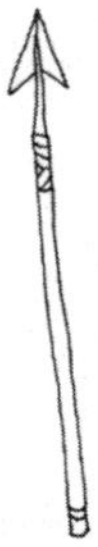

-eat

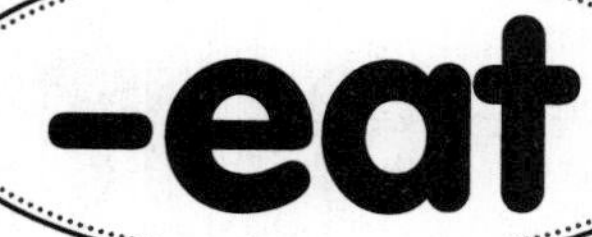

Look at the picture. Then build the word.

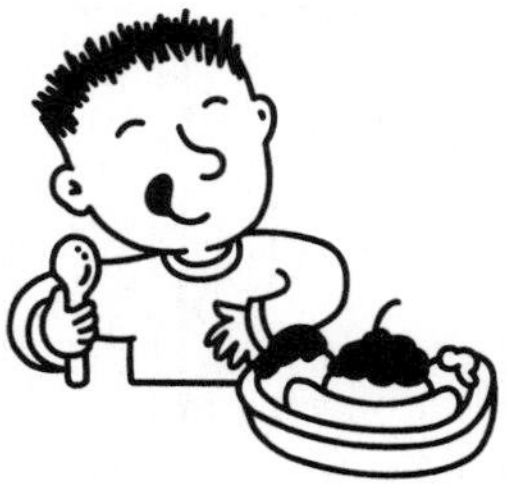

e	a	t

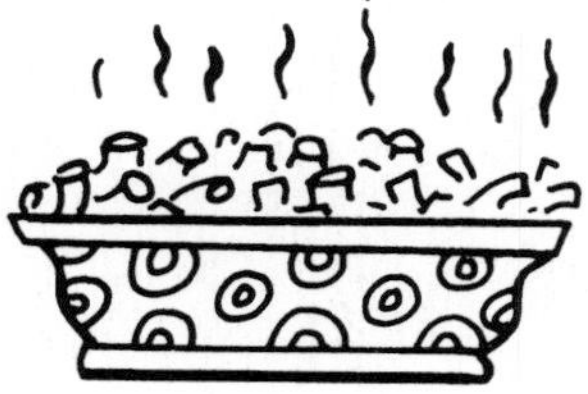

h	e	a	t

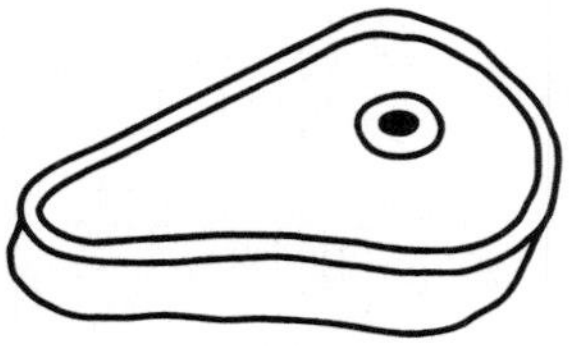

m	e	a	t

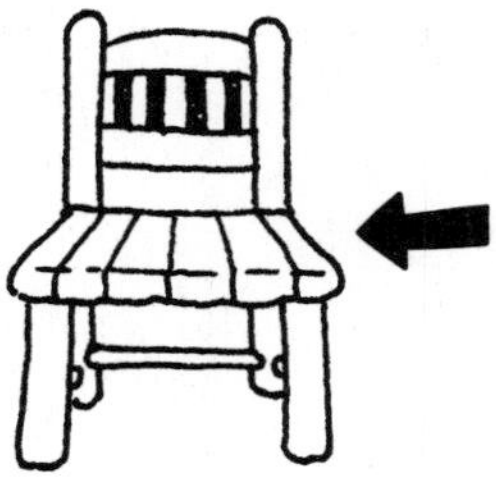

s	e	a	t

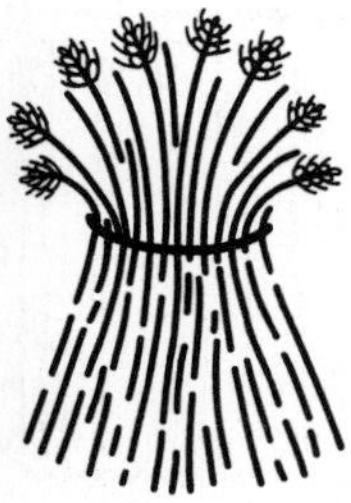

w	h	e	a	t

-eat

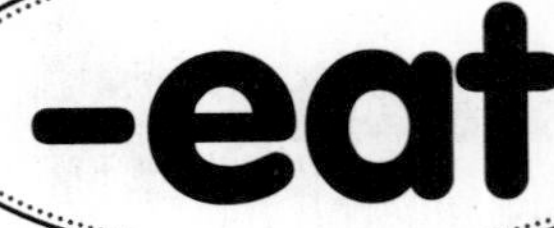

Look at the picture. Then build the word.

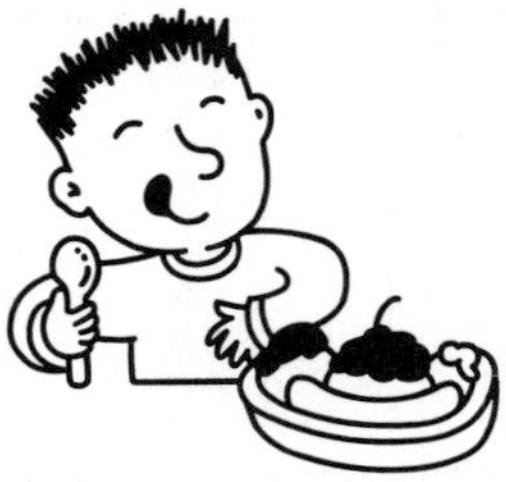

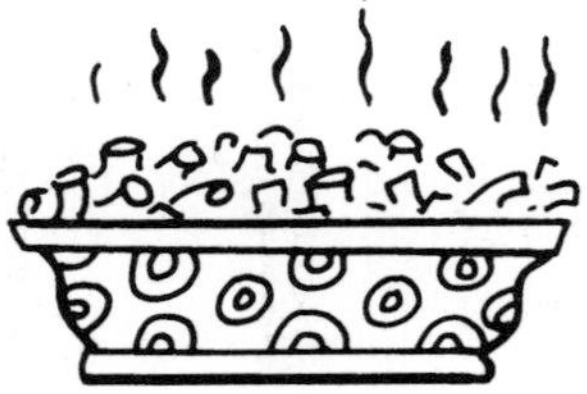

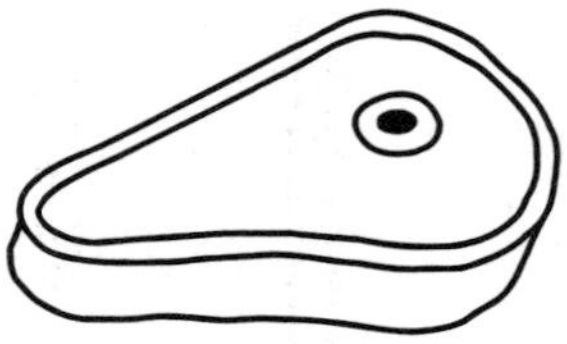

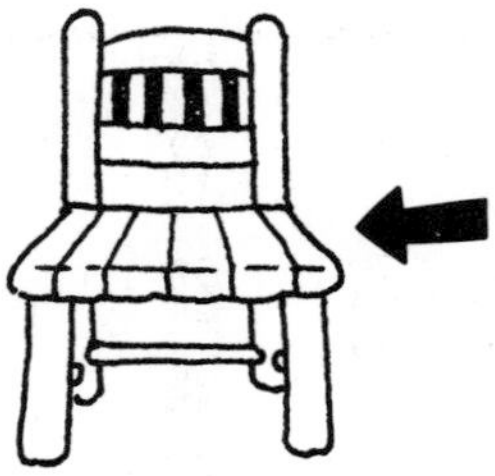

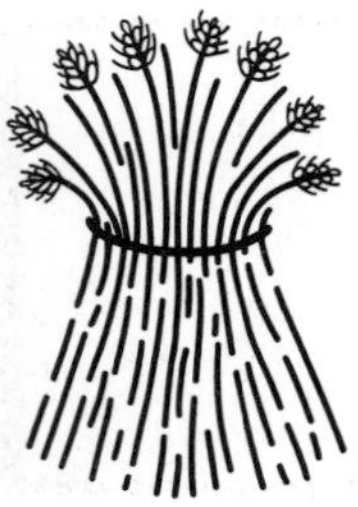

-eel

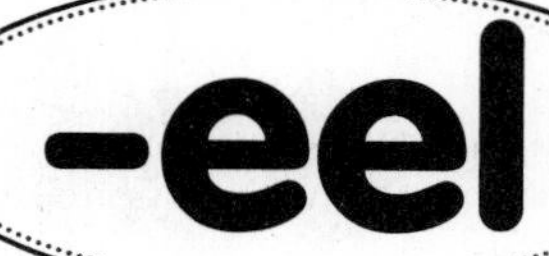

Look at the picture. Then build the word.

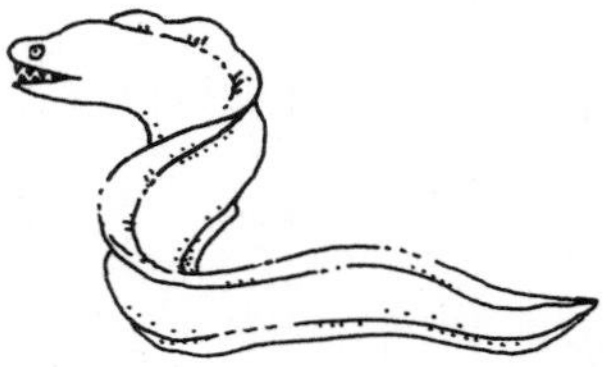

| e | e | l |

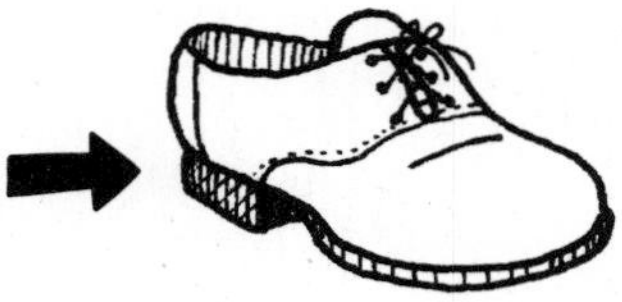

| h | e | e | l |

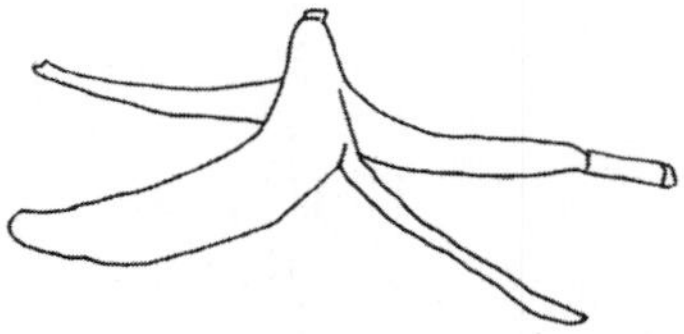

| p | e | e | l |

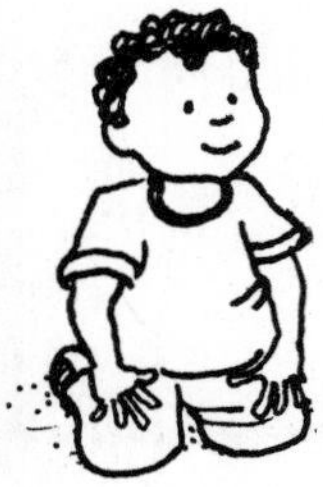

| k | n | e | e | l |

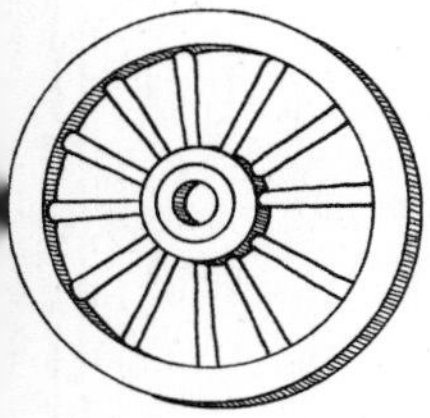

| w | h | e | e | l |

-eel

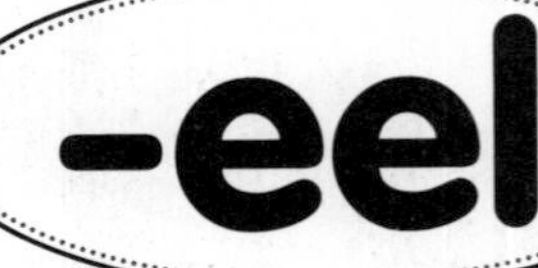

Look at the picture. Then build the word.

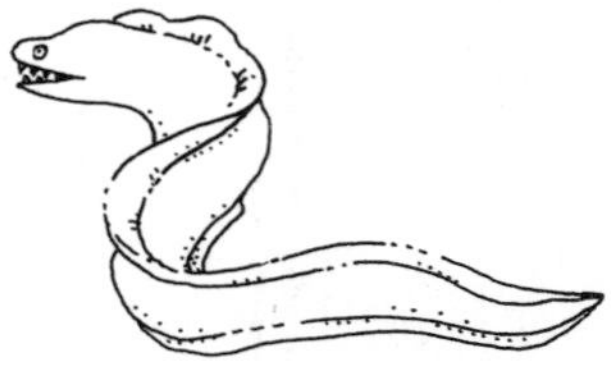

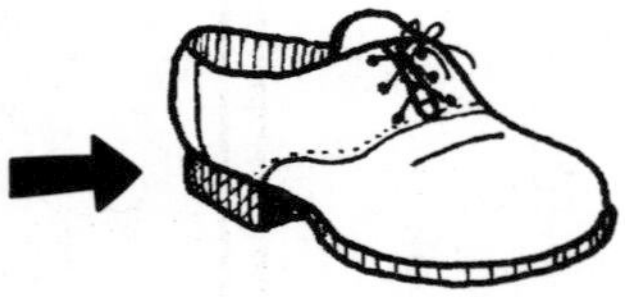

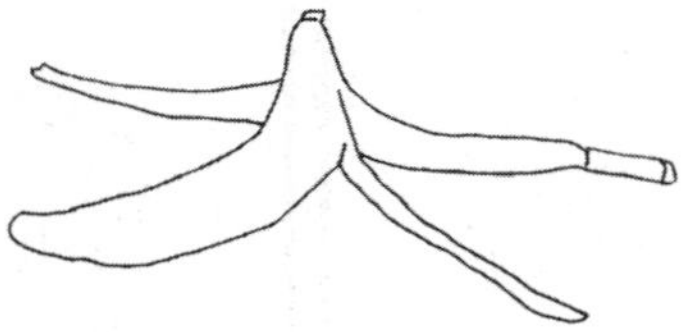

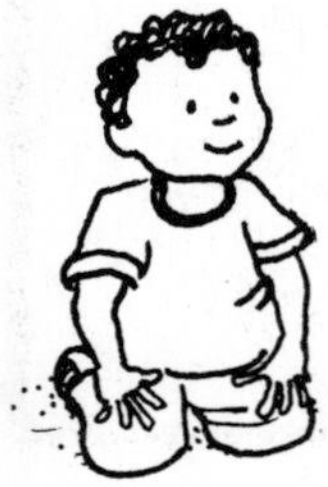

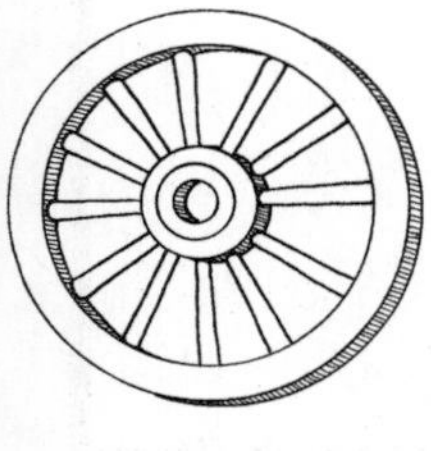

Look at the picture. Then build the word.

-eep

Look at the picture. Then build the word.

   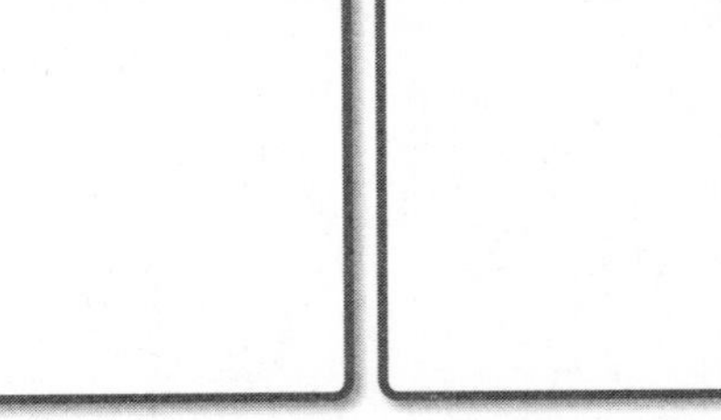

-ell

Look at the picture. Then build the word.

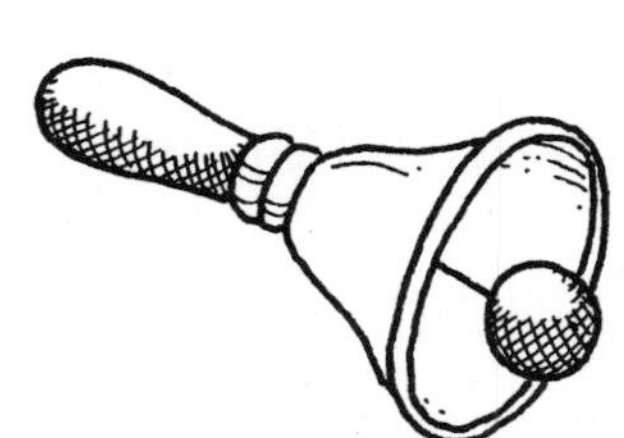

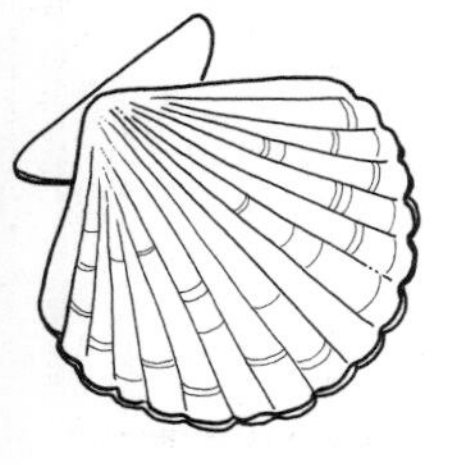

-ell

Look at the picture. Then build the word.

Look at the picture. Then build the word.

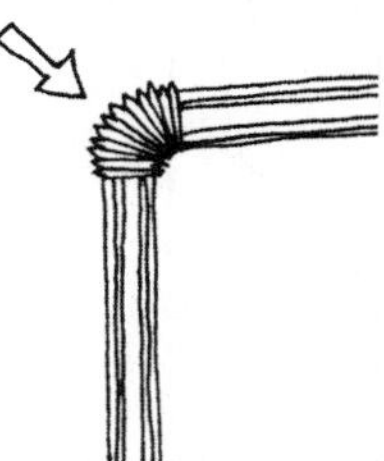

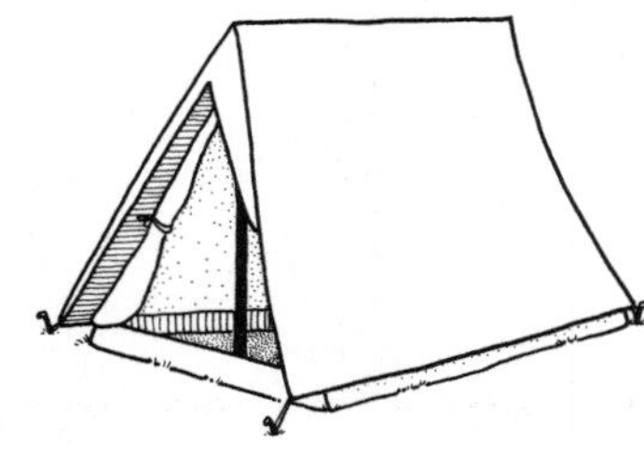

-ent

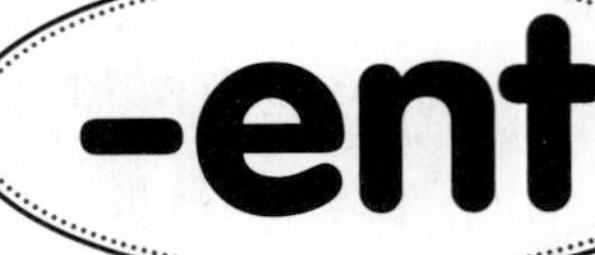

Look at the picture. Then build the word.

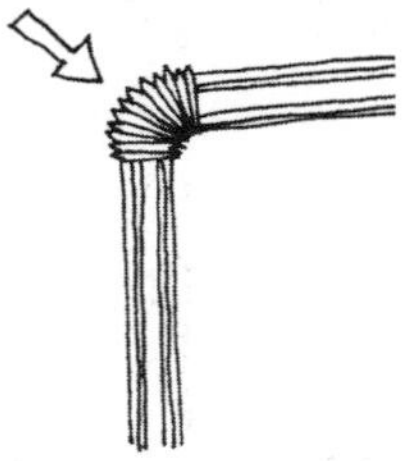

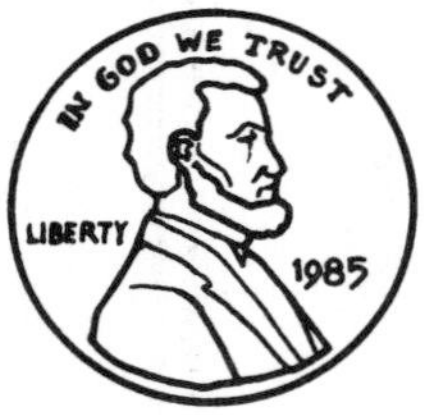

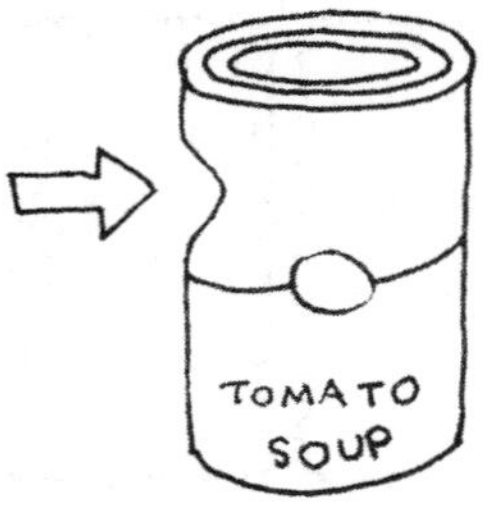

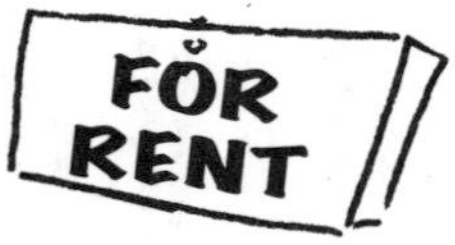

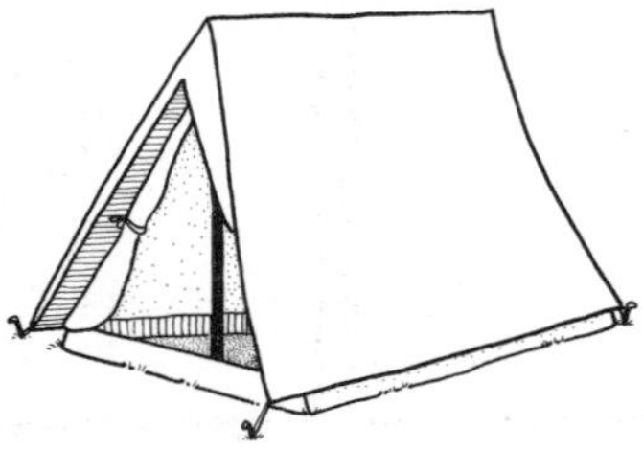

-est

Look at the picture. Then build the word.

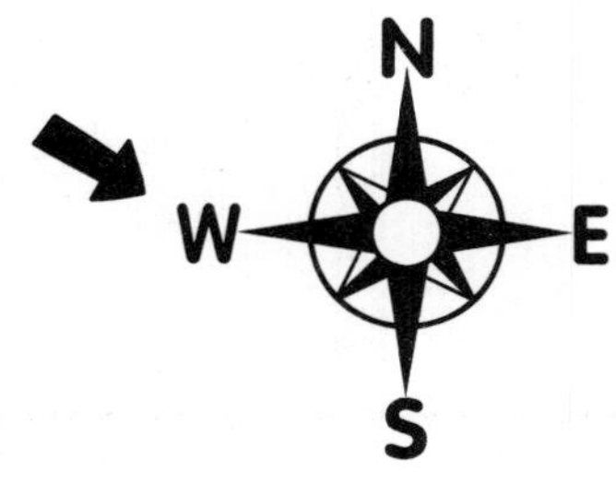

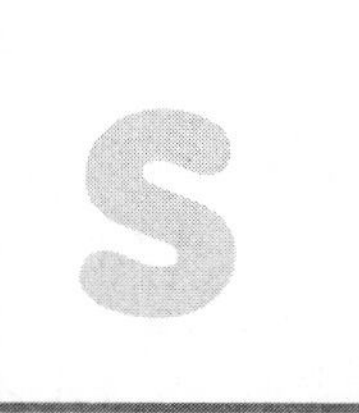

-est

Look at the picture. Then build the word.

-id

Look at the picture. Then build the word.

k i d

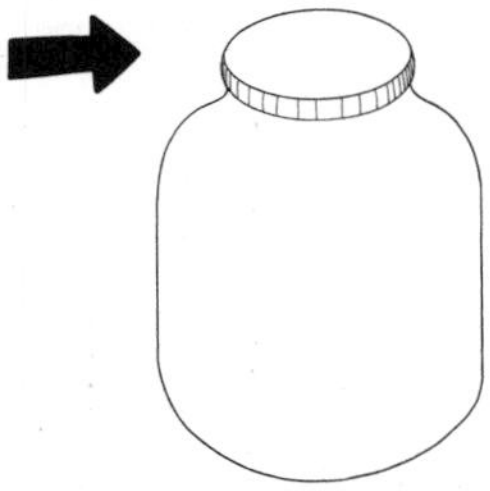

l i d

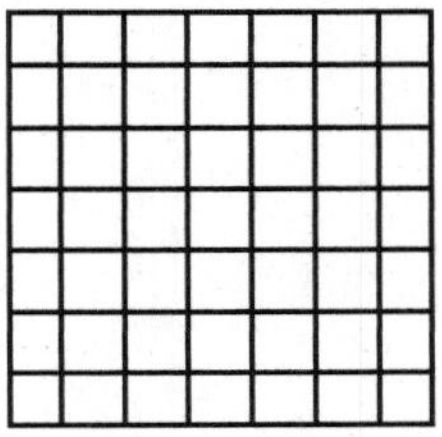

g r i d

s l i d

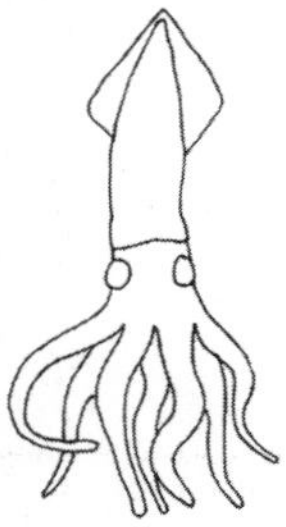

s q u i d

-id

Look at the picture. Then build the word.

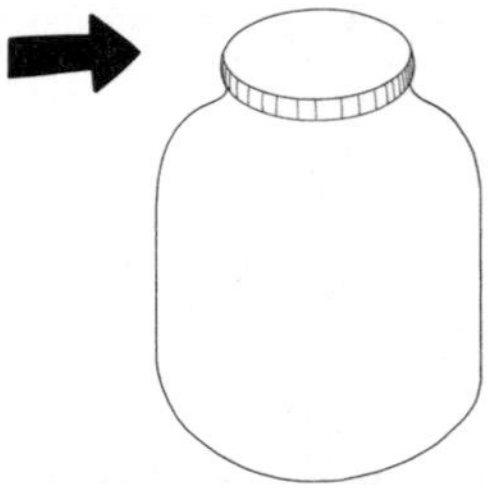

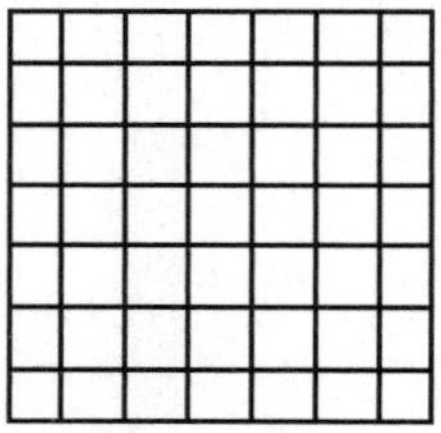

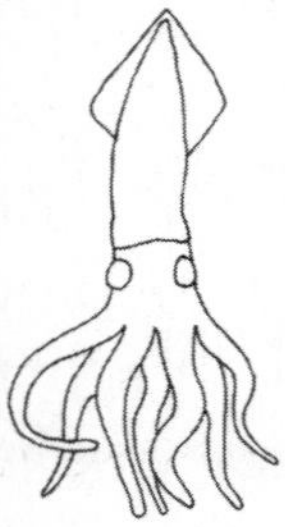

-ig

Look at the picture. Then build the word.

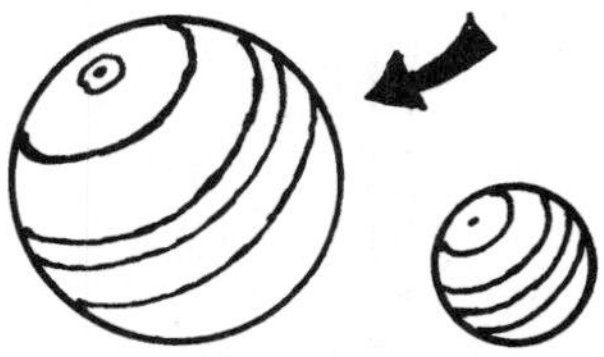

b	i	g
d	i	g
p	i	g
w	i	g

t	w	i	g

-ig

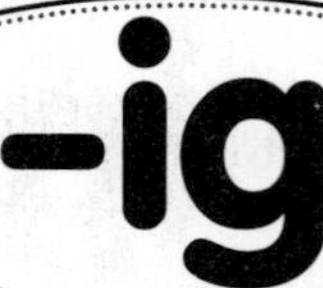

Look at the picture. Then build the word.

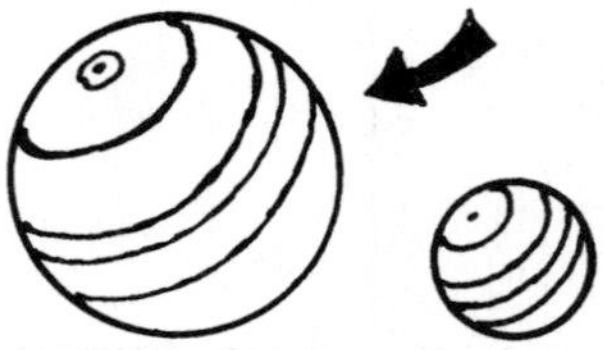

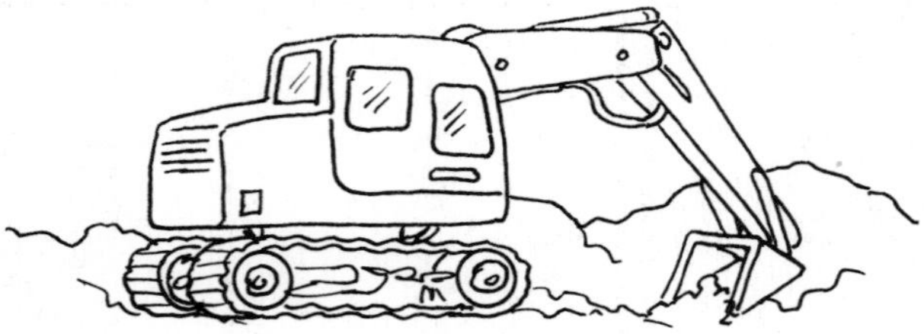

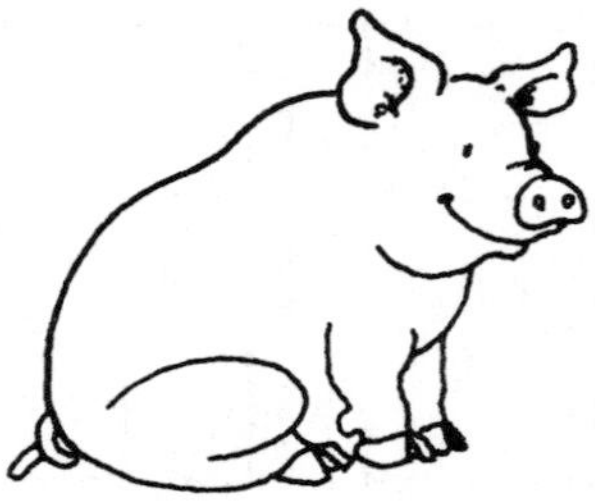

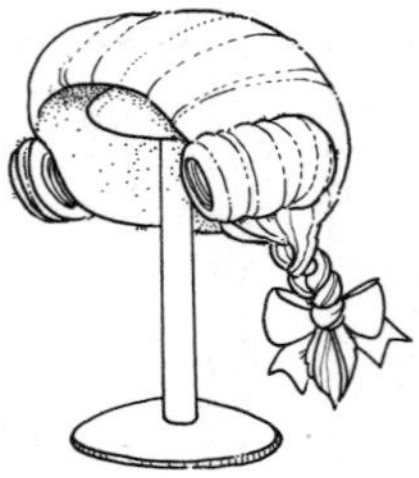

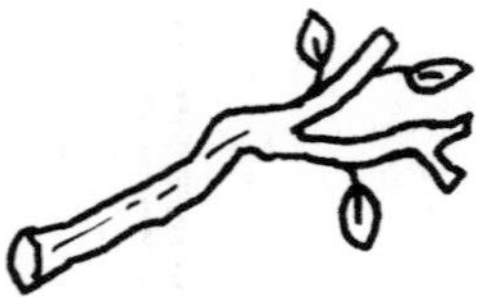

Look at the picture. Then build the word.

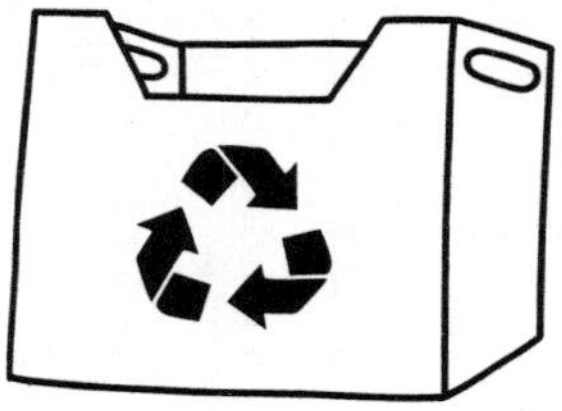

	b	i	n
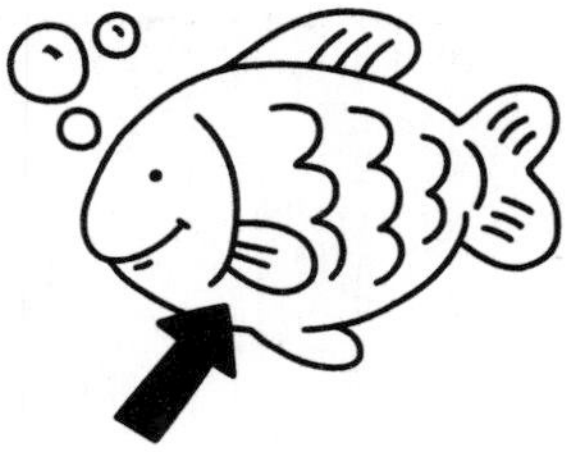	f	i	n
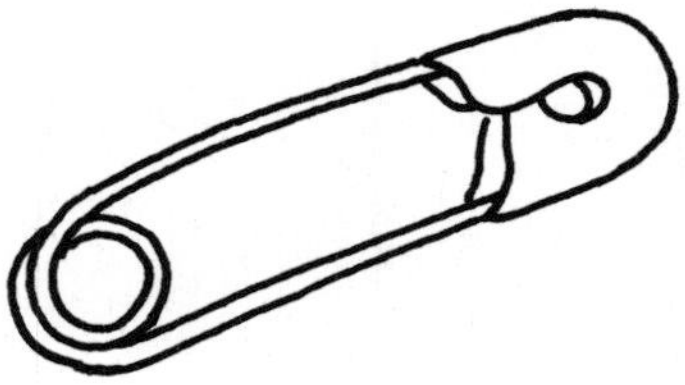	p	i	n
c	h	i	n
s	p	i	n

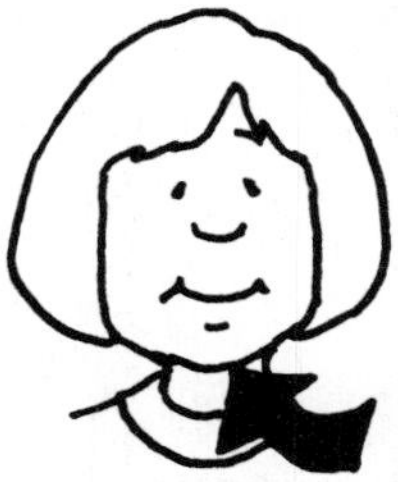

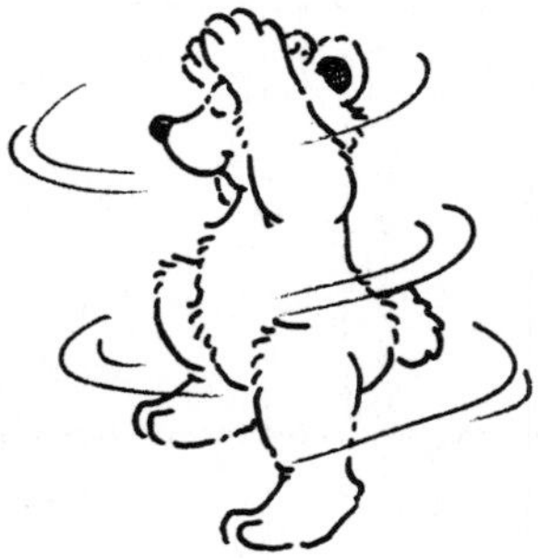

-in

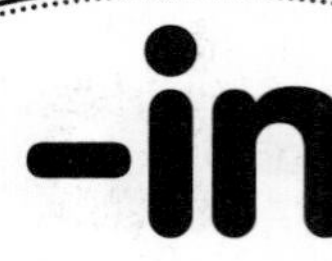

Look at the picture. Then build the word.

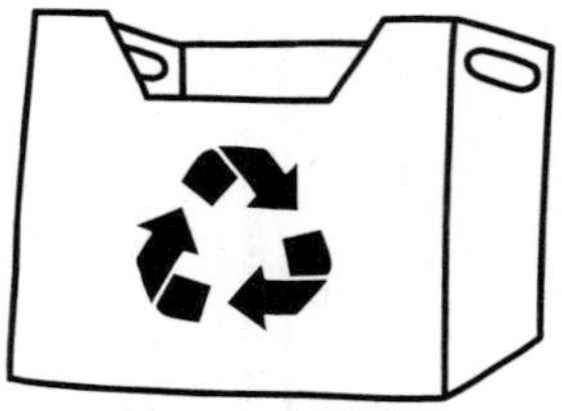

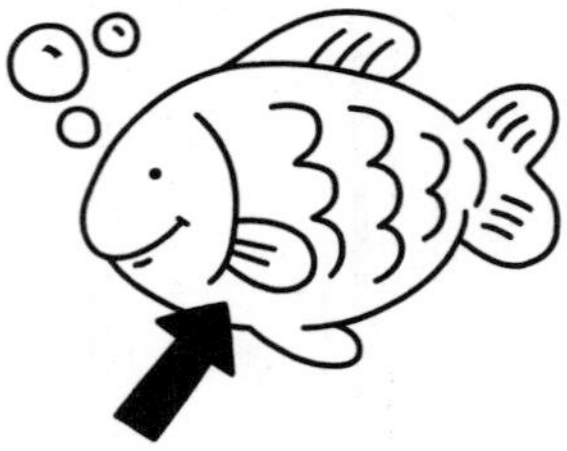

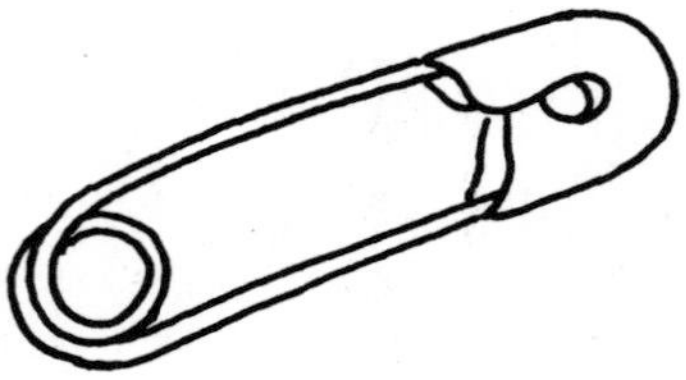

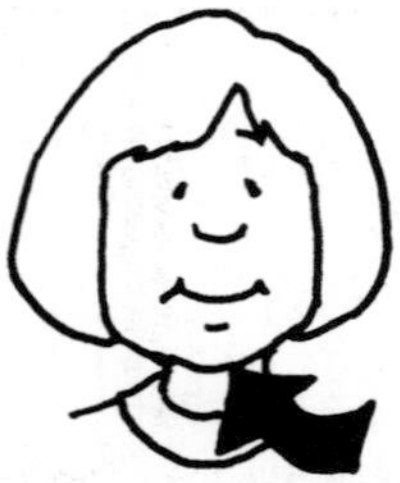

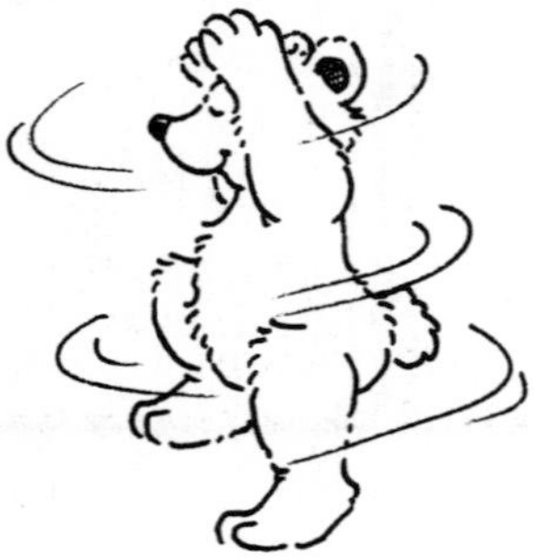

-ip

Look at the picture. Then build the word.

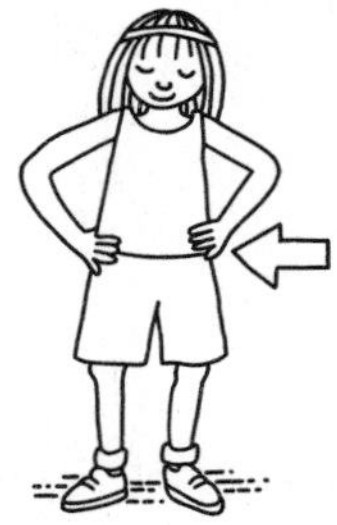

h	i	p

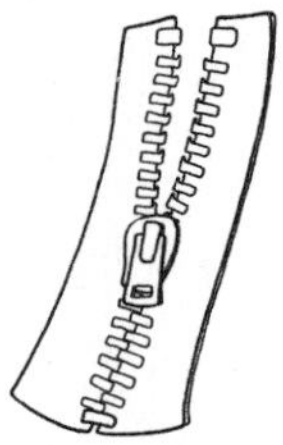

z	i	p

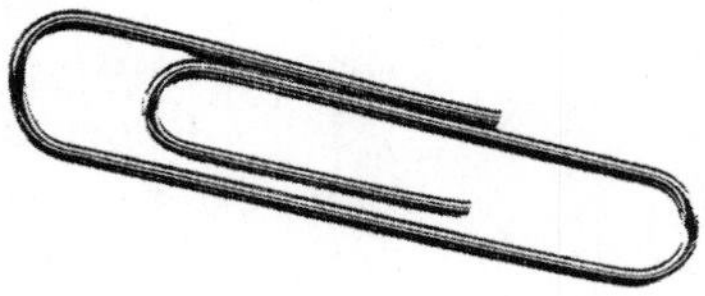

c	l	i	p

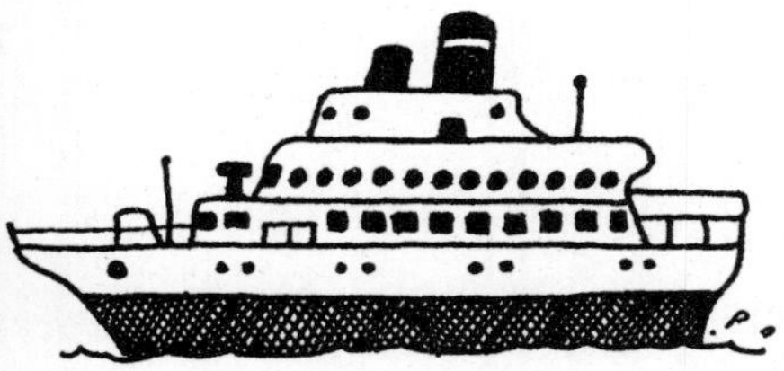

s	h	i	p

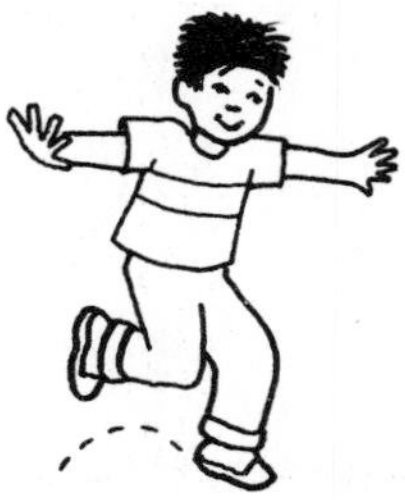

s	k	i	p

-ip

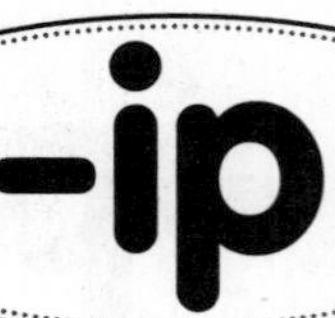

Look at the picture. Then build the word.

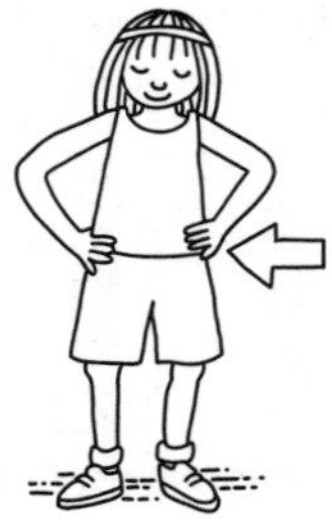

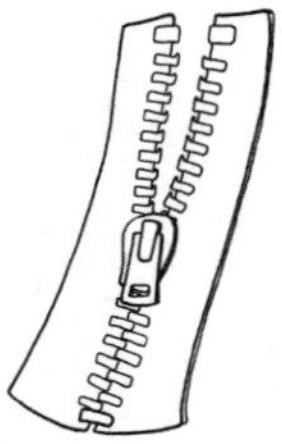

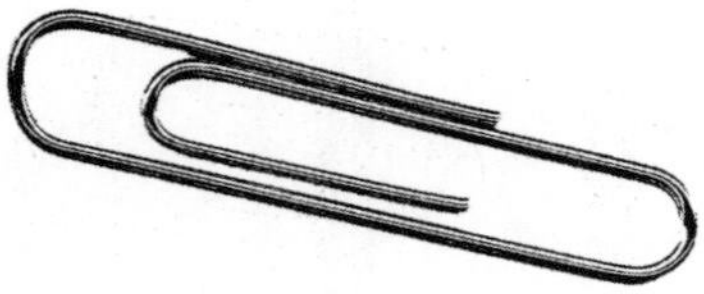

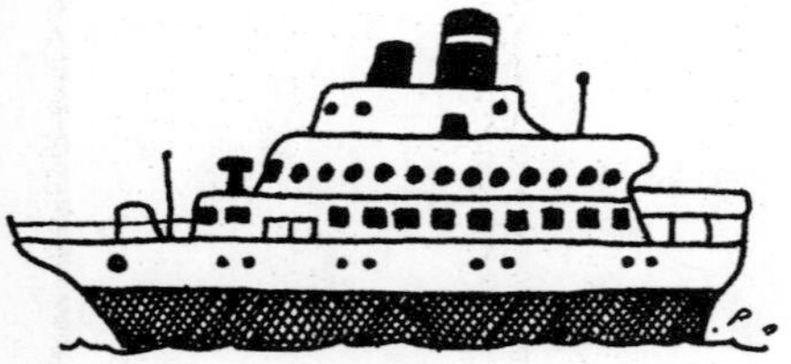

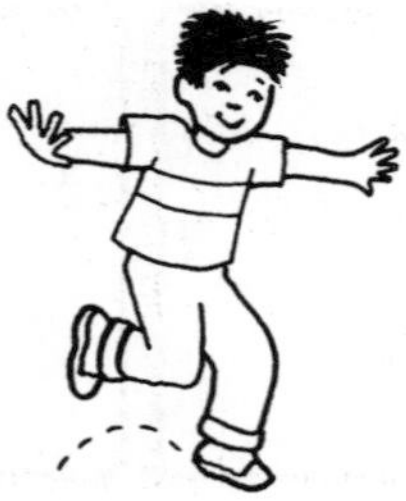

Look at the picture. Then build the word.

b	i	t
h	i	t
k	i	t
l	i	t
s	i	t

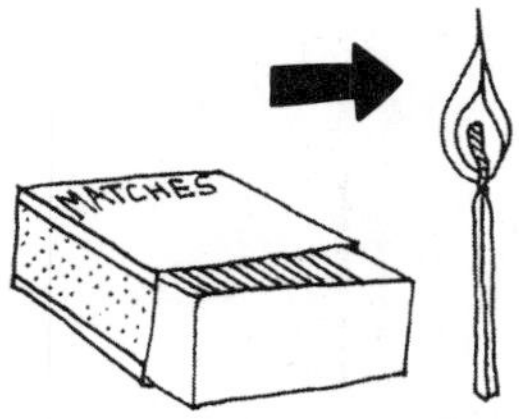

MATCHES

-it

Look at the picture. Then build the word.

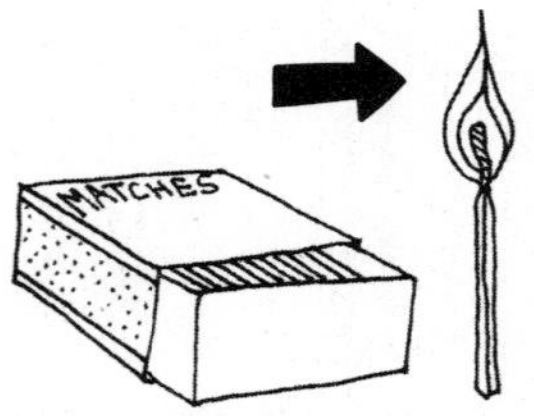

Look at the picture. Then build the word.

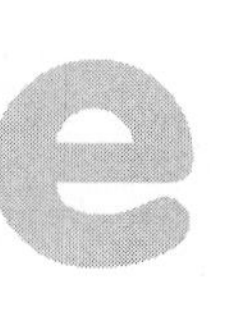

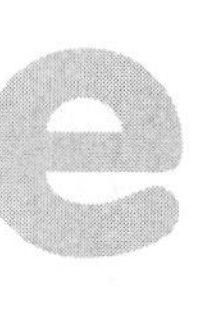

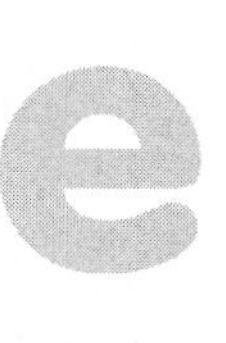

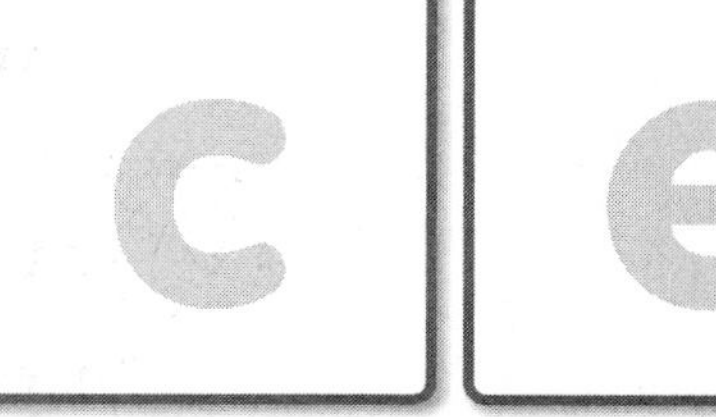

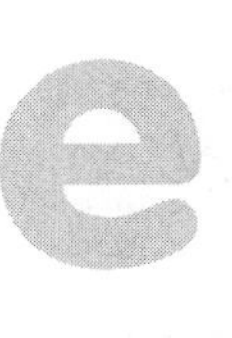

-ice

Look at the picture. Then build the word.

-ick

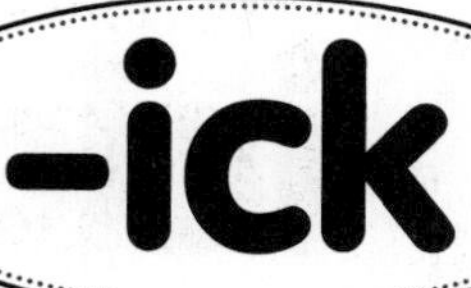

Look at the picture. Then build the word.

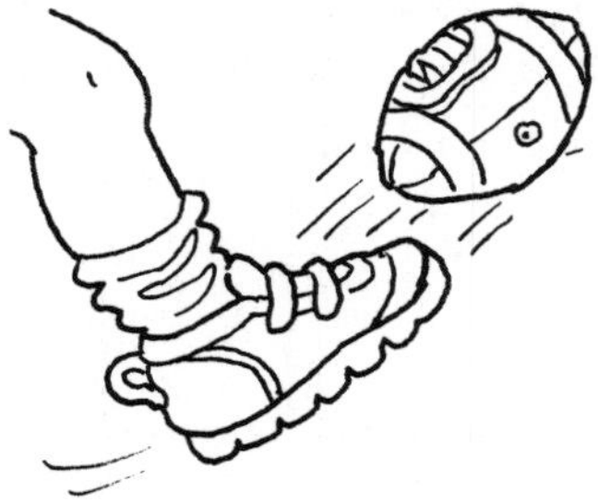

k i c k

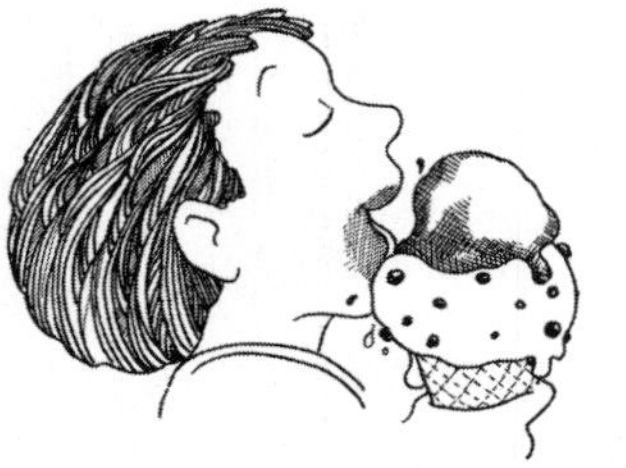

l i c k

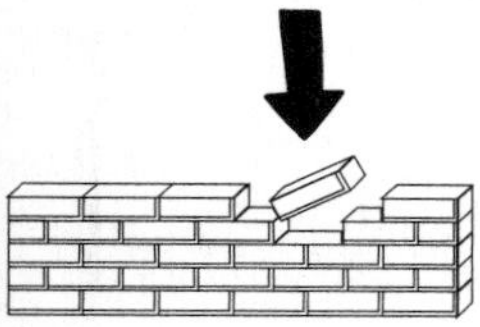

b r i c k

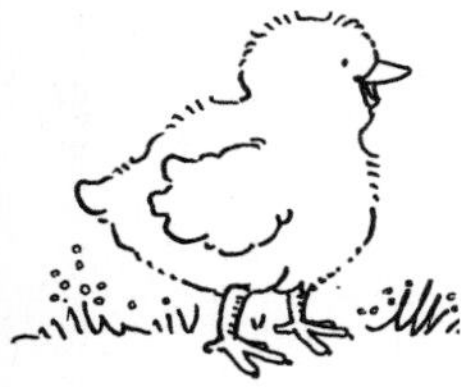

c h i c k

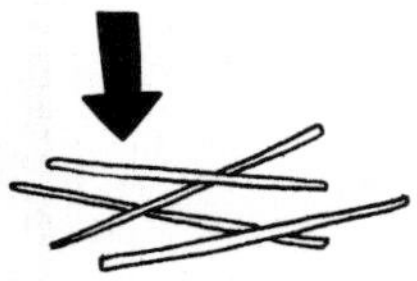

s t i c k

-ick

Look at the picture. Then build the word.

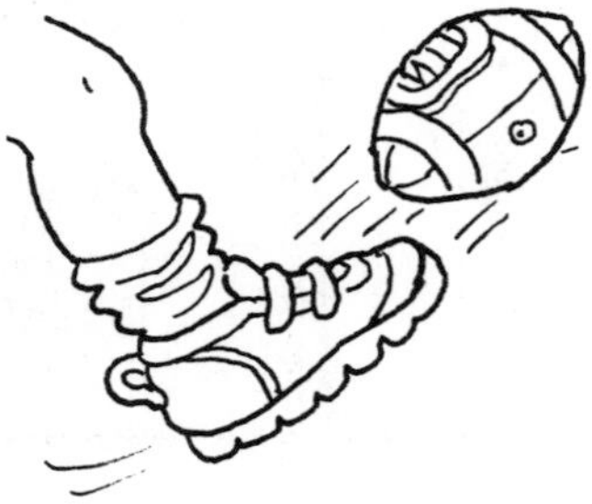

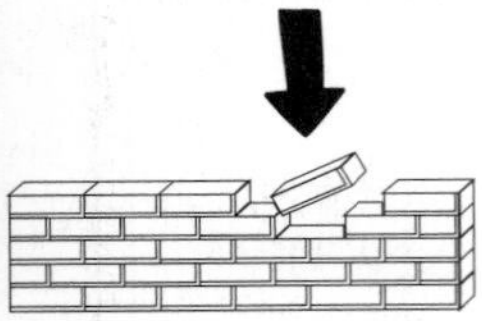

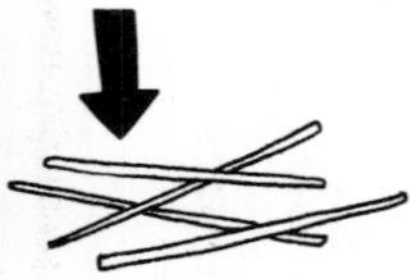

Look at the picture. Then build the word.

h i d e

r i d e

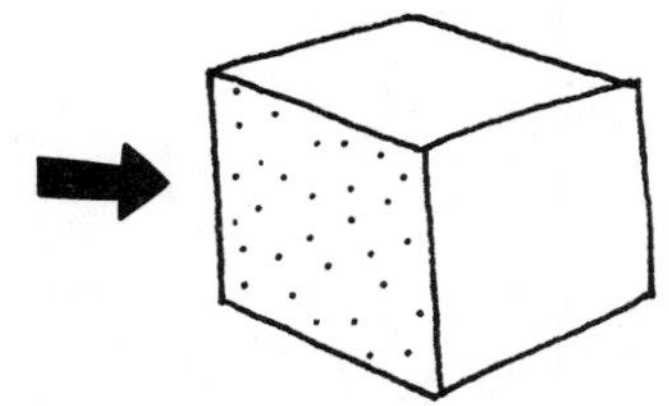

s i d e

b r i d e

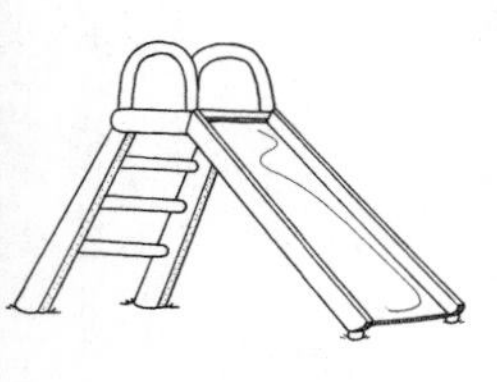

s l i d e

-ide

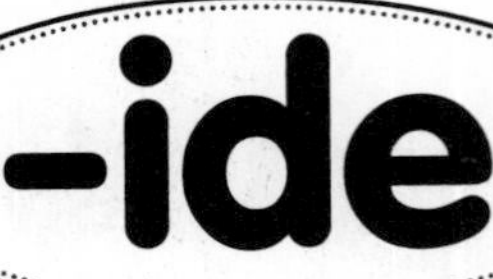

Look at the picture. Then build the word.

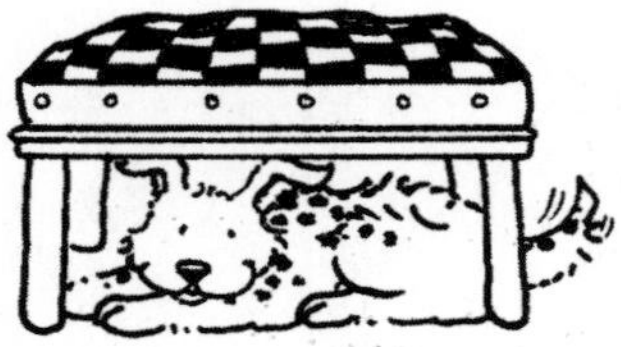

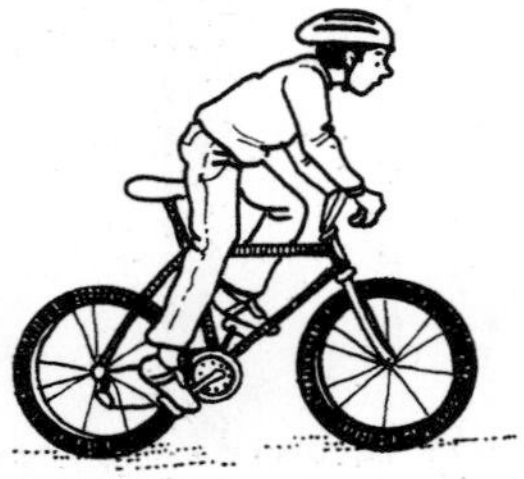

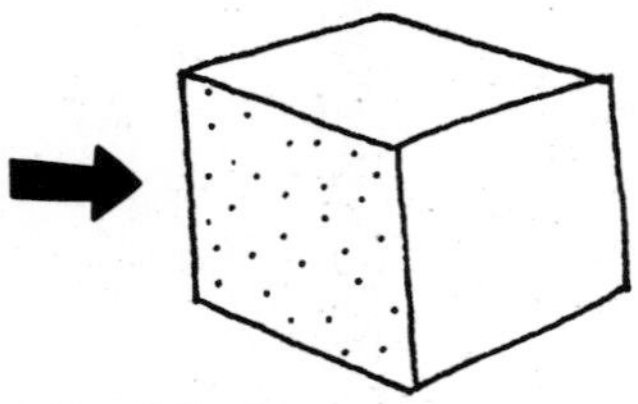

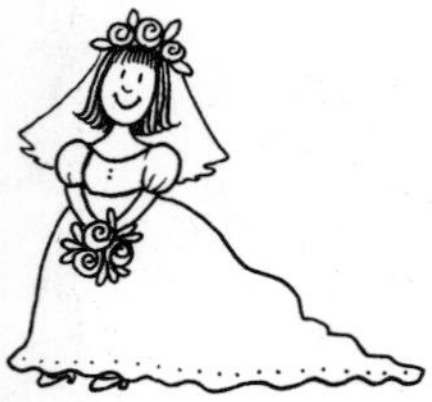

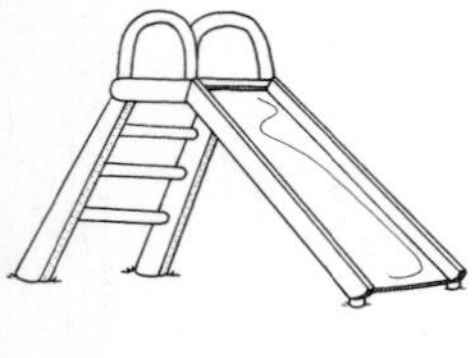

-ill

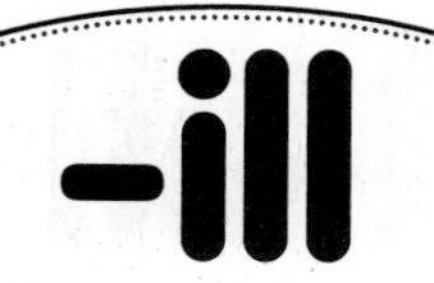

Look at the picture. Then build the word.

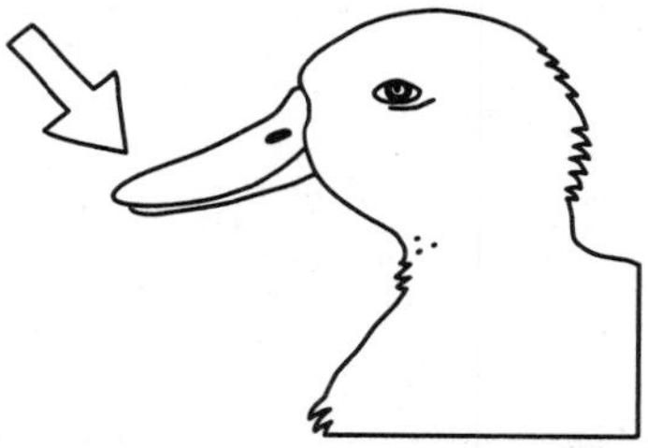

b	i	l	l

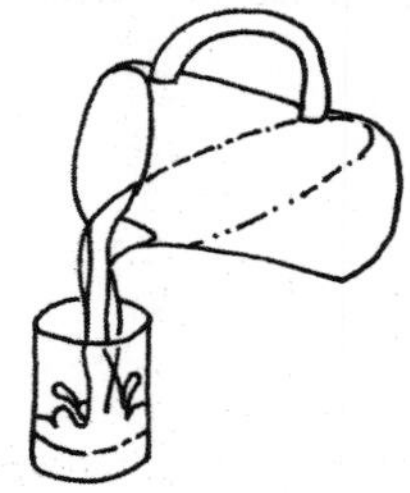

f	i	l	l

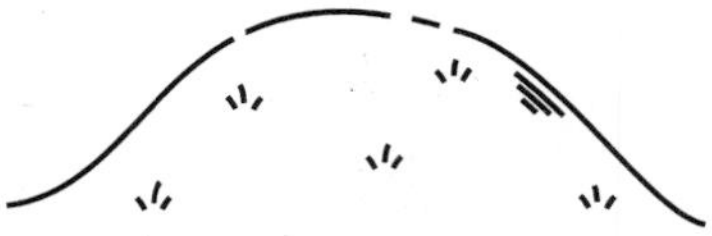

h	i	l	l

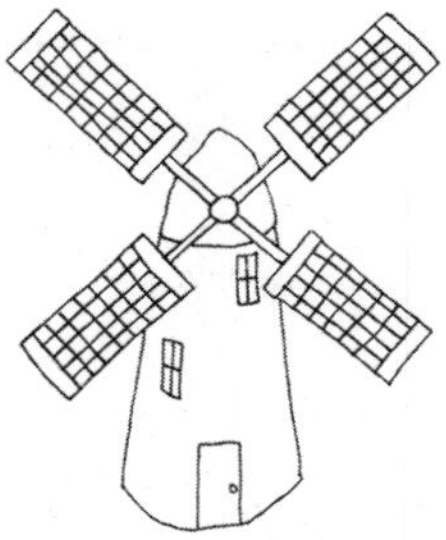

m	i	l	l

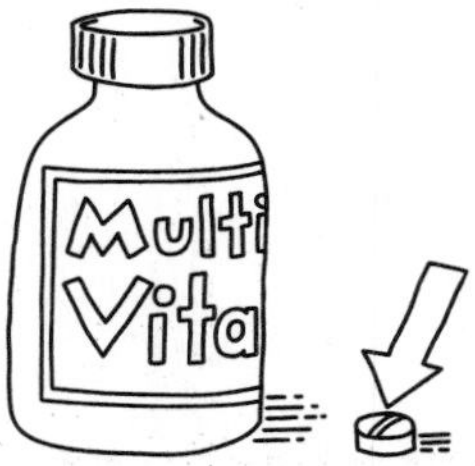

p	i	l	l

-ill

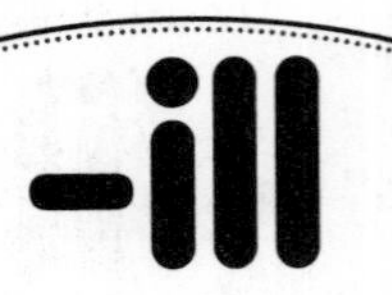

Look at the picture. Then build the word.

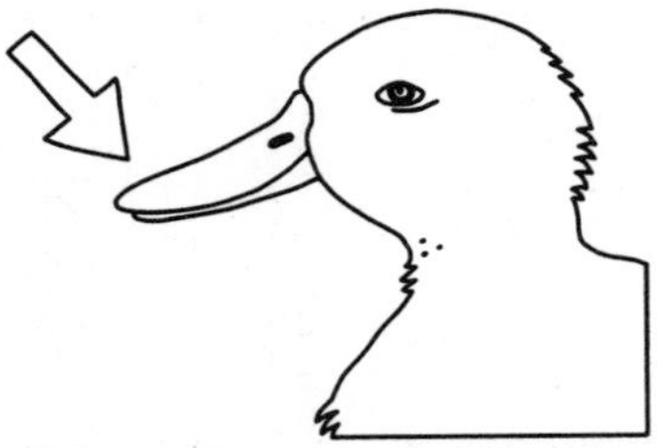

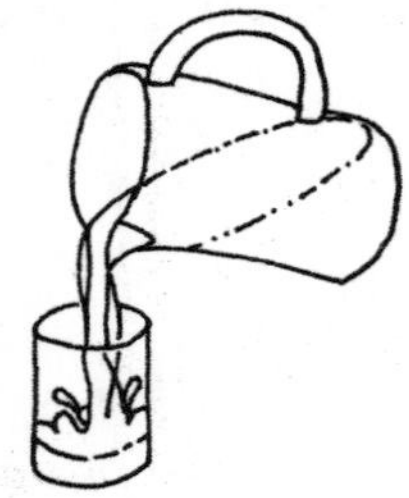

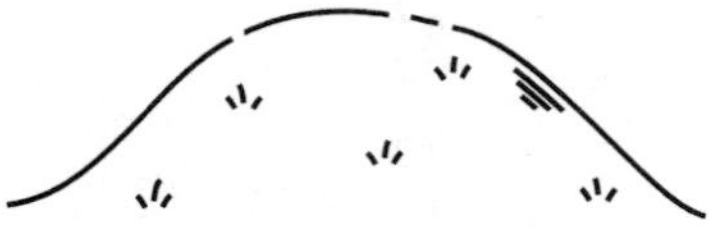

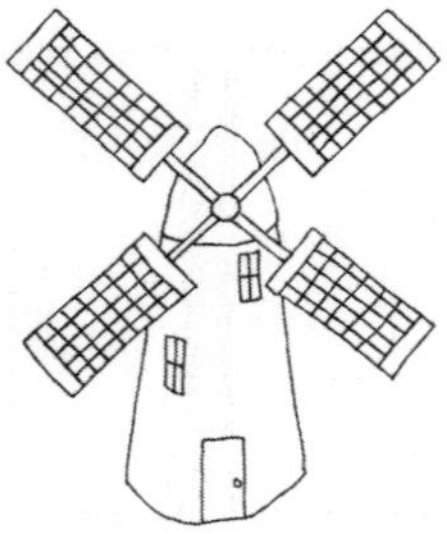

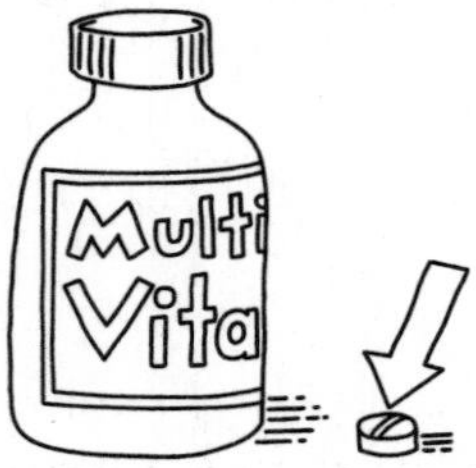

-ine

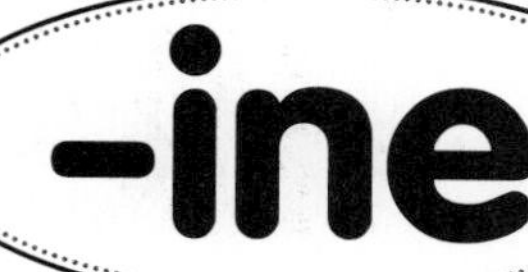

Look at the picture. Then build the word.

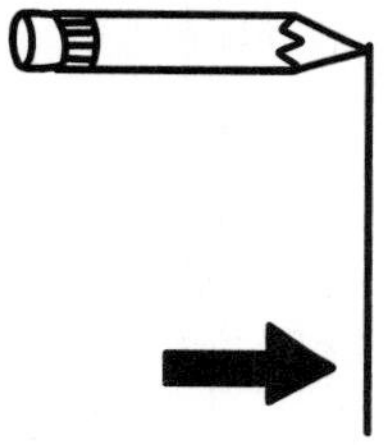

| l | i | n | e |

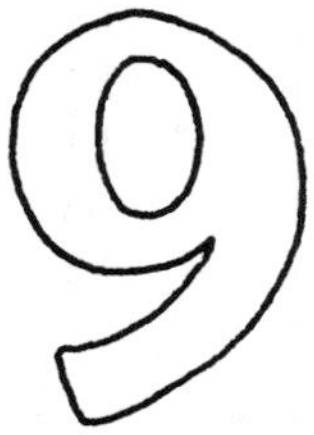

| n | i | n | e |

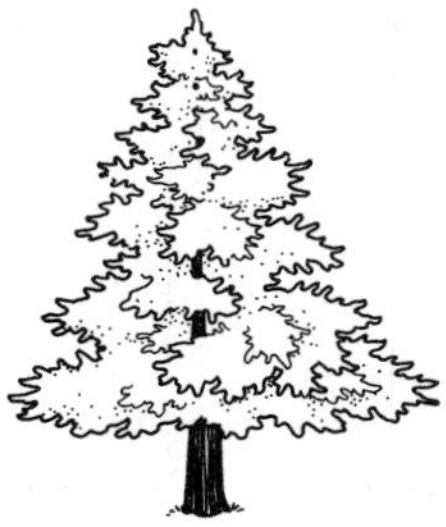

| p | i | n | e |

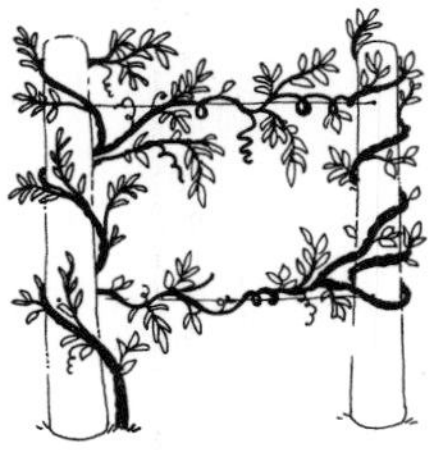

| v | i | n | e |

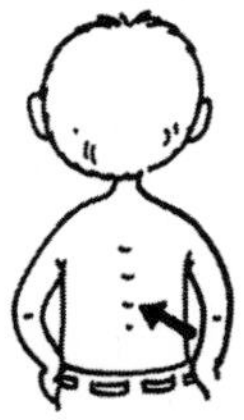

| s | p | i | n | e |

-ine

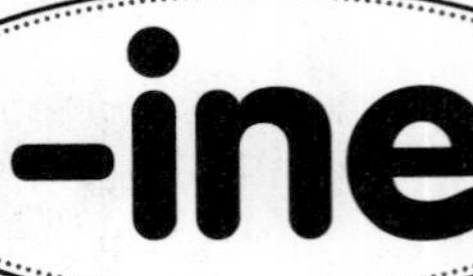

Look at the picture. Then build the word.

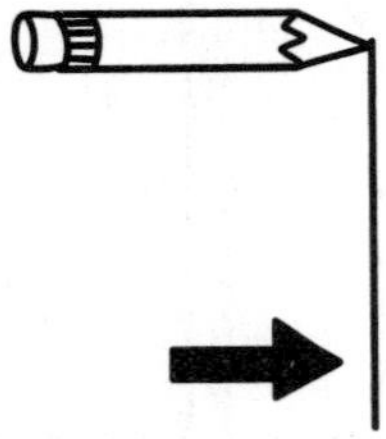

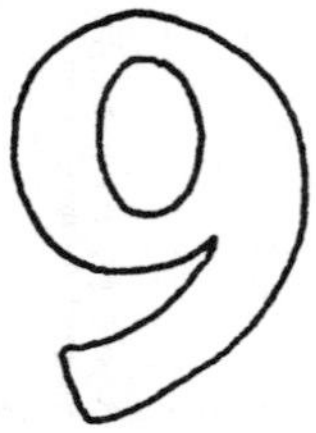

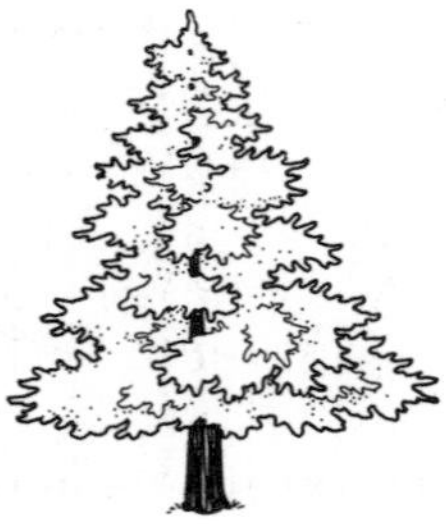

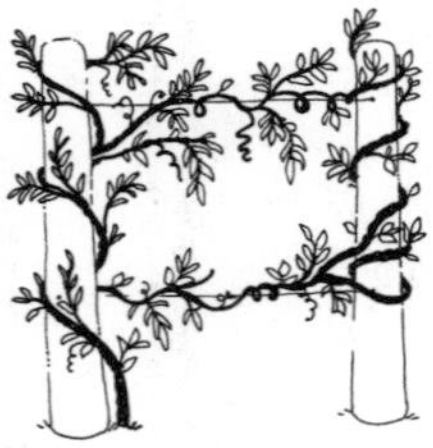

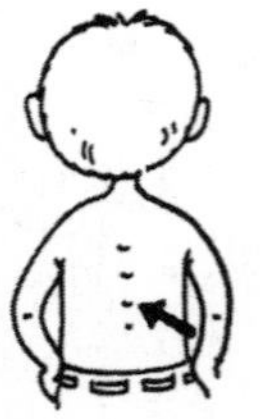

Look at the picture. Then build the word.

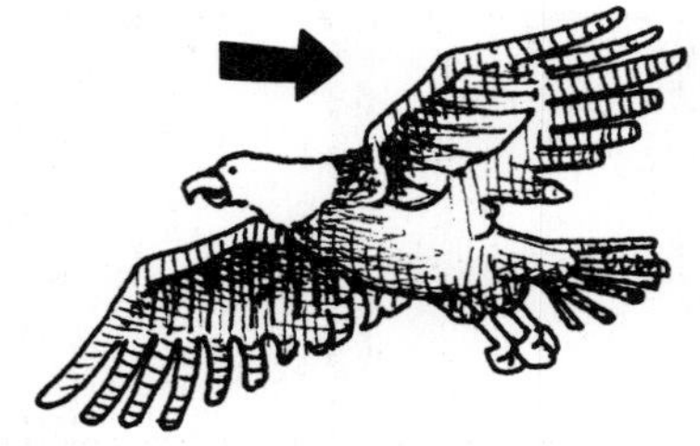

-ing

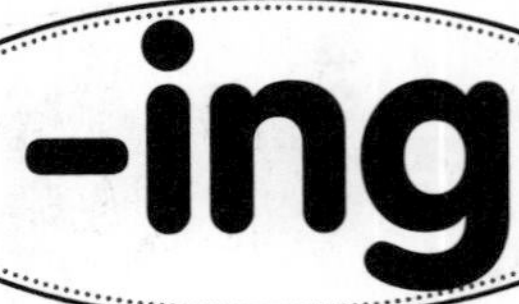

Look at the picture. Then build the word.

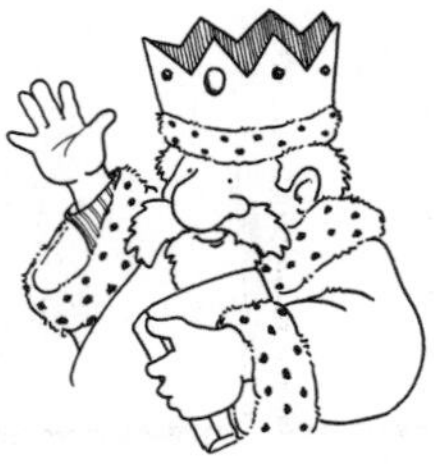

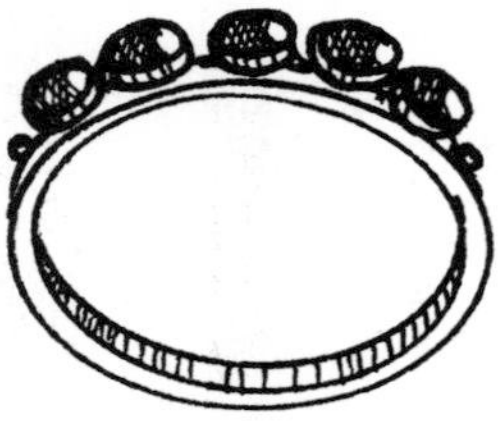

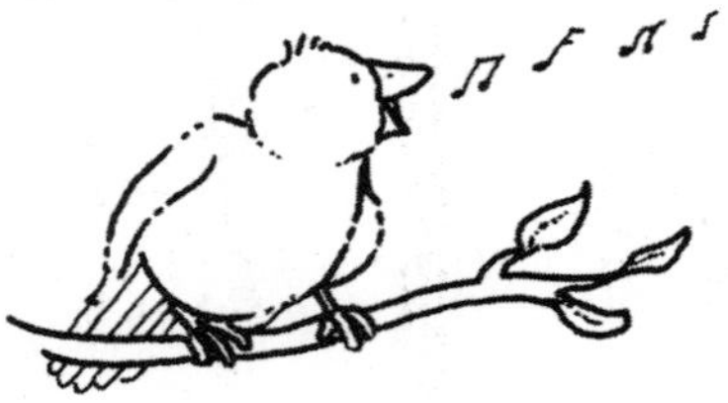

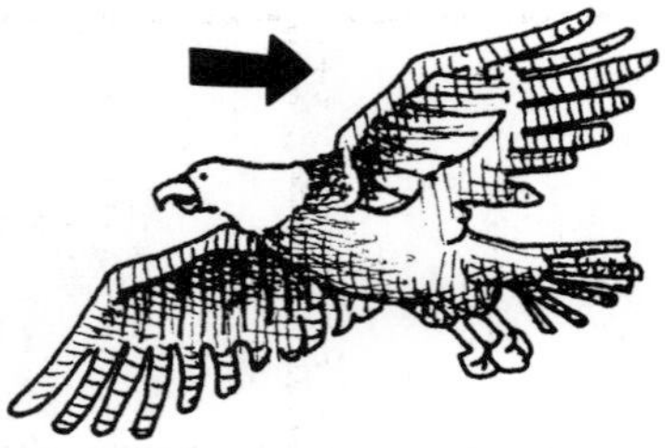

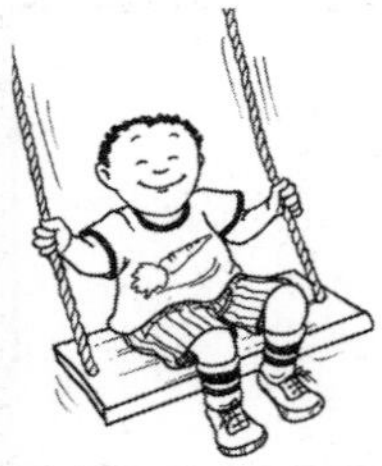

-ink

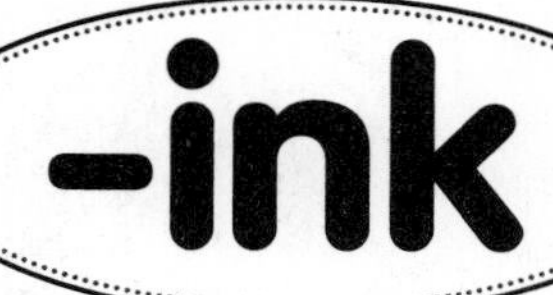

Look at the picture. Then build the word.

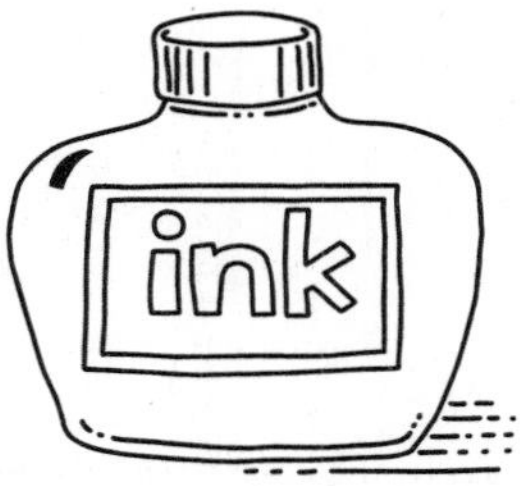

i n k

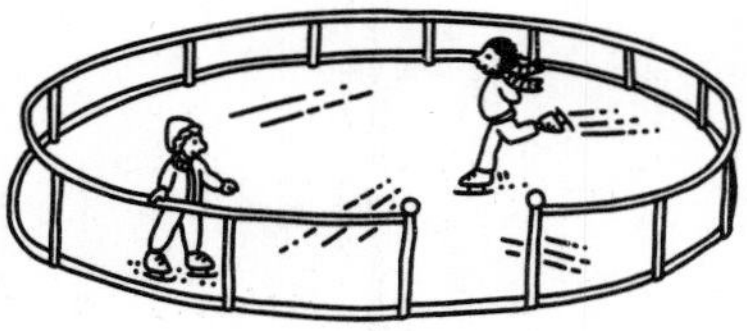

r i n k

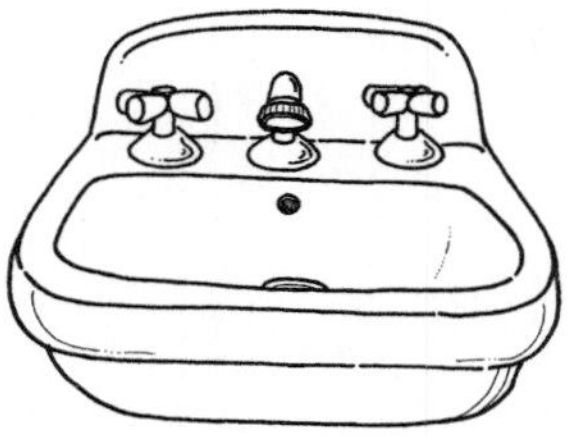

s i n k

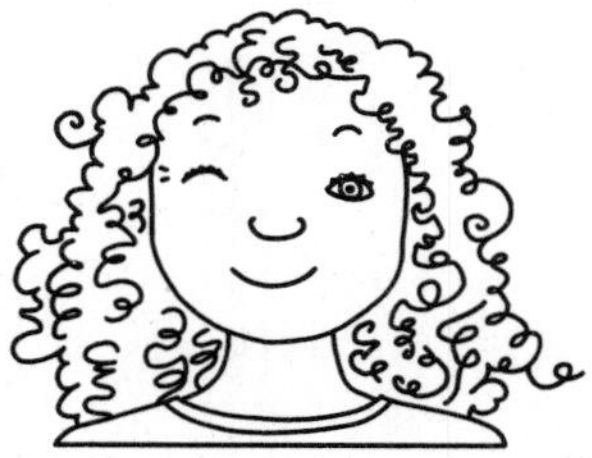

w i n k

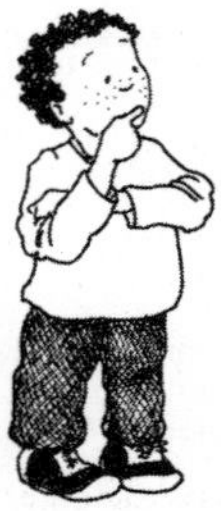

t h i n k

-ink

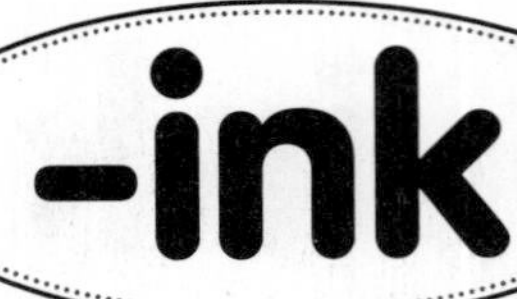

Look at the picture. Then build the word.

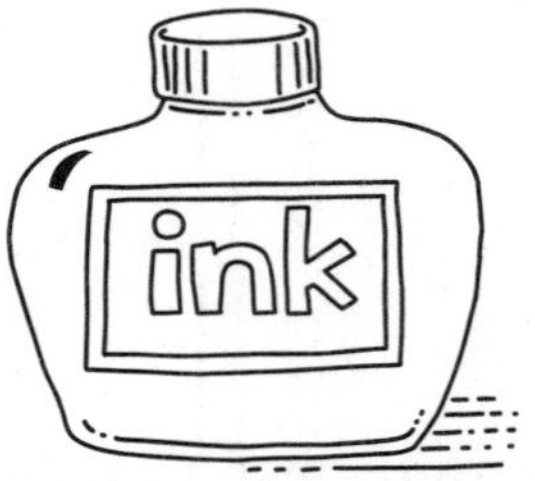

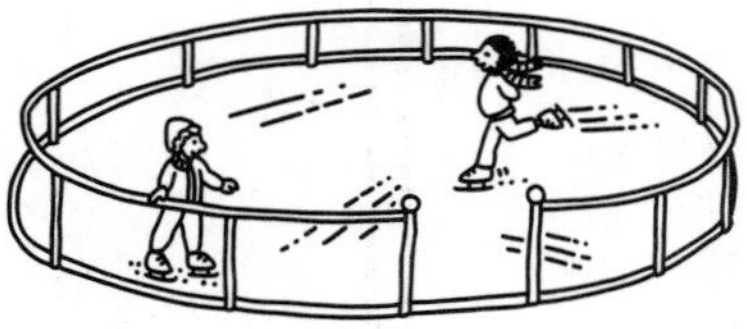

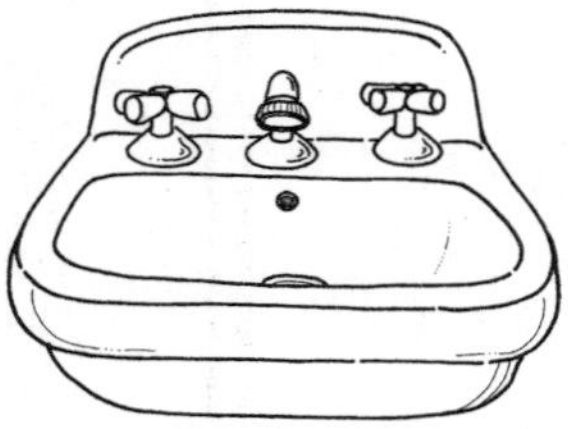

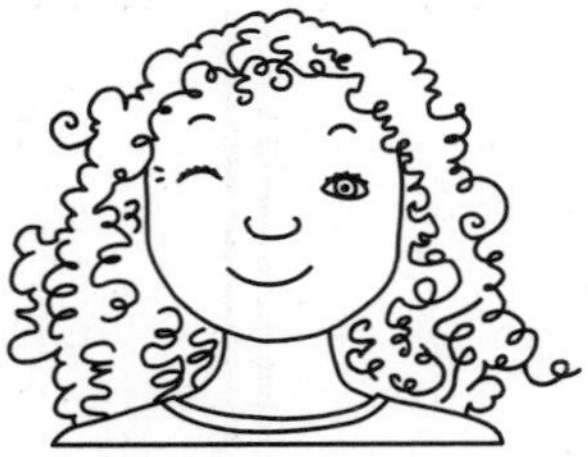

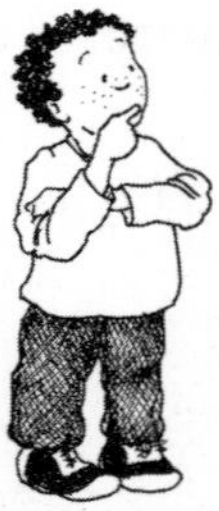

-ob

Look at the picture. Then build the word.

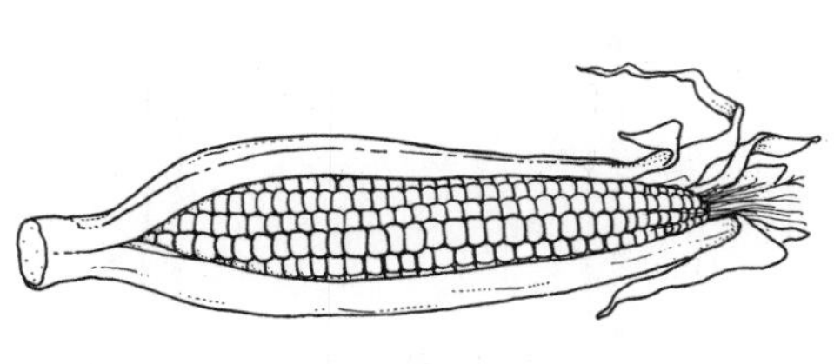

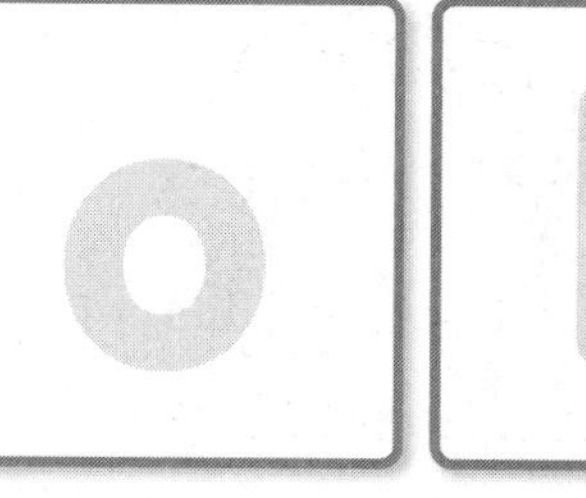

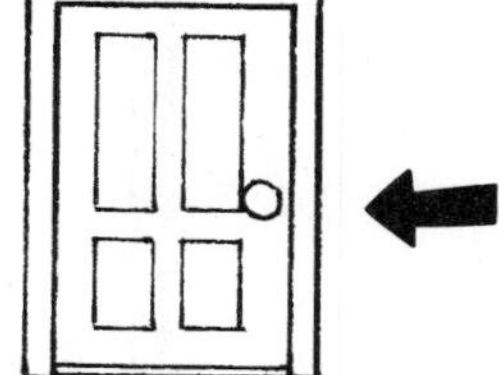

-ob

Look at the picture. Then build the word.

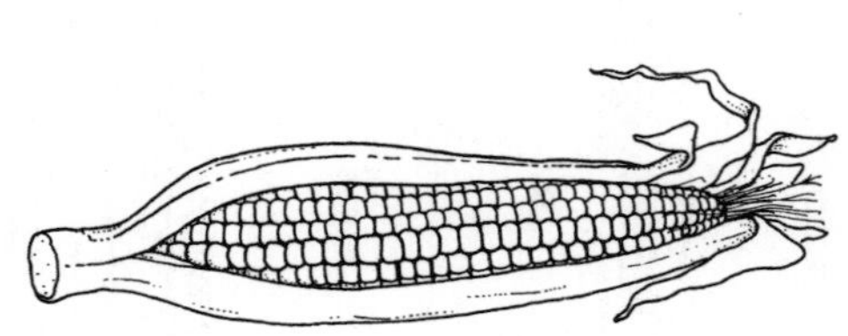

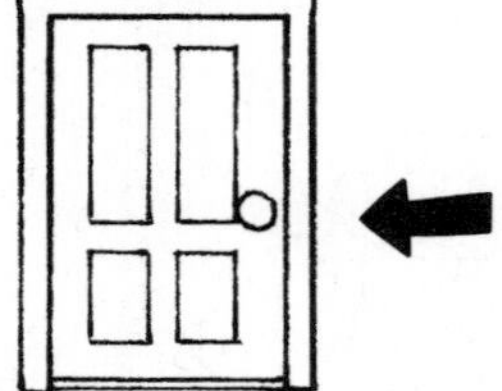

-og

Look at the picture. Then build the word.

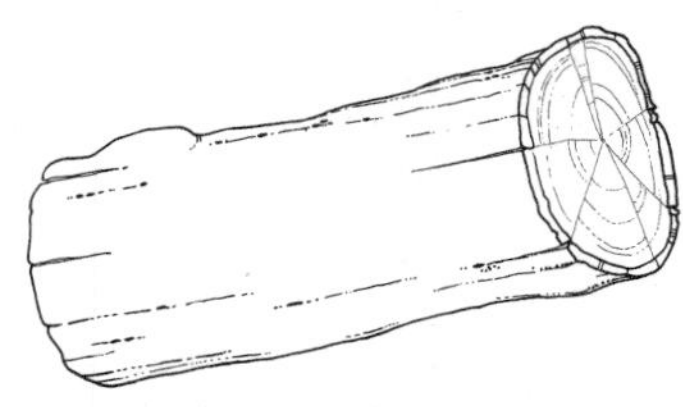

-og

Look at the picture. Then build the word.

Look at the picture. Then build the word.

c o p

h o p

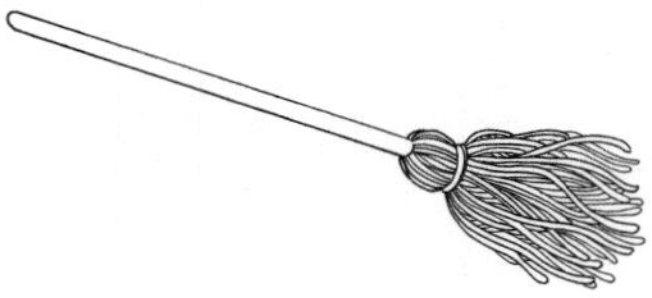

m o p

t o p

STOP

s t o p

-op

Look at the picture. Then build the word.

-ot

Look at the picture. Then build the word.

-ot

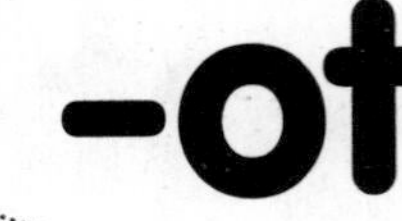

Look at the picture. Then build the word.

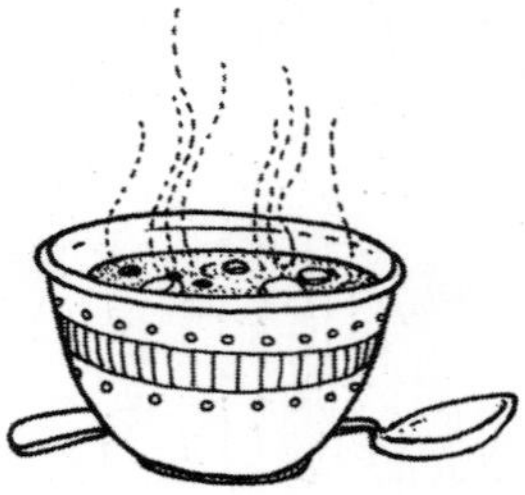

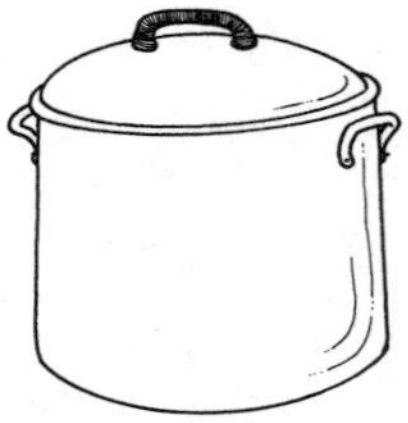

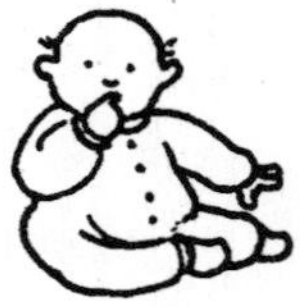

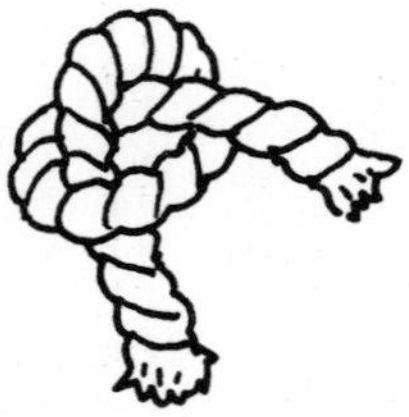

-ow

Look at the picture. Then build the word.

-ow

Look at the picture. Then build the word.

Look at the picture. Then build the word.

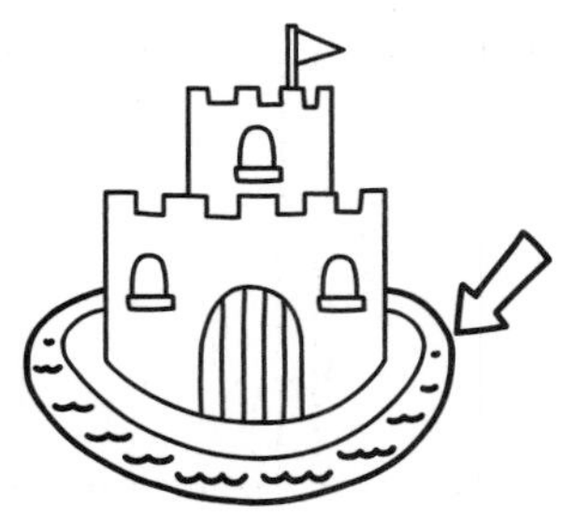    

-oat

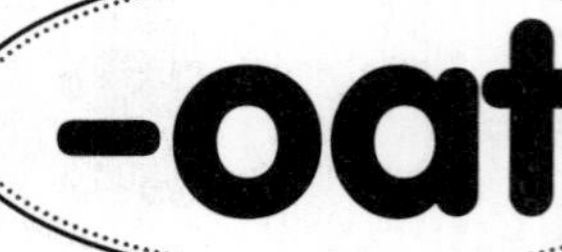

Look at the picture. Then build the word.

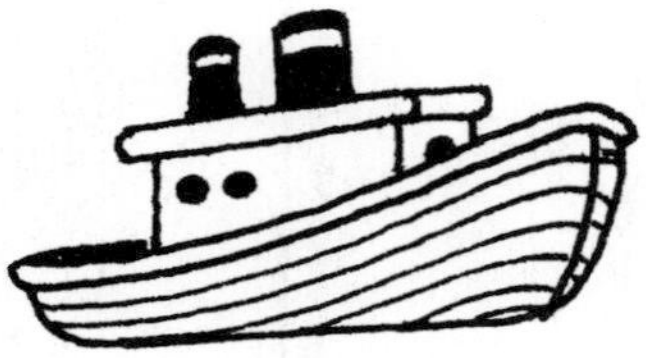

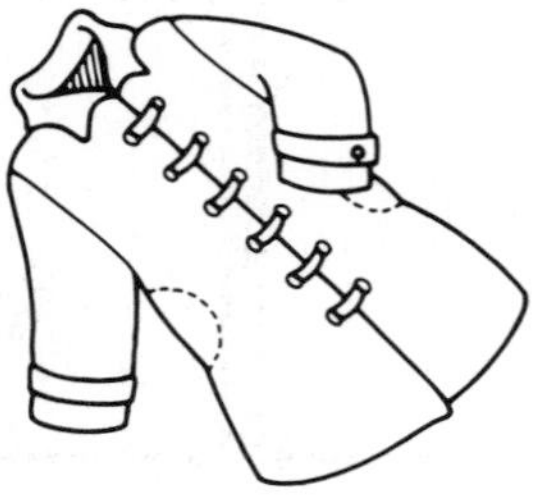

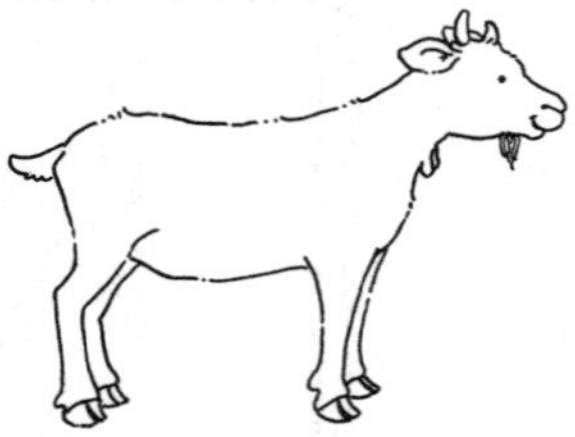

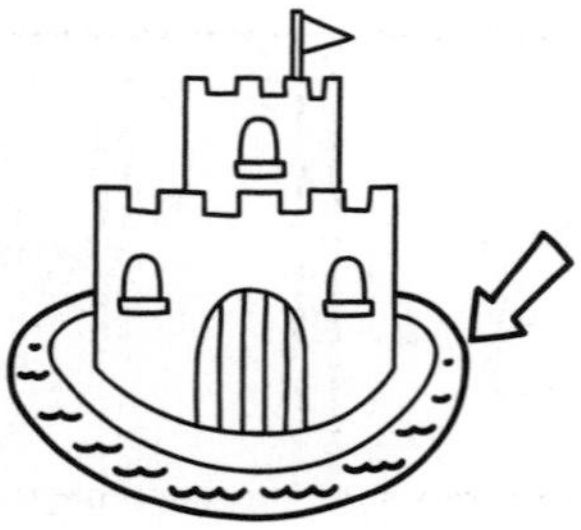

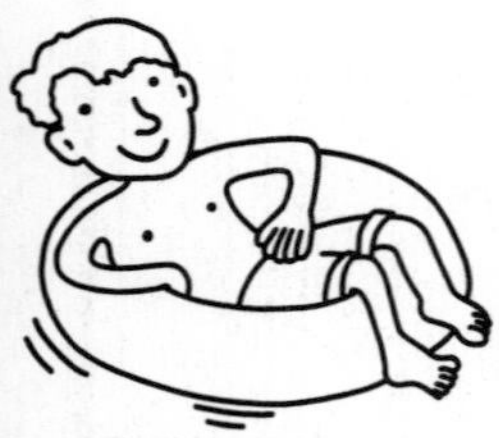

Look at the picture. Then build the word.

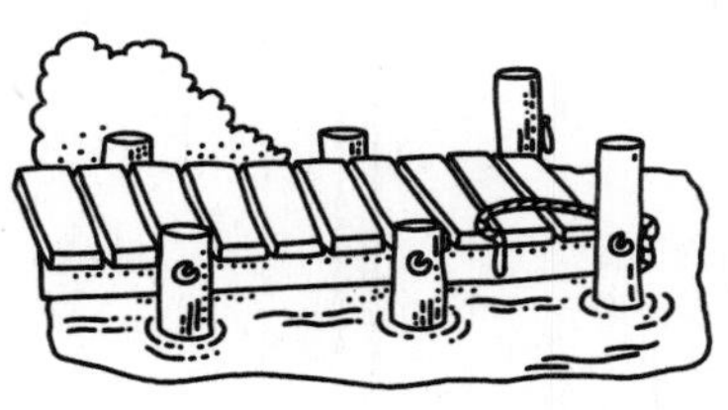

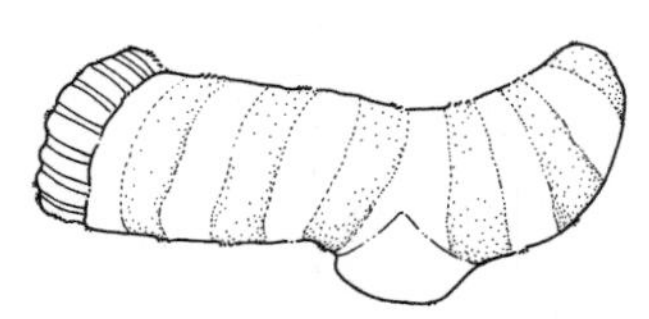
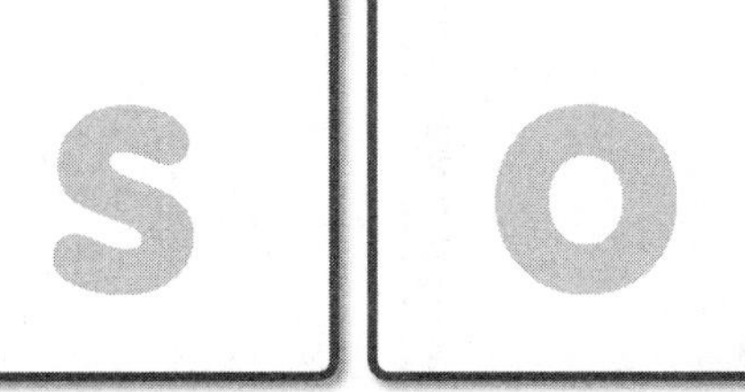

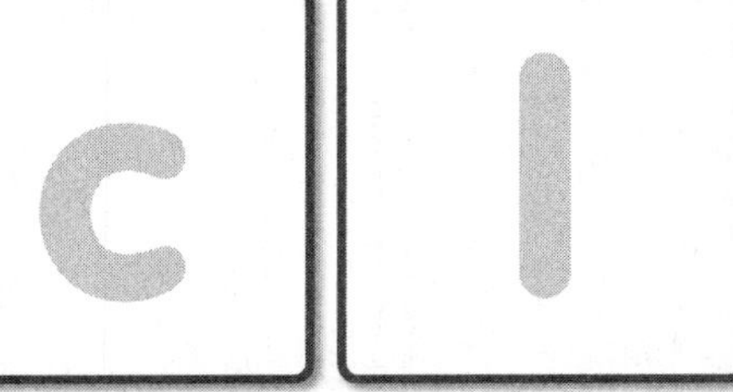

Look at the picture. Then build the word.

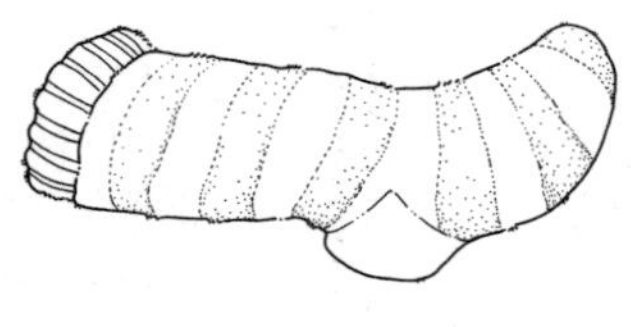  

-oke

Look at the picture. Then build the word.

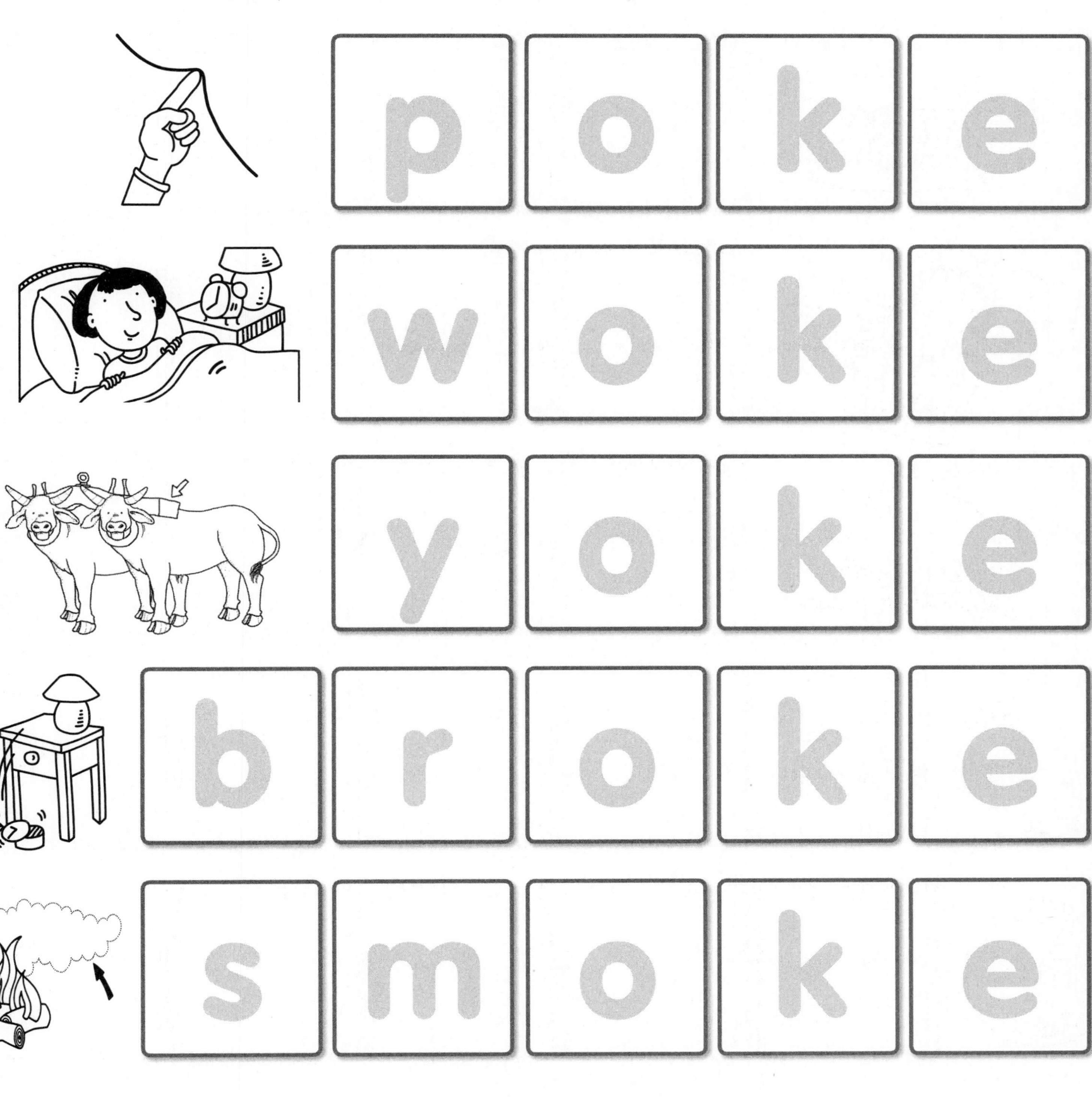

-oke

Look at the picture. Then build the word.

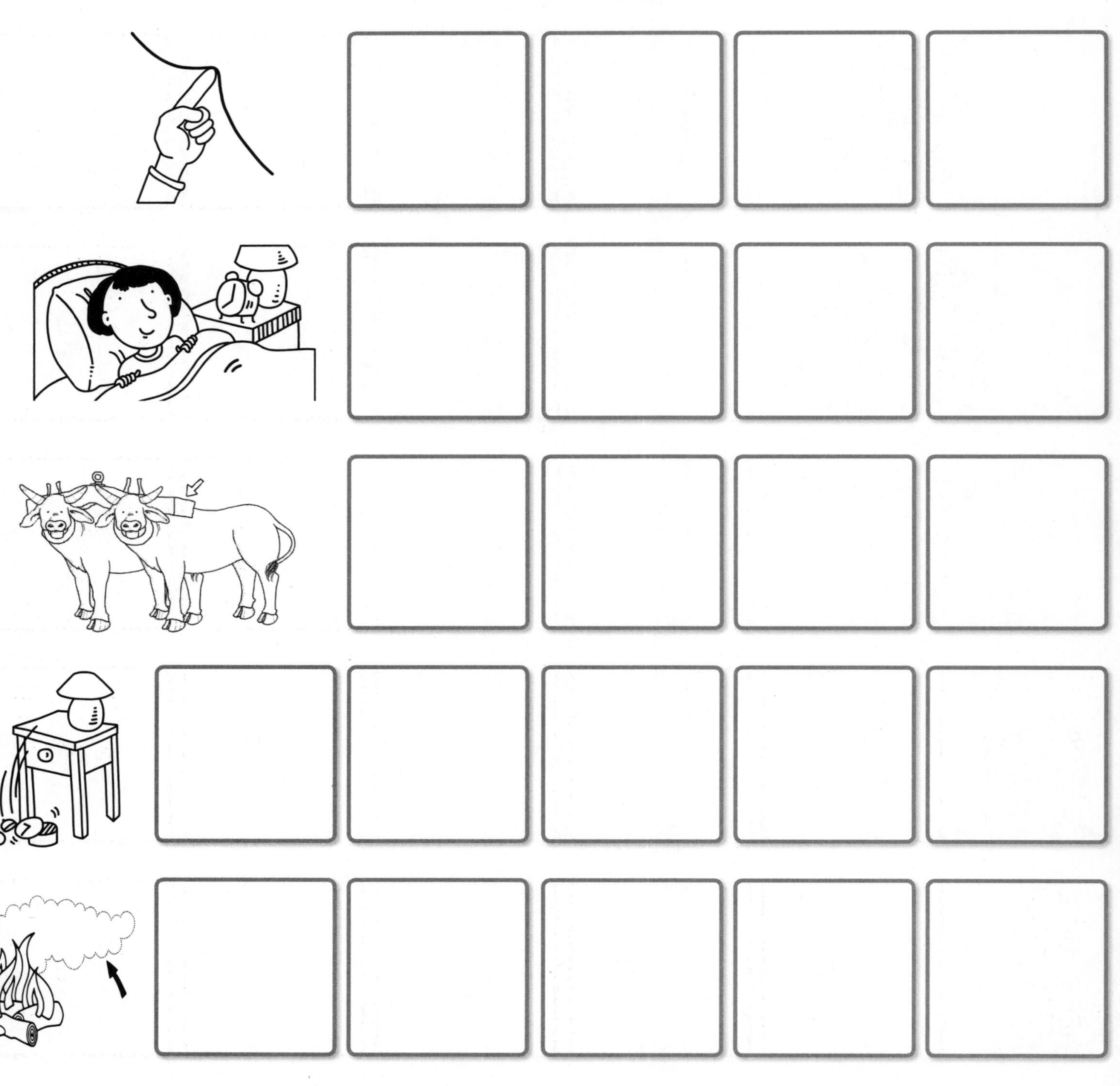

-ook

Look at the picture. Then build the word.

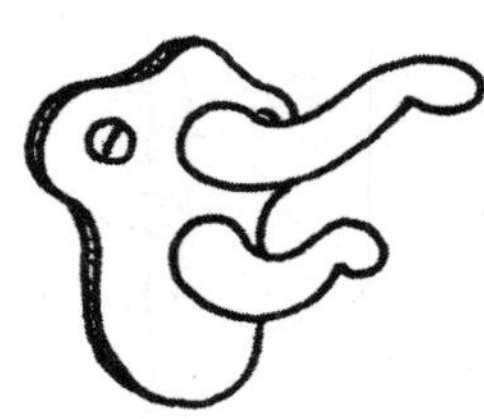    

-ook

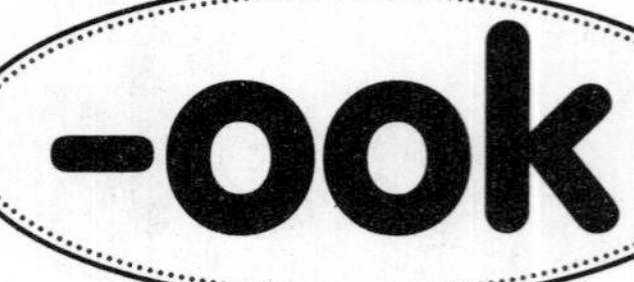

Look at the picture. Then build the word.

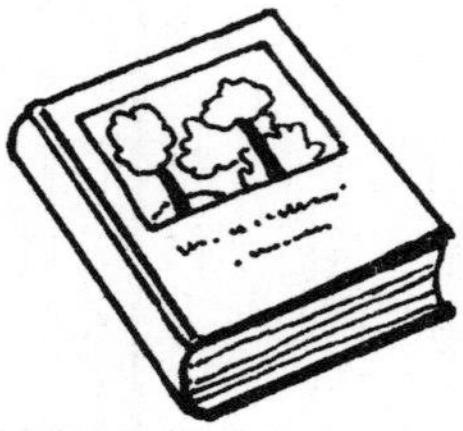

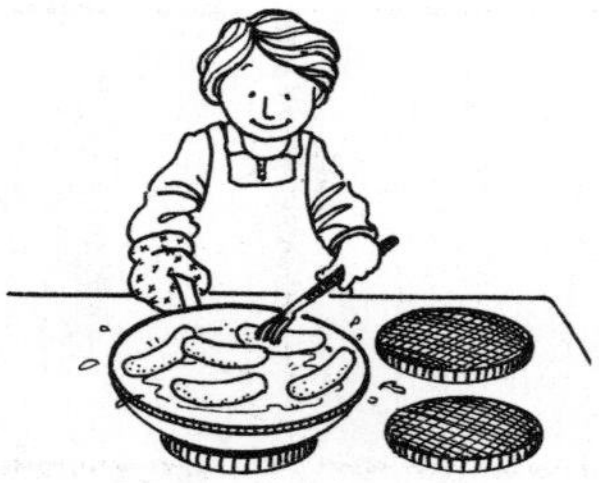

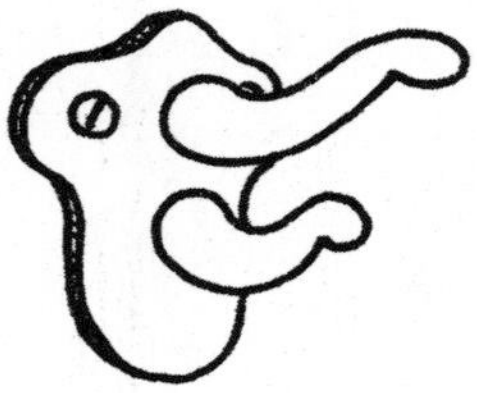

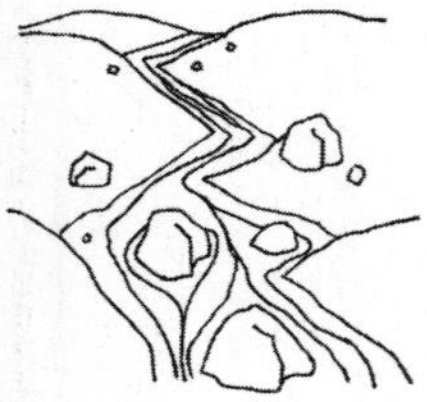

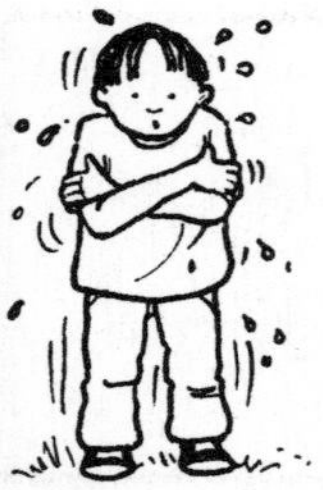

-ub

Look at the picture. Then build the word.

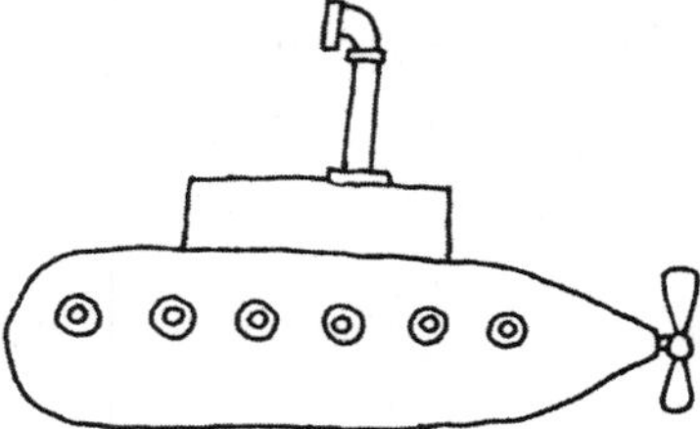

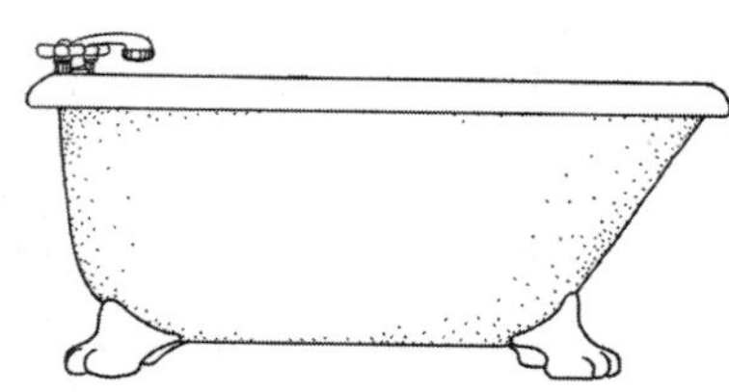

-ub

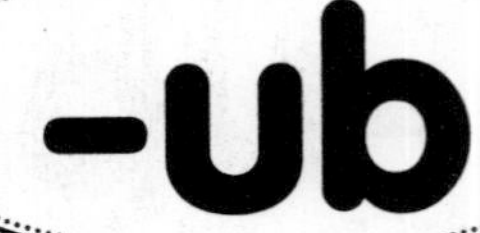

Look at the picture. Then build the word.

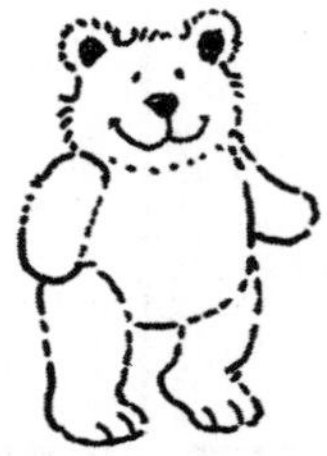

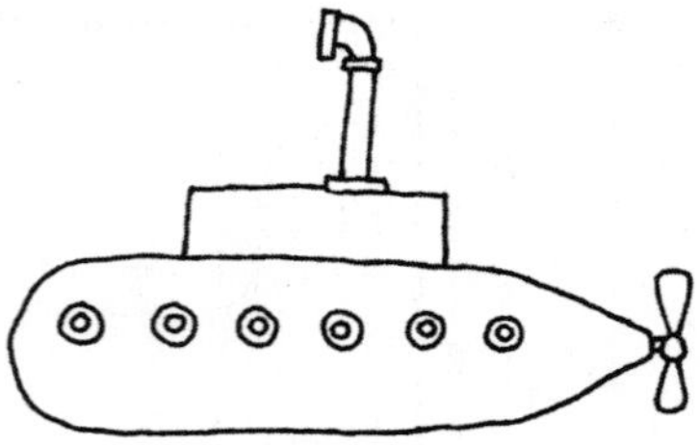

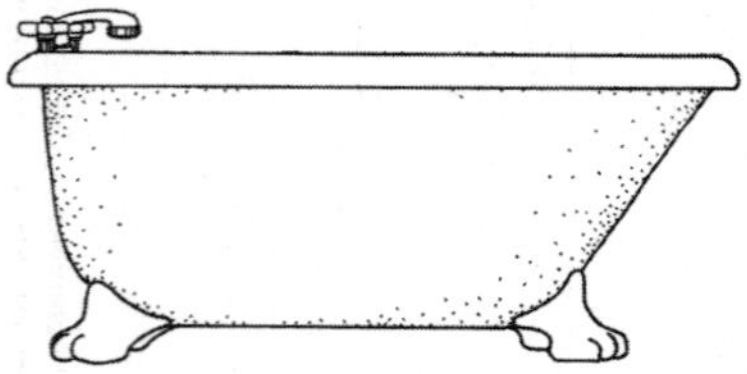

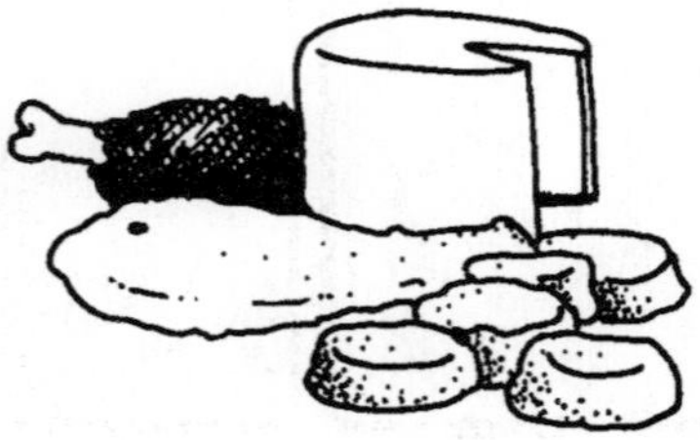

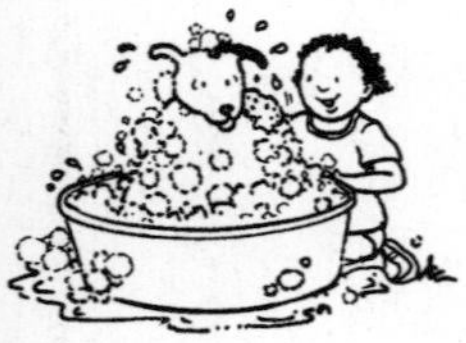

-ug

Look at the picture. Then build the word.

-ug

Look at the picture. Then build the word.

Look at the picture. Then build the word.

g u m

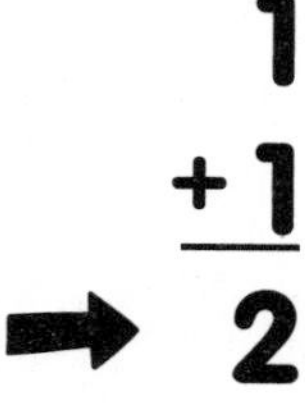

s u m

m

m

Look at the picture. Then build the word.

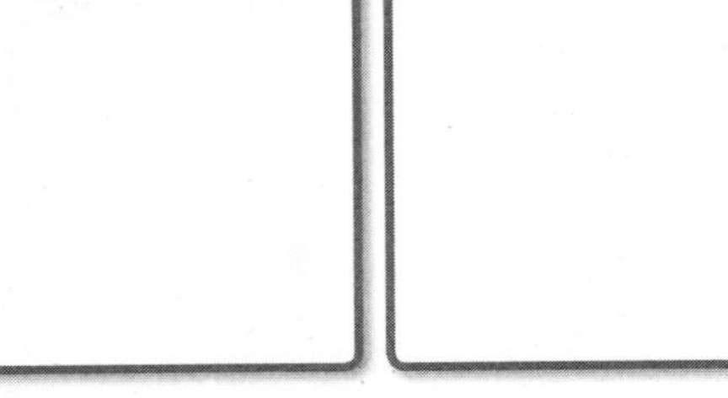

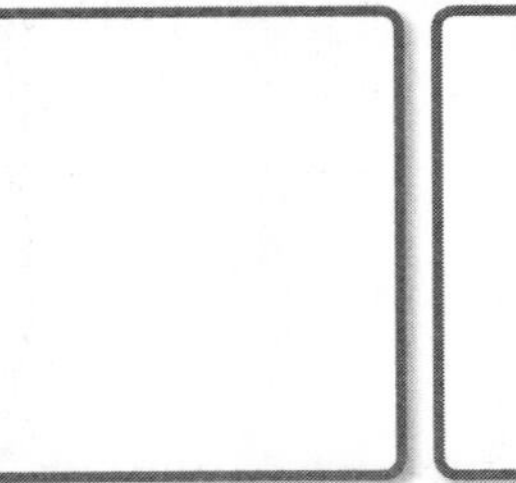

-uck

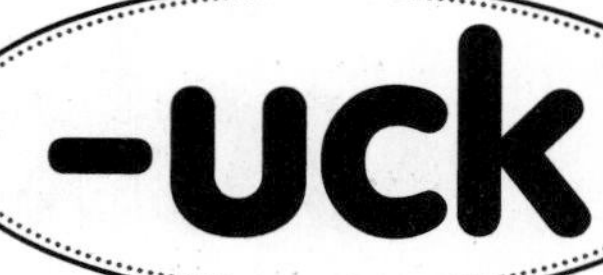

Look at the picture. Then build the word.

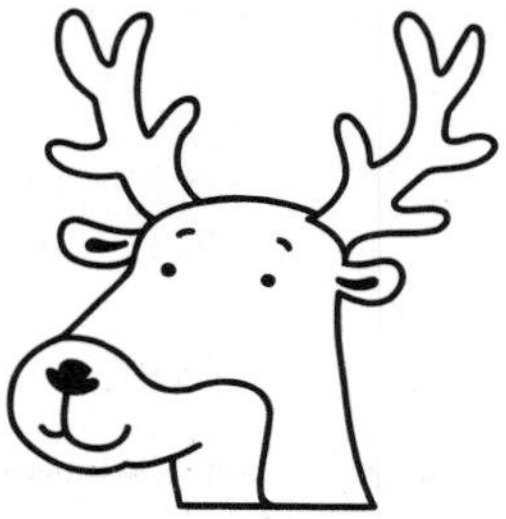

| b | u | c | k |

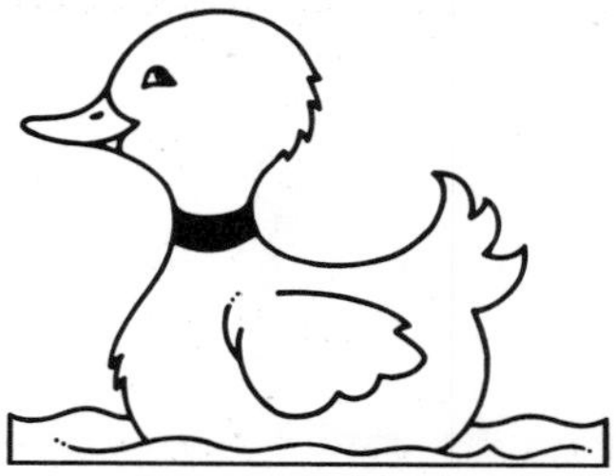

| d | u | c | k |

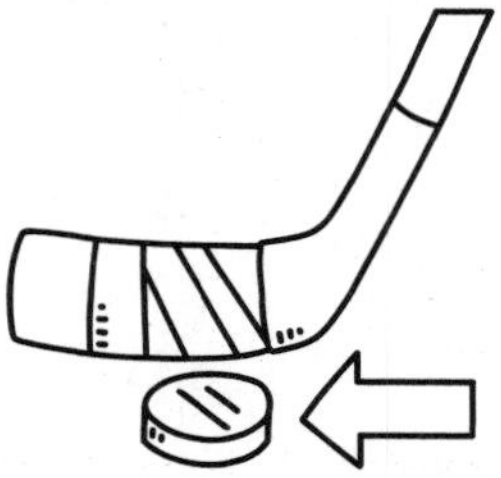

| p | u | c | k |

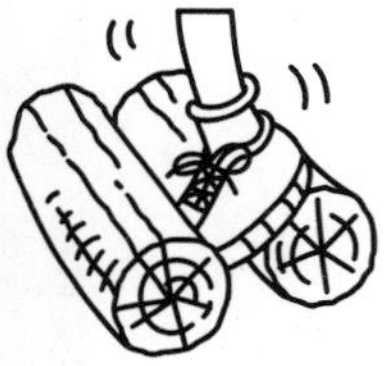

| s | t | u | c | k |

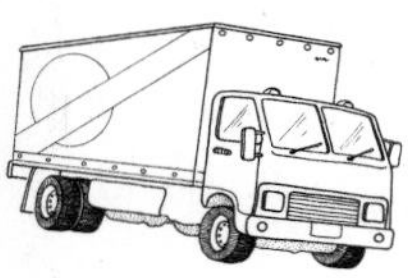

| t | r | u | c | k |

-uck

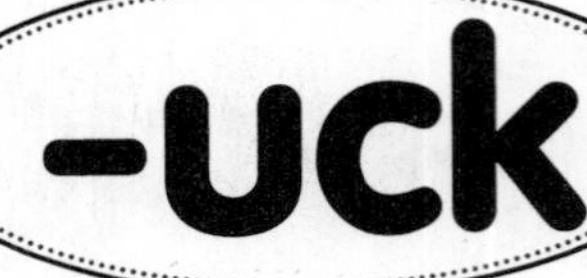

Look at the picture. Then build the word.

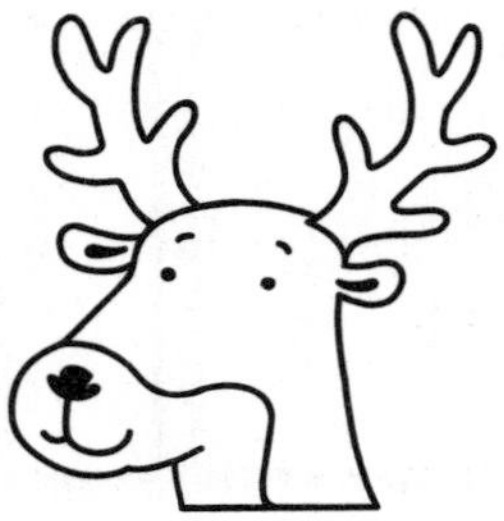

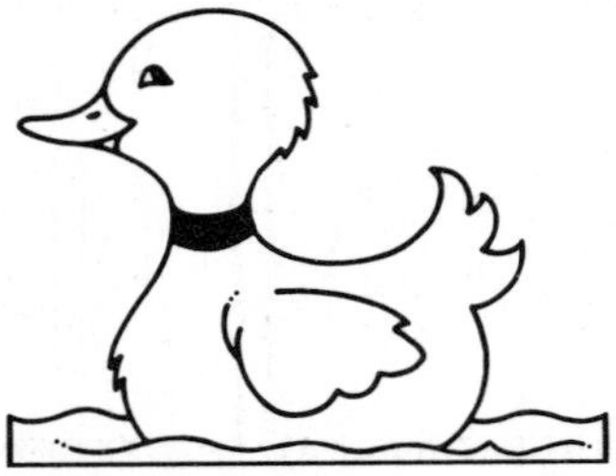

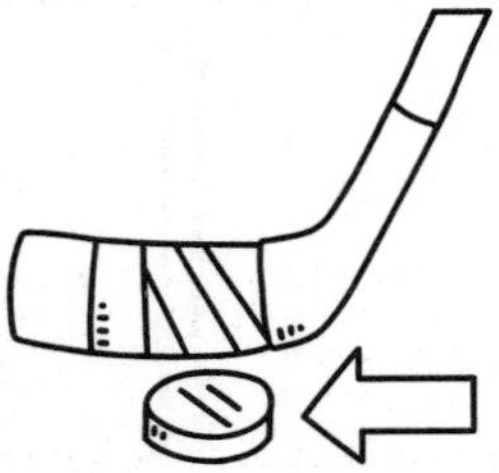

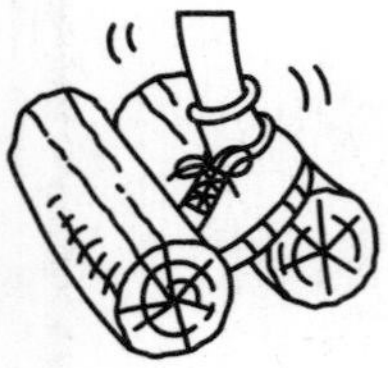

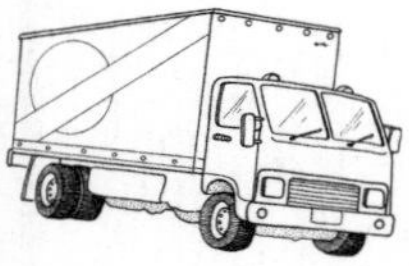

Look at the picture. Then build the word.

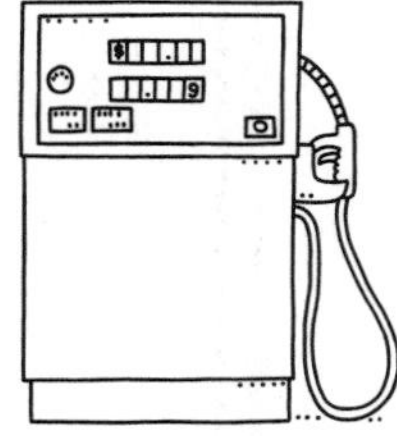

-ump

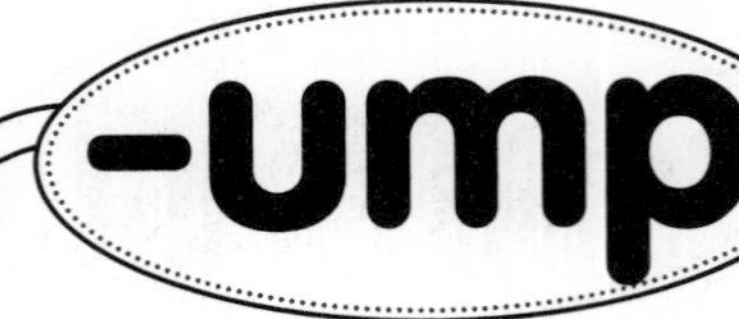

Look at the picture. Then build the word.

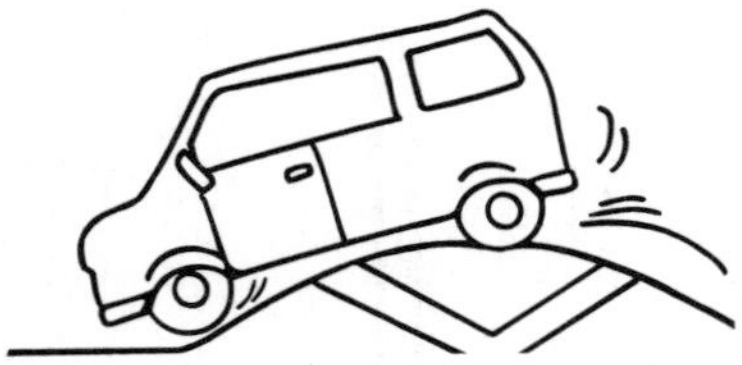

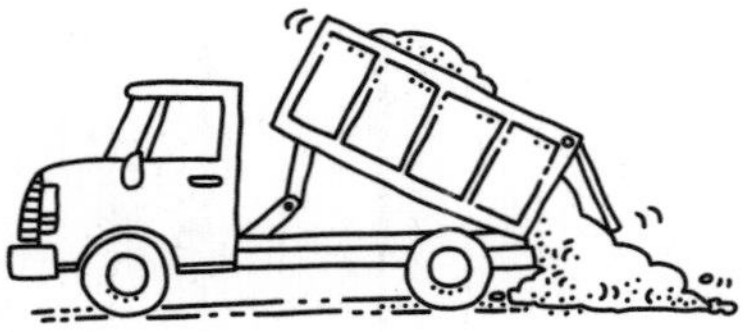

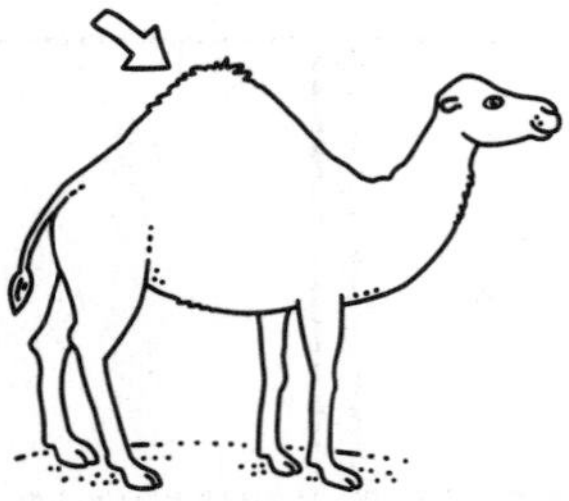

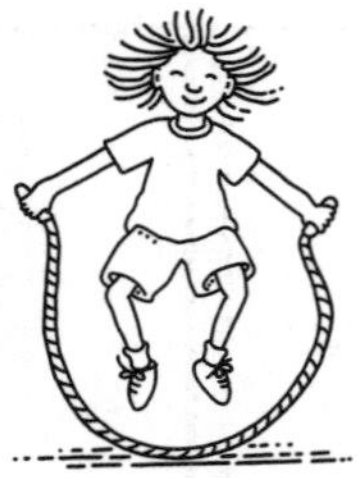

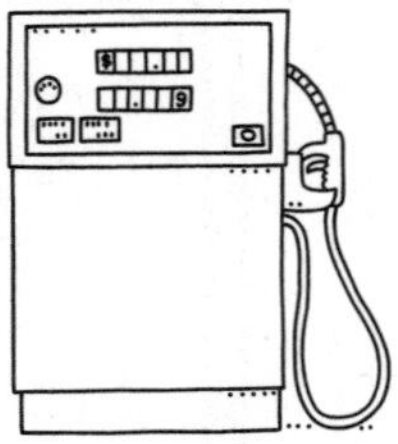

-unk

Look at the picture. Then build the word.

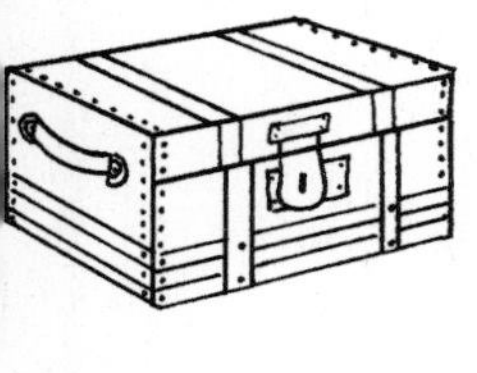

-unk

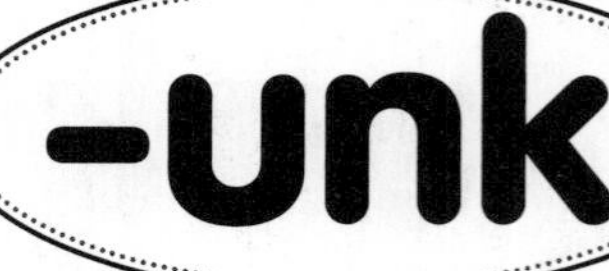

Look at the picture. Then build the word.

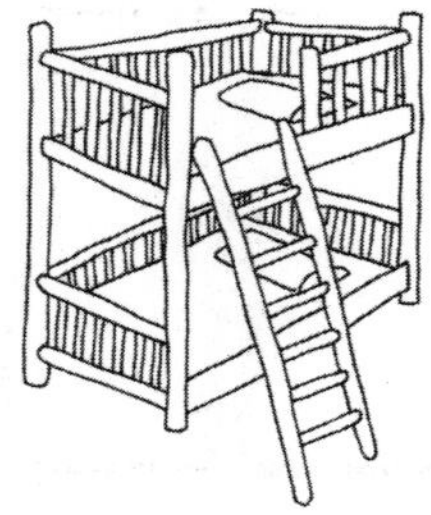

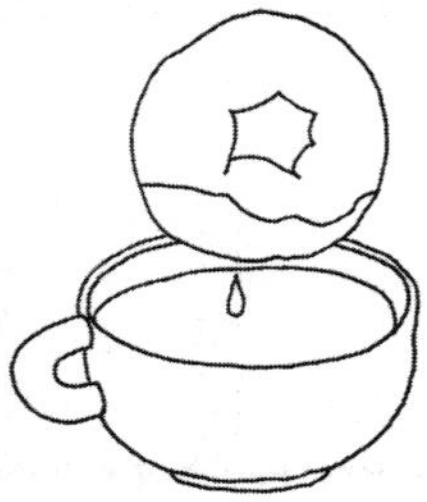

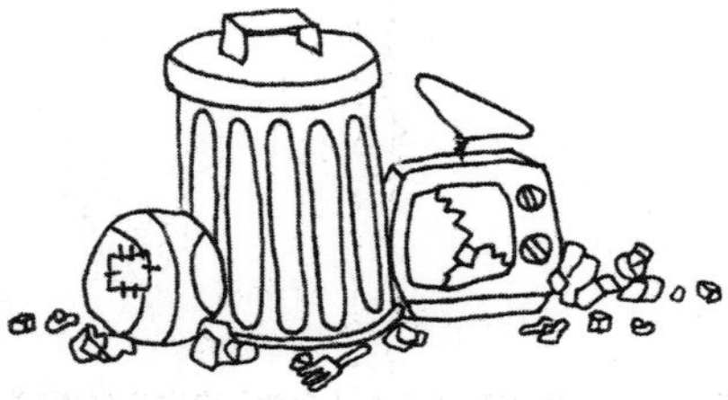

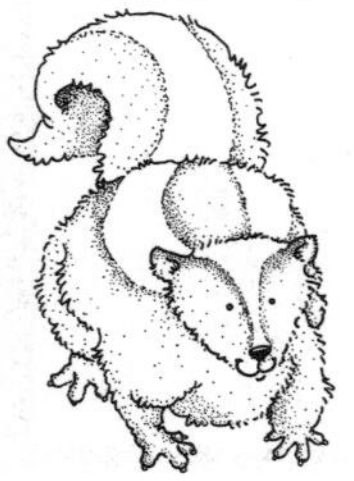

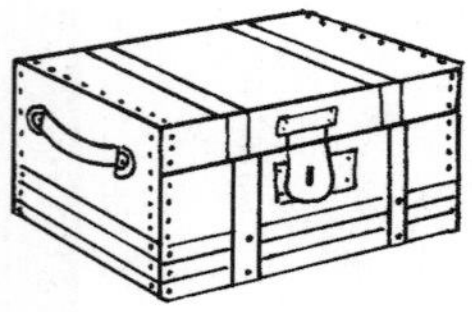

-y

Look at the picture. Then build the word.

c	r	y
f	l	y
f	r	y
s	k	y
s	p	y

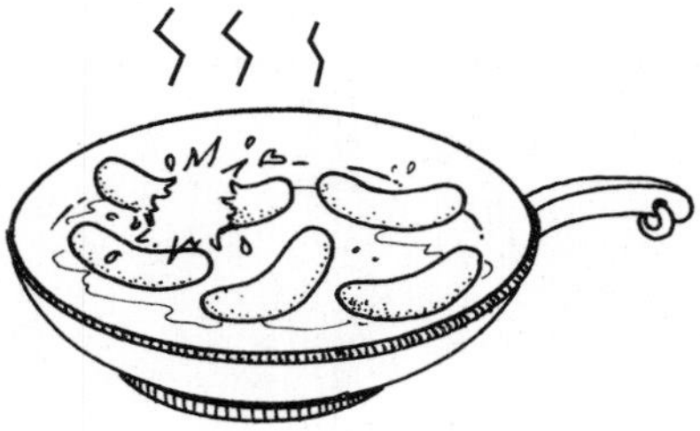

-y

Look at the picture. Then build the word.

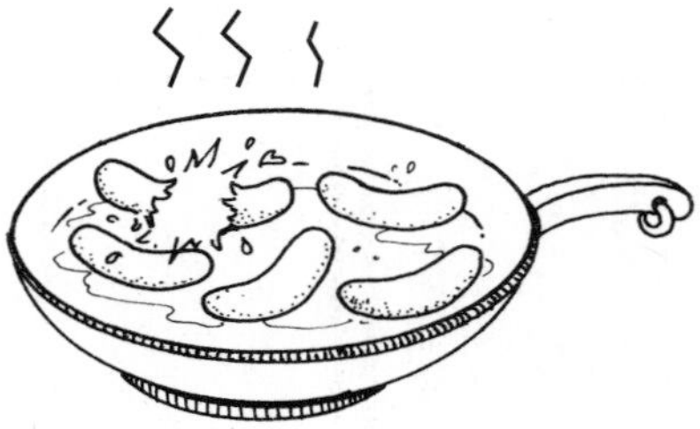

Look at the picture. Then build the word.

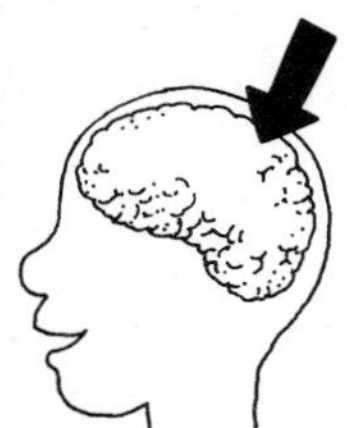

b

a

b

b

b

b

br

Look at the picture. Then build the word.

Look at the picture. Then build the word.

c	h	i	n

c	h	a	i	n

c	h	a	i	r

c	h	e	s	t

c	h	i	c	k

ch

Look at the picture. Then build the word.

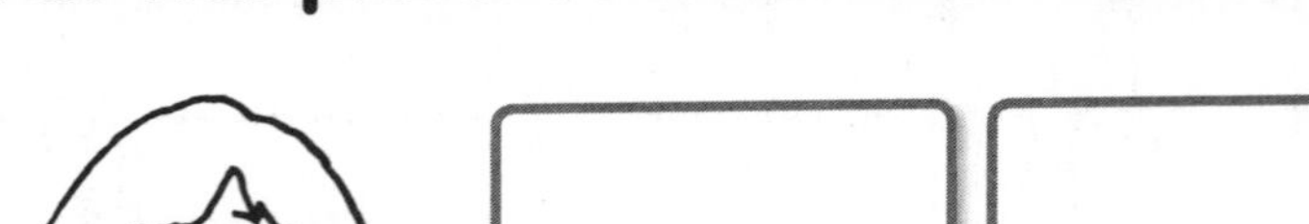

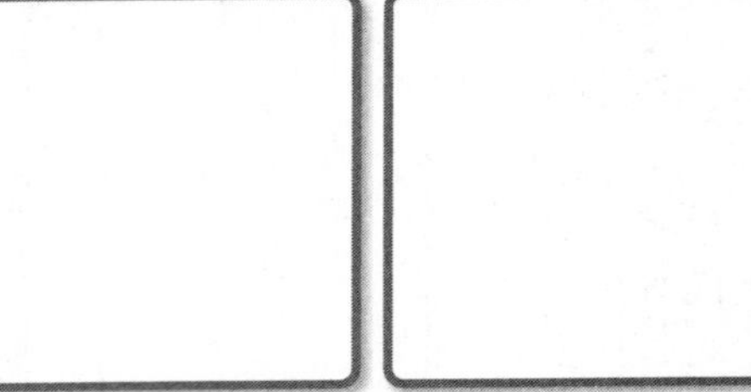

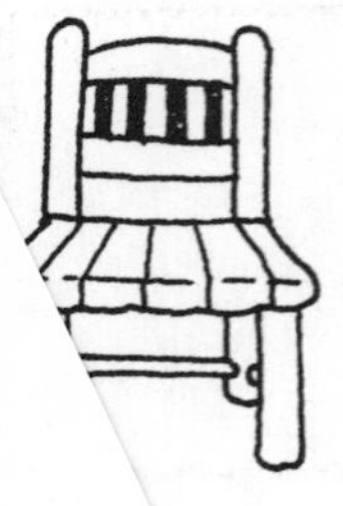

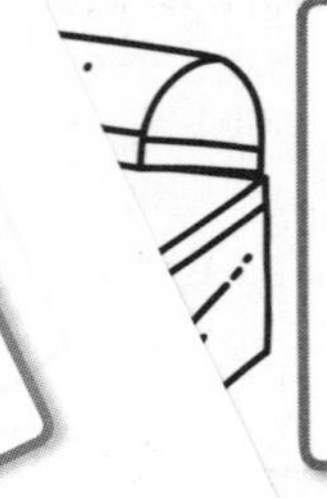

cl

Look at the picture. Then build the word.

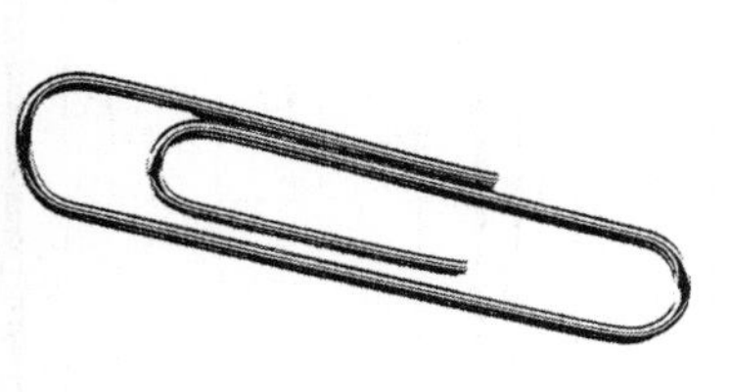

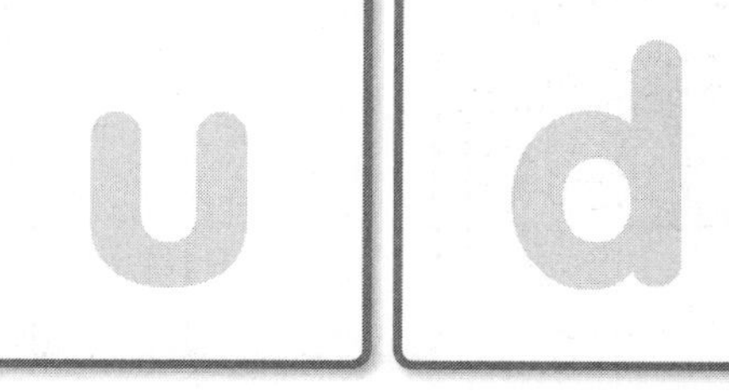

cl

Look at the picture. Then build the word.

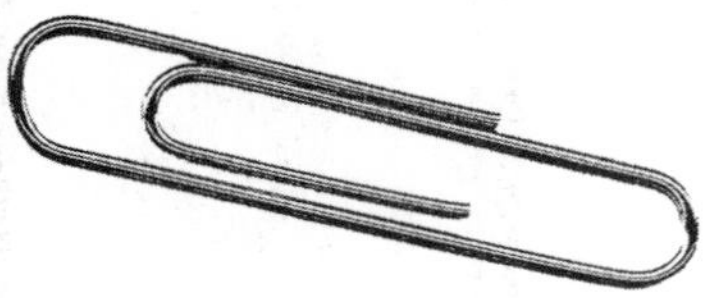

Look at the picture. Then build the word.

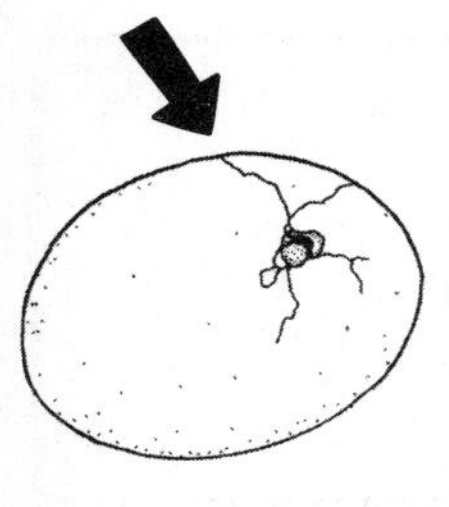

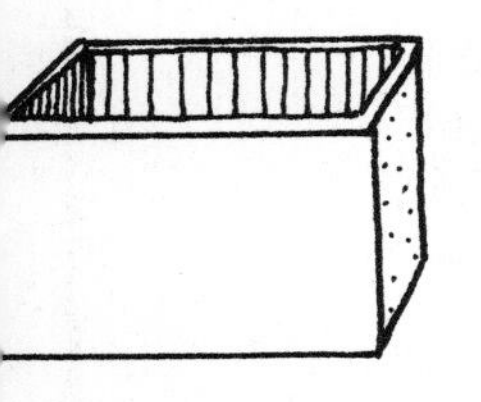

cr

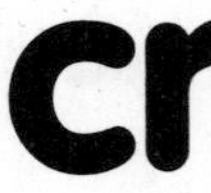

Look at the picture. Then build the word.

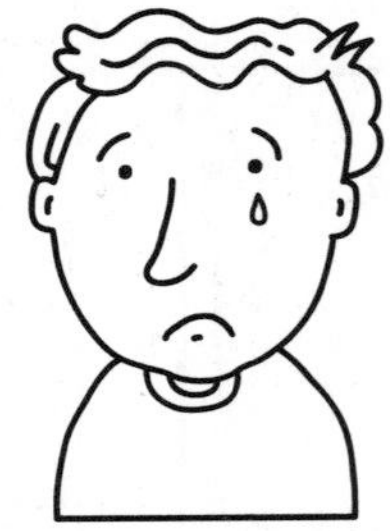

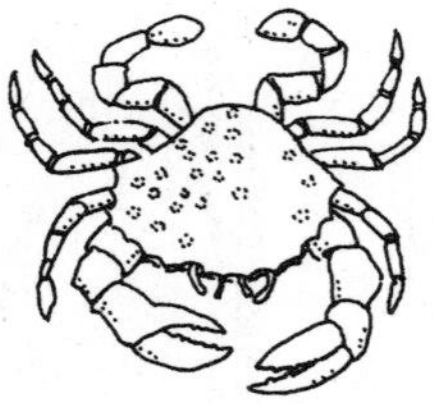

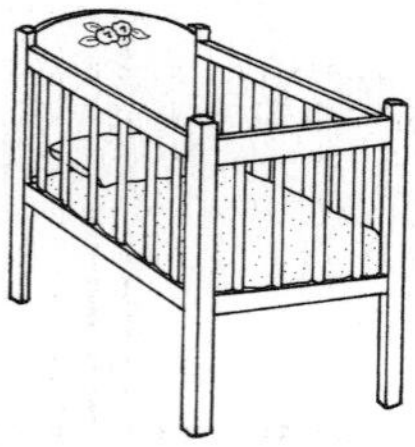

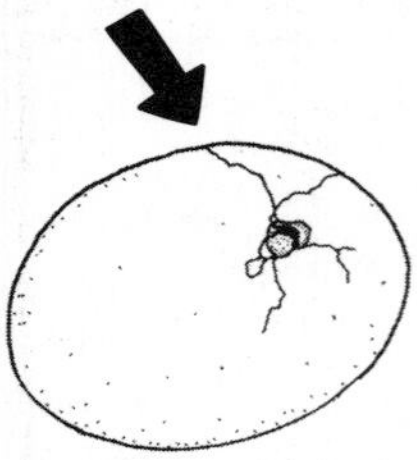

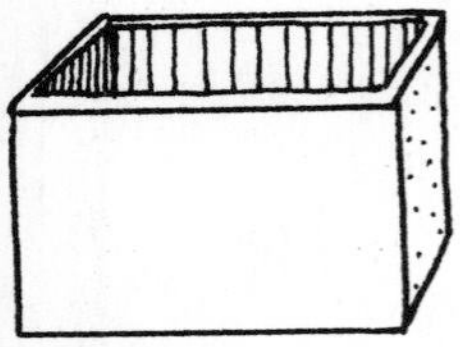

fl

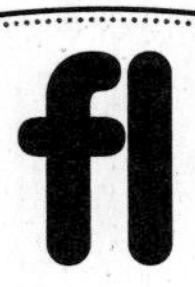

Look at the picture. Then build the word.

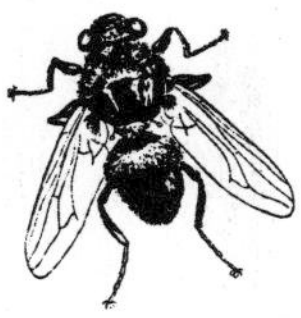

f l y

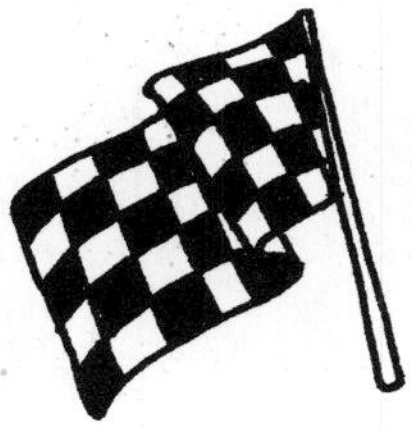

f l a g

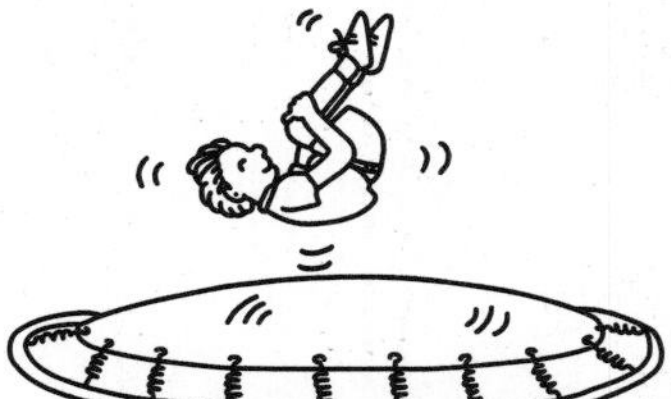

f l i p

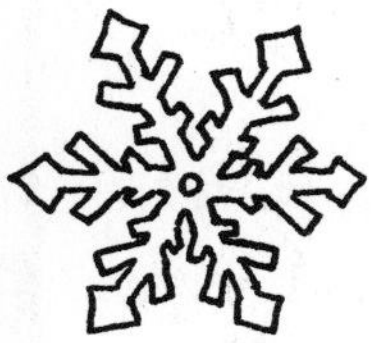

f l a k e

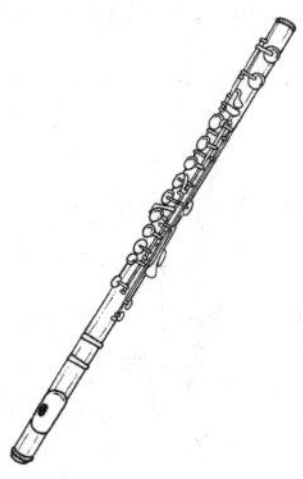

f l u t e

fl

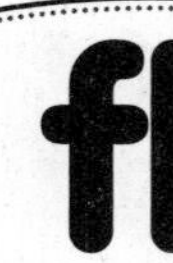

Look at the picture. Then build the word.

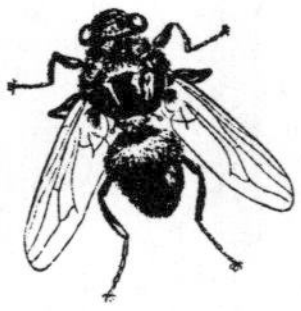

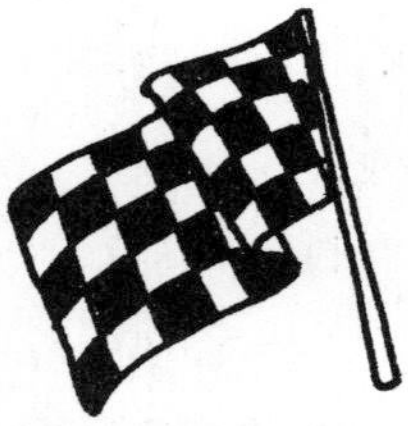

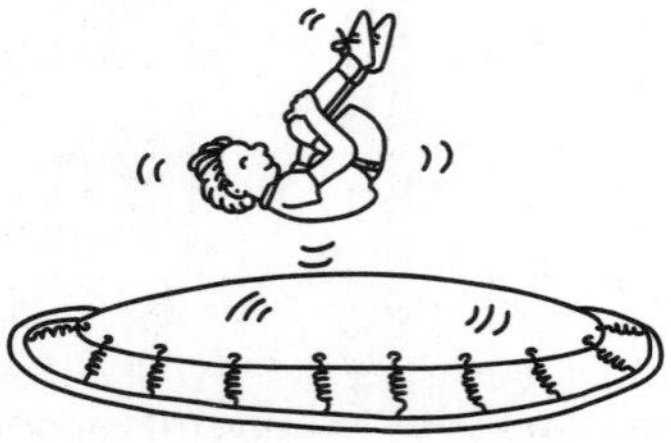

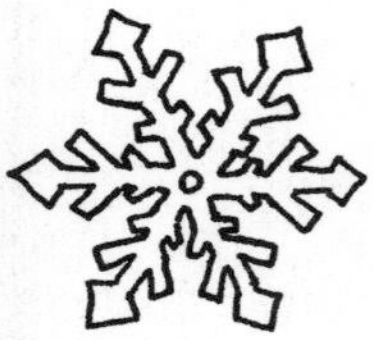

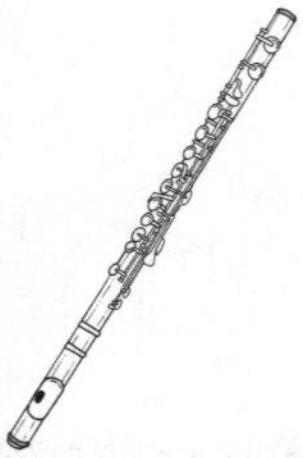

gl

Look at the picture. Then build the word.

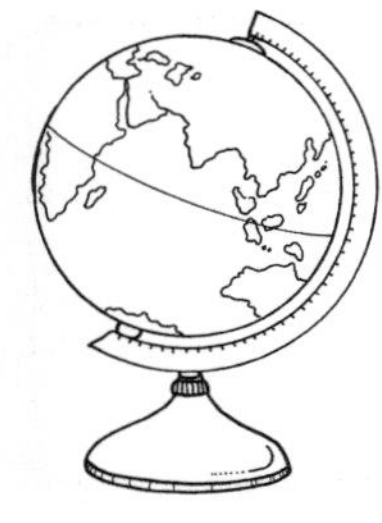

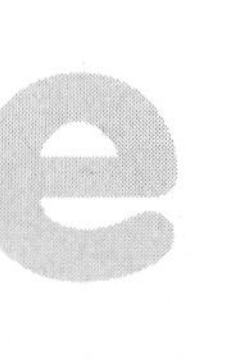

gl

Look at the picture. Then build the word.

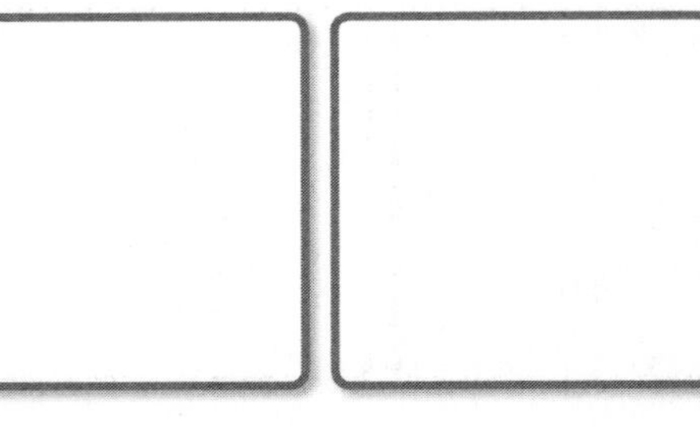

gr

Look at the picture. Then build the word.

g r i n

g r a p e

g r a s s

g r e e n

g r i l l

 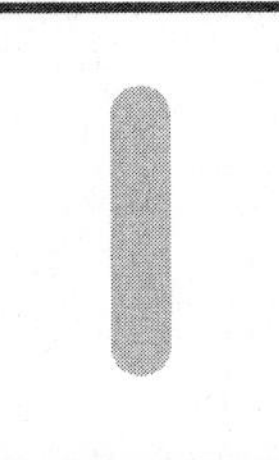 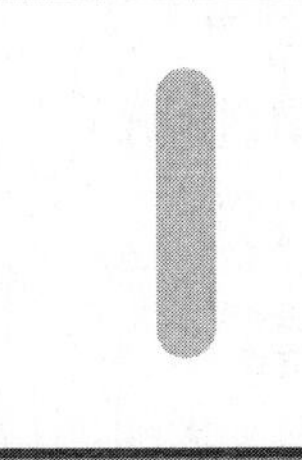

gr

Look at the picture. Then build the word.

pl

Look at the picture. Then build the word.

  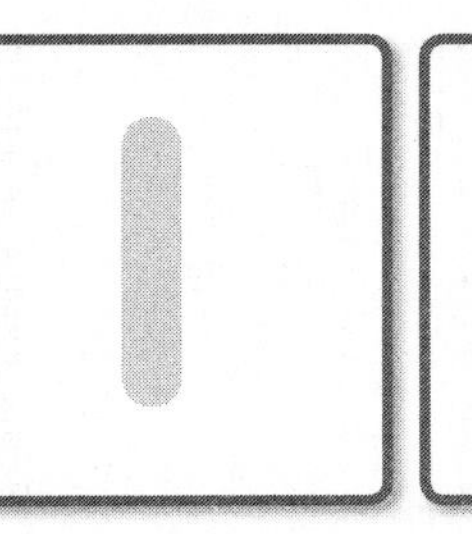 

p l u m

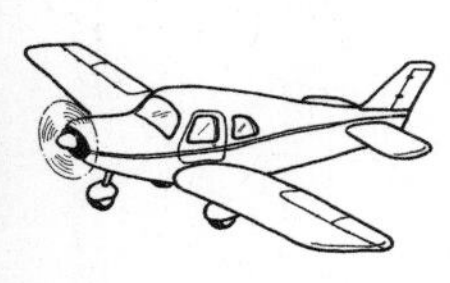   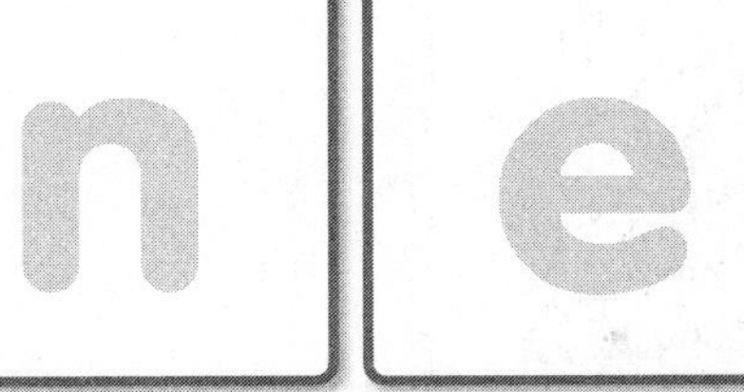

p l a n e

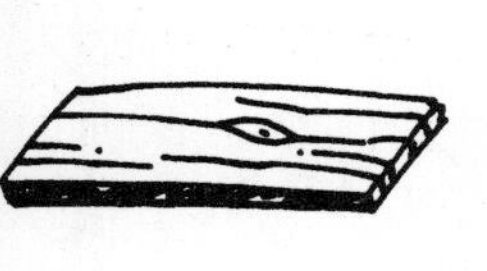   

p l a n k

p l a n t

p l a t e

pl

Look at the picture. Then build the word.

sh

Look at the picture. Then build the word.

s h i p

s h o e

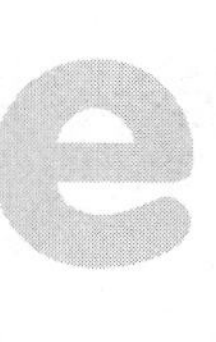

s h e e p

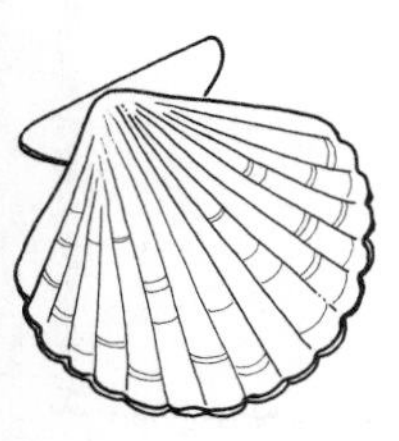

s h e l l

s h i r t

sh

Look at the picture. Then build the word.

sk

Look at the picture. Then build the word.

sk

Look at the picture. Then build the word.

sl

Look at the picture. Then build the word.

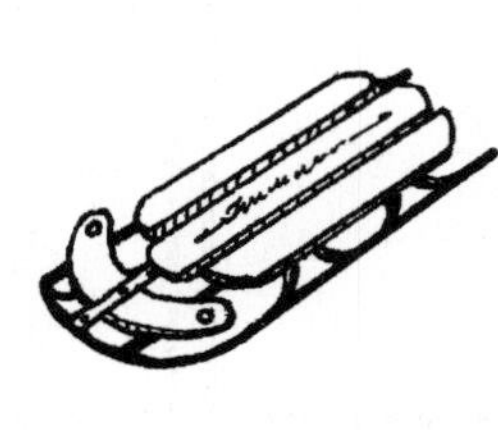

sl

Look at the picture. Then build the word.

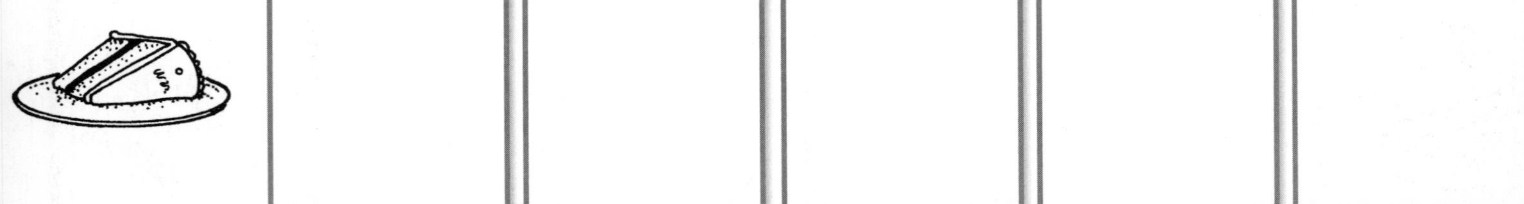

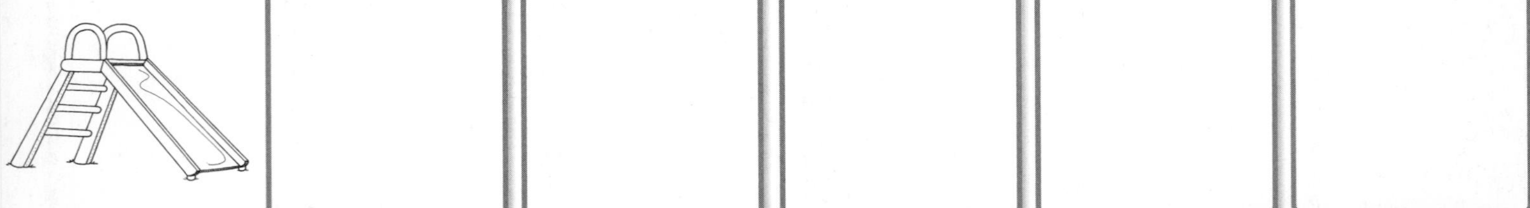

sn

Look at the picture. Then build the word.

s n a p

s n o w

s n a i l

s n a k e

s n i f f

sn

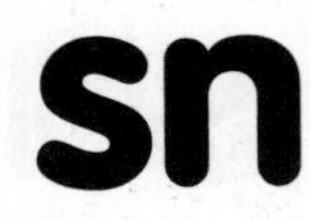

Look at the picture. Then build the word.

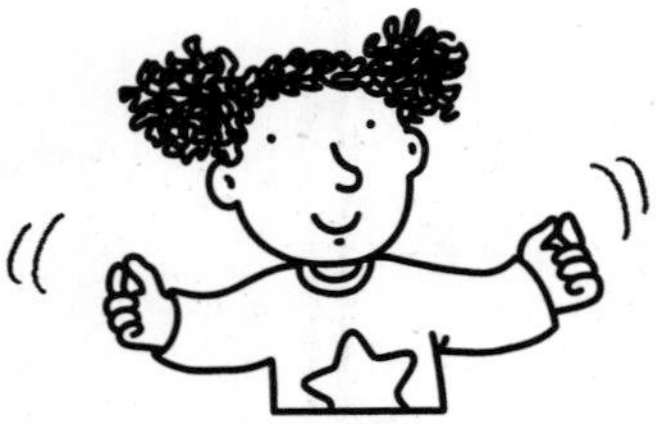

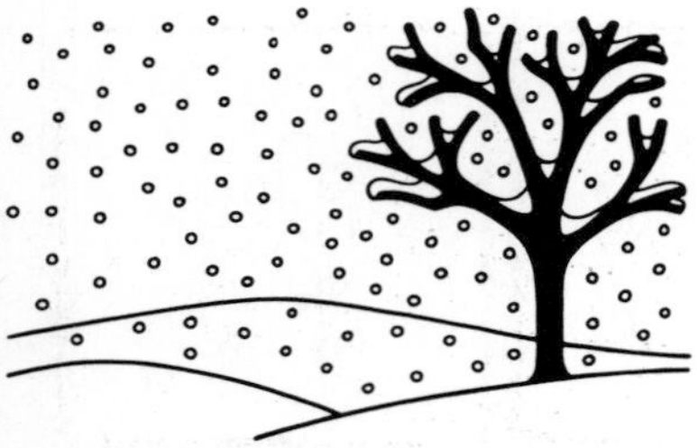

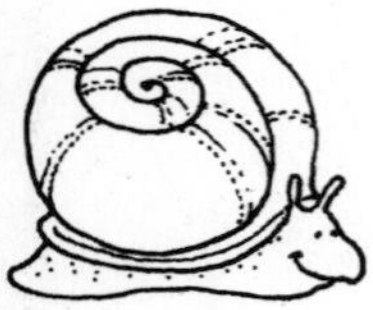

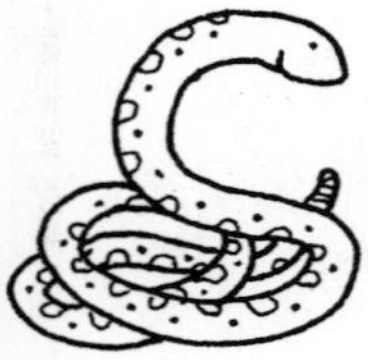

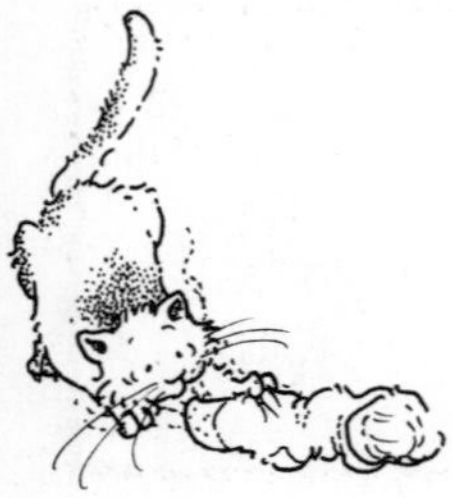

st

Look at the picture. Then build the word.

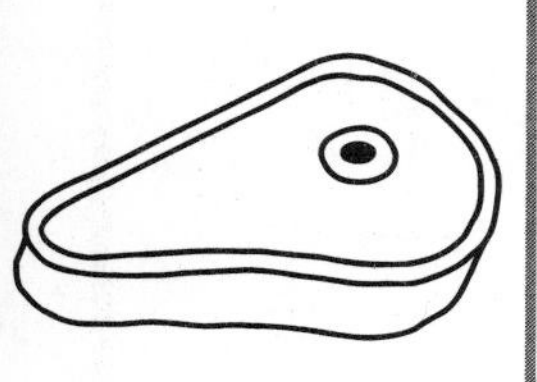

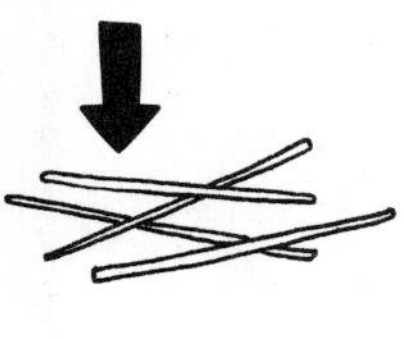

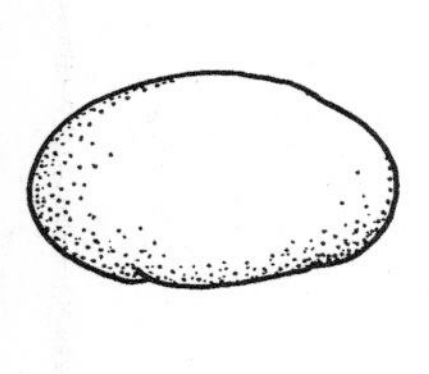

st

Look at the picture. Then build the word.

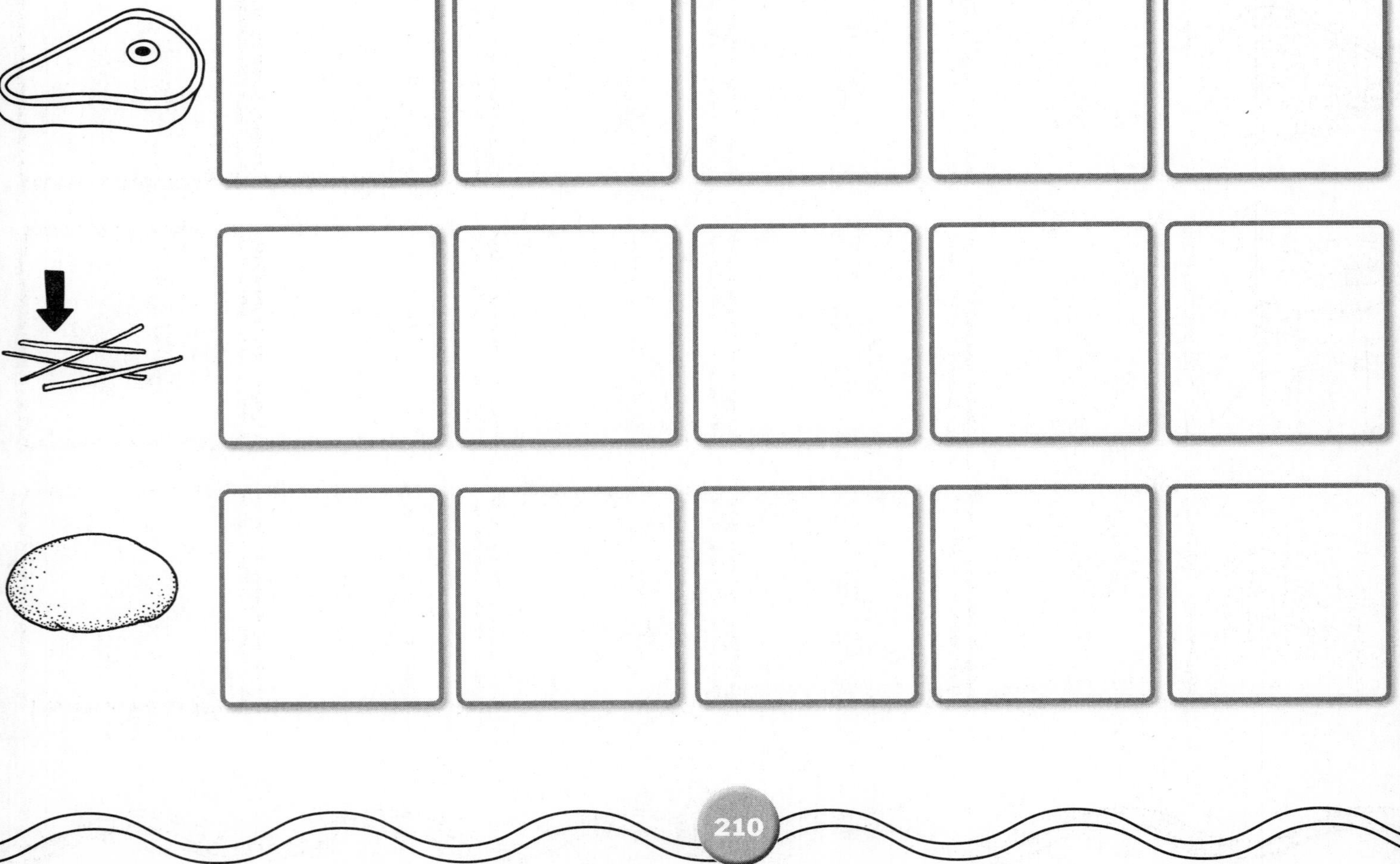

Look at the picture. Then build the word.

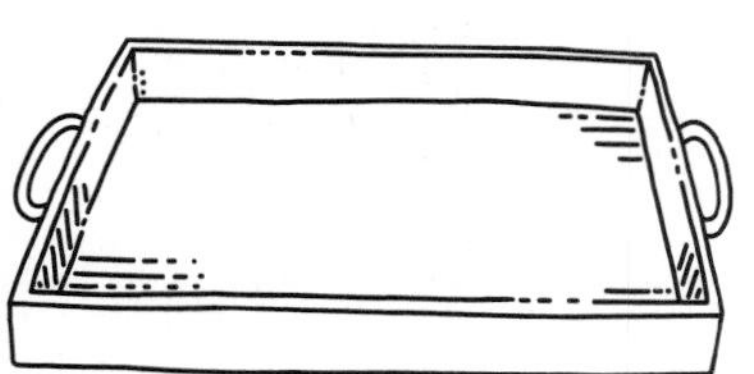

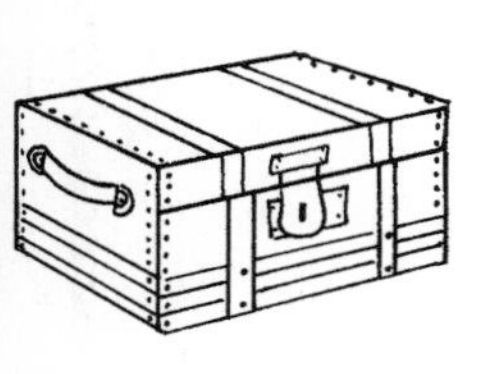

tr

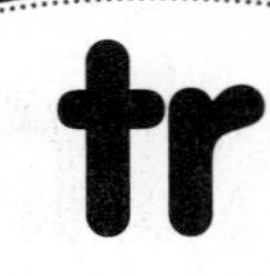

Look at the picture. Then build the word.

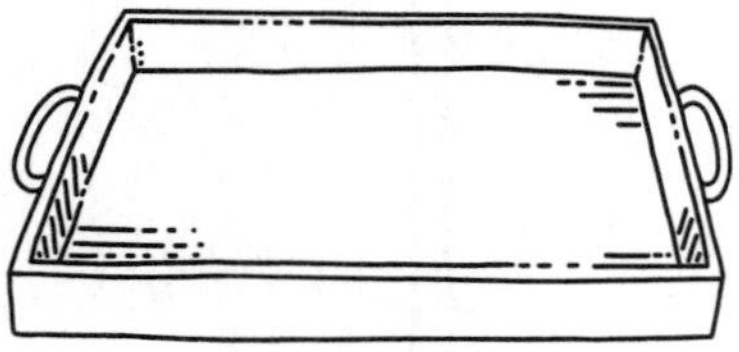

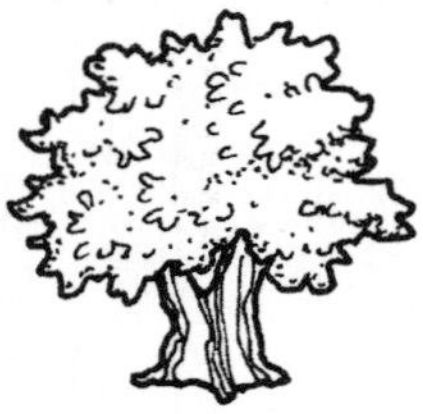

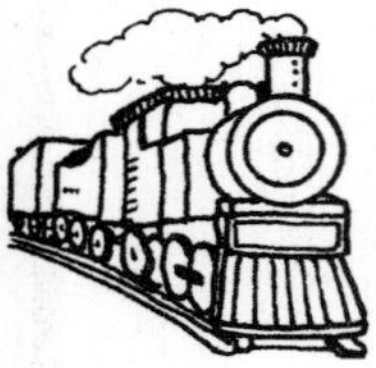

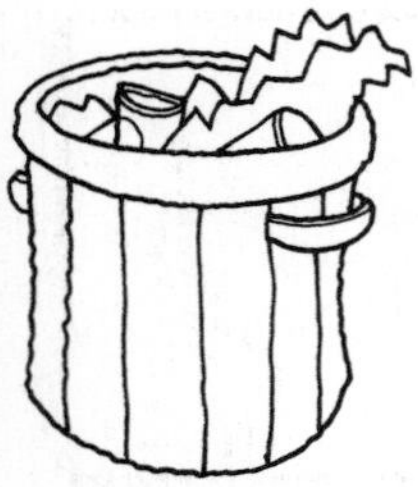

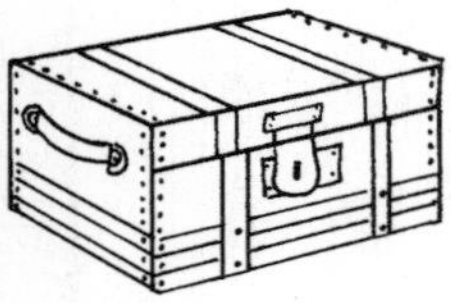

oo

Look at the picture. Then build the word.

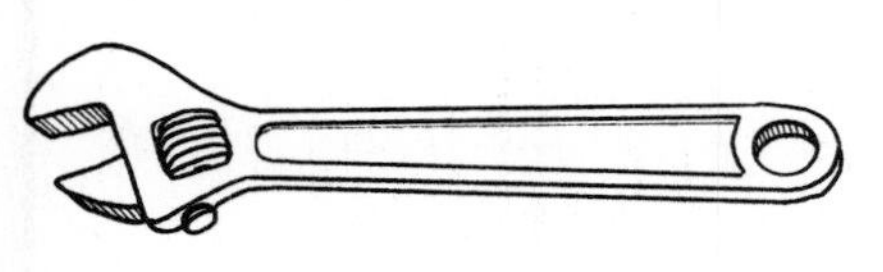

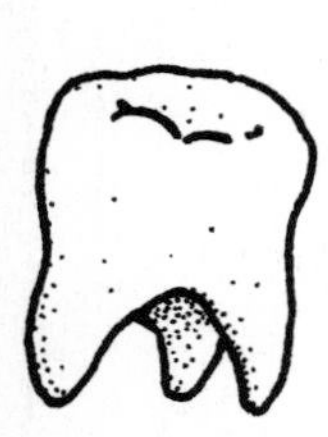

oo

Look at the picture. Then build the word.

oo

Look at the picture. Then build the word.

oo

Look at the picture. Then build the word.

Look at the picture. Then build the word.

 c    

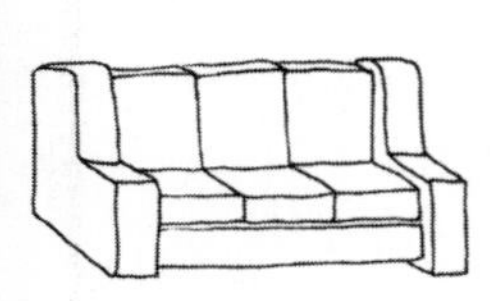     

     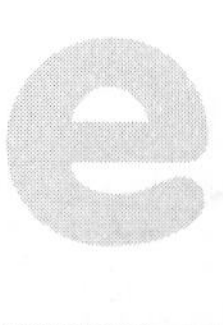

ou

Look at the picture. Then build the word.

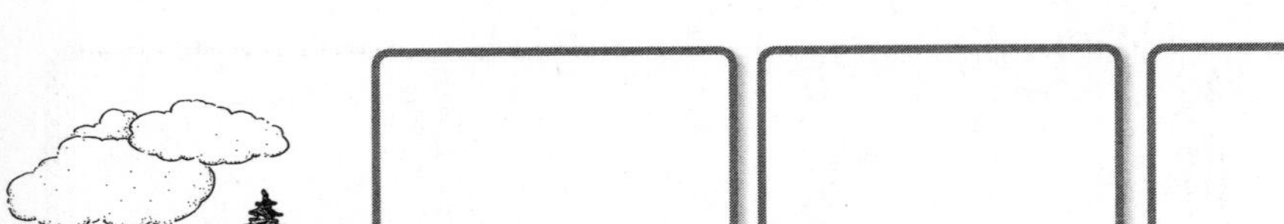

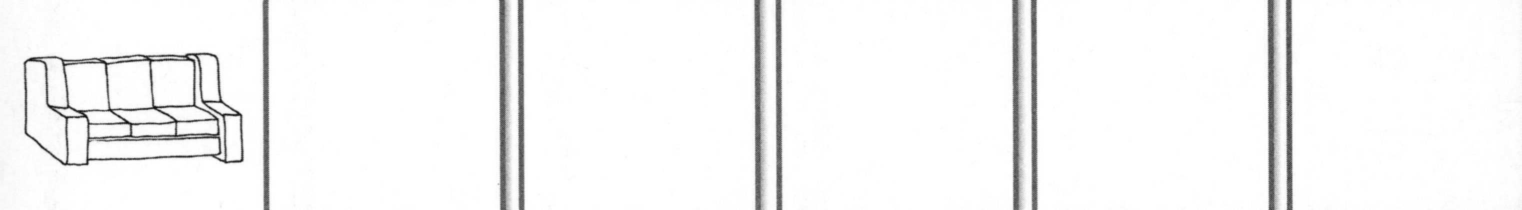

Look at the picture. Then build the word.

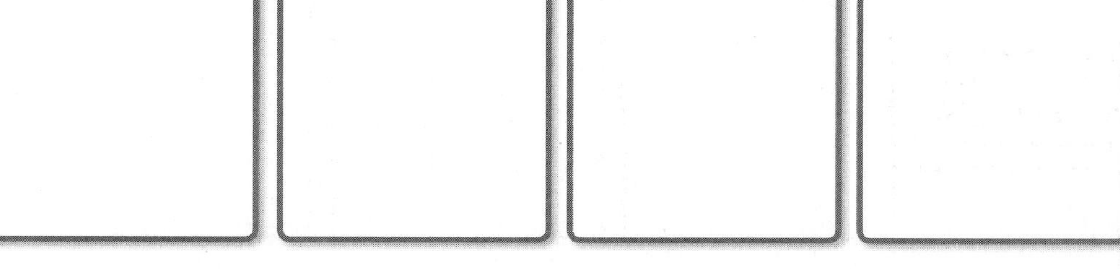

Look at the picture. Then build the word.

a	e	i	o	u	y
a	e	i	o	u	y
a	e	i	o	u	y
a	e	i	o	u	y
a	e	i	o	u	y
a	e	i	o	u	y
a	e	i	o	u	y

b	b	c	c	d	d
f	f	g	g	h	h
j	j	k	k	l	l
m	m	m	n	n	n
p	p	q	r	r	r
s	s	s	t	t	t
v	v	w	w	x	z

A	E	I	O	U	Y
A	E	I	O	U	Y
A	E	I	O	U	Y
A	E	I	O	U	Y
A	E	I	O	U	Y
A	E	I	O	U	Y
A	E	I	O	U	Y

B	B	C	C	D	D
F	F	G	G	H	H
J	J	K	K	L	L
M	M	M	N	N	N
P	P	Q	R	R	R
S	S	S	T	T	T
V	V	W	W	X	Z